Managing Information

Titles in the Chartered Management Institute Series

Managing Information

Third edition

IT for Business Processes

David A. Wilson

chartered
management
institute

BUTTERWORTH
HEINEMANN

OXFORD   AMSTERDAM   BOSTON   LONDON   NEW YORK   PARIS
SAN DIEGO   SAN FRANCISCO   SINGAPORE   SYDNEY   TOKYO

Butterworth-Heinemann
An imprint of Elsevier Science
Linacre House, Jordan Hill, Oxford OX2 8DP
225 Wildwood Avenue, Woburn MA 01801-2041

First published 1993
Second edition 1997
Third edition 2002

British Library Cataloguing in Publication Data
A catalogue record for this book is available from the British Library

ISBN 0 7506 5621 2

For information on all Butterworth-Heinemann publications
visit our website at www.bh.com

Typeset by Keyword Typesetting Services Ltd, Wallington, Surrey
Printed and bound in Great Britain

Contents

CONTENTS

CONTENTS

CONTENTS

Preface

Information and knowledge are the key resources in business. All other resources are widely available, and cannot on their own deliver competitive advantage. Having the right information technology and using it appropriately is therefore crucial to business success.

This book is written for business students, not computer scientists. My target reader is aged between nineteen and thirty-five years, studying for a management qualification at Certificate, Diploma, Degree or Masters level. My reader wants to understand the business benefits, not the technical details. If that sounds like you, read on.

You may be doing, or aspire to, a job in marketing, accounting or general management. You need to pass several modules and computing may not be your favourite. I hope to change that by satisfying your interests in every day language, and avoid the formality of an academic text. It is pointless being definitive about the business use of computers – things move too fast. The picture has changed by the time you print it. The past is history, and the future is more important than the present.

That said, computers are useless without people to operate them, and people in some organizations change slowly. Some organizations in protected markets have changed little, while others have changed beyond recognition. Also, history is important (only back to 1960: before that is pre-history for the business computer) because it affects the way people view the world and how they behave. And historical trends can provide a guide to the future.

There is a theme – almost a story line running through the book. The computer is just a tool that we use in business, but it is a powerful and versatile one. There is a symbiosis: the computer is shaping business and how we conduct it, and business is shaping computer architectures and systems. Computer networks mirror organizational structures: computer architectures must meet business needs and support business processes.

The story starts in the 1960s with the mainframe computer in the classical command and control organization. In the culture of secrecy and mistrust that prevailed then, information was held centrally, and only released on a strict 'need to know' basis. Now in the twenty first century, networks of computers have become widespread. Hierarchies are being replaced by team-based structures. Information flows more freely throughout the organization, and beyond its boundaries in a more open and trusting environment. We are on the verge of a new era of full, flexible support for business processes.

The book is about how computers help people in organizations to automate, communicate and collaborate. I hope you enjoy the story.

David Wilson
E-mail: david@thetudorhouse.fsnet.co.uk
March 2002

CHAPTER 1

How to win business in the e-economy

Forward, forward let us range,
Let the great world spin for ever down the ringing grooves of change.
'Locksley Hall' (1842), Alfred, Lord Tennyson

IN THIS CHAPTER . . .

- How computers and networks are enabling and driving the fundamental changes taking place in business.
- Why it is essential to keep up to date on information technology (IT).
- A brief history of business computing – spotting the trends.
- What lies ahead?

I WANT THE BEST, I WANT IT NOW, AND I WANT IT FREE

The market behaves like a spoilt child – have you noticed? It always demands more than you gave it last time. Nothing is constant in business any longer, and it's all down to those damned computers.

They speed up the business cycle with automated business processes and instant messaging. And things are bound to get worse as computers get faster and more powerful. Do you ever wonder if you're in the right job? You might do better as a brain surgeon.

When we first started at work, we expected an orderly hierarchy, in which managers held meetings, worked to budgets, planned strategies and then executed them efficiently to make a profit. But what we find now often seems like barely contained chaos: no time to do anything properly, missed targets, crises looming at every turn ... So what went wrong? The problem lies in a business mythology left over from times when the pace of business was more leisurely. Until the 1980s, many big companies had ten or more levels in their organization chart, and everyone had a job description. There was a chain of command and at each level, a span of control. People had one boss, and performed specialist functions in separate departments. Corporate plans looked five years ahead, and customers stood meekly in line, waiting to be served with often mediocre goods or services.

During the 1980s and 1990s, the developed world left behind the industrial age, and moved into the information age. Factory machinery was automated, markets became global, and for the first time ever, markets for most standard products became over-supplied. Customers started complaining about quality, and began shopping around for better value. Business competition intensified. The rules changed: meticulous planning no longer worked. It was more important to be fast and flexible.

So what's the situation at the start of the new century? A mixed picture, I guess. As the pace accelerated, some organizations pulled ahead, stretching out the pack. The leaders are now flat, lean, agile organizations, making full use of technology to deliver high quality goods and services on demand at low prices. Two examples spring to mind: Dell Computers, and Ryanair. Meanwhile, other organizations are trailing the field and seem not to have changed. For instance, some business schools and some book publishers (who both deal in information) have scarcely begun to use technology to deliver a better, faster, cheaper service.

And what can we expect in this first decade? As we shall discuss shortly, further developments are in the pipeline and the pace will accelerate. Technology will eventually penetrate most sectors, some first movers will win huge advantage and some laggards will cease to be competitive. But in the end, technology is just a tool. It is groups of people in your enterprise who must collaborate to achieve goals, and groups of people, your customers, who will judge how well you achieve those goals. The trick is to get people using the tools to automate, to communicate and to collaborate.

And when you can do that, you can be proud to call yourself a manager.

COMPUTERS CHANGE ORGANIZATIONS

Back in the 1980s when PCs were first being adopted by business, department managers could justify purchasing stand-alone PCs purely on short payback cost savings: these new machines could save money by automating clerical tasks, and save time and space by replacing paper files with databases. Later, many of these departmental 'islands of automation' in the organization were found to contain the same information, very often not accurately replicated, but in different, conflicting versions. The solution was to connect up the PCs in an organization-wide network, thus avoiding the cock-ups caused by different departments working with different versions of the same data. Speed and efficiency were also improved by allowing data and information to flow accurately and instantaneously between departments, instead of being typed out and passed by hand through the mail system.

Up to this point computers simply automated and speeded up existing business processes, which was good – so long as your business processes were appropriate for the circumstances. If not, computers just hastened your demise. In fact, computers were not only exposing weak business processes, but also making possible completely new ways of organizing work and doing business. Managers in different departments who had never communicated before now began to co-operate because they shared data through the same network. The watertight walls between departments were beginning to crumble. Then, in 1990, business process re-engineering (BPR) became the hot new topic, offering not ten per cent but ten-fold improvements, by redesigning the whole business organization from the ground up with computers in mind. Suddenly the tree-like structure for organizing a business no longer looked appropriate, and organizational theorists were scrambling to suggest new ways of organizing in teams, and teams of teams, instead of departments.

THE INTERNET

That was more than enough change to be going on with, but in the 1990s a world-wide computer network for researchers called the Internet was opened up to commerce, and made accessible by user-friendly software. The opportunities and threats seemed limitless, and spurred widespread, frenetic business activity which ultimately led to the dotcom bubble that finally burst at the beginning of the new millennium. The legacy, however, is a much-improved infrastructure for digital communications of all types, and this has permanently changed the business landscape. Secrecy, mistrust and lack of communication do not help a company to deliver goods and services that are fine-tuned to the needs of customers. Couple Internet technology with a new spirit of openness and trust, and the old win-lose games that businesses played with their suppliers and customers are over for good. Companies discovered that when they co-operate with suppliers, customers, and even competitors (co-opetition), all parties can win because customers get what they want and are prepared to pay a premium for that.

The importance of business information continues to grow. It is the key to better management, survival and success.

THE VALUE OF INFORMATION

When you want a sandwich for lunch, do you buy the cheap one from the crummy tray – or will you pay a bit more for one that is carefully packed and looks fresh and appetizing? With growing expectations and disposable income, more people will pay for quality, as affirmed by the success of, say, Starbucks and Pret-a-Manger.

Quality, design and branding are clearly very important factors in determining price. It is true for trivial items such as sandwiches and it is also true for major purchases such as cars. For example, take two similar small hatchback cars, the Daewoo Lanos and the Audi A2 SE. The Daewoo costs £8975 and the Audi costs 75 per cent more at £15,620. On the face of it (see Figure 1.1) these two hatchbacks are very similar.

So what do these examples tell us? If we assume that customers are not complete idiots with more money than sense, then from their point of view the Audi represents a far more attractive combination of raw materials than the Daewoo. In other words, starting with the

Figure 1.1
Specifications of
two 1.4 litre
5-door hatchbacks
(Source: *What
Car?*, December
2001)

Model	Power (bhp)	Length (mm)	Width (mm)	Height (mm)	Weight (kg)	Max Speed (mph)	Accel. (0–60) (secs)	Fuel Cons. (mpg)
Daewoo Lanos 1.4 5dr	74	4064	1854	1422	1005	98	12.3	35.6
Audi A2 SE 1.4 5dr	75	3826	1676	1549	990	107	12.0	47.1

same kinds of input – similar amounts of similar materials and labour
– one car manufacturer or sandwich maker builds in more know-how
and thereby adds more value than the other. Know-how of course
includes different types of information, for instance design information, quality information, production information and marketing or
branding information. Presumably the manufacturers of the Daewoo
would like to know how to produce a more attractive car and charge
more for it and thus it seems their problem is directly related to how
they manage information.

HOW TO MANAGE INFORMATION

All organizations must manage information, just as all businesses
must make a profit, but for a chief executive to tell you to improve
your information management, like telling you to improve profits, is
no help at all. What you need is more specific direction on the route
to those overall goals, and that is what this book aims to do.

Is it fair to suggest that managing information is as important as
making a profit? However well you manage information, without
profits your business will fail. But profits depend upon good decisions
based on accurate information. Decision-making is central to every
manager's role, so we are told by authors Herbert Simon and Peter
Drucker. They helped create perhaps the most important school of
management thought – the decision-making school.

Decisions are impossible without information and managers are
constantly seeking more and better information to support their decision-making. Hence the growth of information systems – a term that
generally means networks of computers, but strictly speaking should
also include non-computerized channels of communication such as
regular meetings, the in- and out-trays full of memos and reports and

of course the phone. To survive, every organization must have an information system. All organizations must be able to collect information, communicate it internally and process it so that managers can make decisions quickly and effectively in pursuit of organizational objectives in a changing, competitive environment. The information system is the nervous system that allows an organization to respond to opportunities and avoid threats. To be effective it must reach every part of the organization, and beyond, into the furthest extremities of the extended enterprise.

THE ROLE OF COMPUTERS

Information technology (i.e. computers and electronic communications networks) is destined to play an ever-bigger role in the handling of information for four reasons:

- Processing. Computers are more accurate, and cheaper than people.
- Communication. Electronic messaging is faster, and cheaper than paper.
- Storage. Electronic files are more accessible, and cheaper than paper.
- Collaboration. Team results are better and quicker when supported by computer networks.

Cheap, accurate processing

In banking, for instance, computers have brought massive permanent savings by completely removing the need for large amounts of routine paperwork and the army of clerks who process it. An early example was the decline of the chequebook. Your bank statements show many more automatic entries such as card purchases, direct debits and automated cash, and fewer cheque entries. Not long ago thousands of millions of cheques where drawn annually in the UK. Each cheque had to be physically transported to the recipient's bank for cashing, then returned to its home bank for deducting from the drawer's account. Machines were used for automatically sorting and processing, but this could only be done after each individual cheque had been manually encoded to make them machine-readable. Banking personnel did this with magnetic character inscribers. It cost the banks literally millions of man- and woman-hours on clearing cheques – a strong incentive for them to replace the paper-based cheque system with electronic funds transfer, wherever possible.

More recently, direct line or telephone banking has made it possible to do our banking without having to travel in to town and queue to speak to a cashier. When you phone in, the call centre operator already knows who is calling before you speak. Computer-telephony integration (CTI) allows a computer to check your phone number and use it to find and display your account details so the operator can respond immediately to your requests. Thus the bank wins by saving on branch operating costs, and the customer wins by gaining a quicker, more convenient service.

It's a small step then to automate the whole procedure by allowing self-service banking via the Internet, better known as e-banking. The banks will never close all their High Street branches, but e-banking and direct line banking seem set to take an increasing share of day-to-day retail banking. Some customers will always prefer to do their banking face to face in a branch, and many customers will always need the solid presence of a branch before they can trust an Internet bank with their money. One of the first Internet-only banks in the UK with no branches was first-e, who were never able to secure a viable customer base. Eventually in the autumn of 2001 they returned their customers' money before closing their virtual doors forever. In banking it seems that mouse clicks will never completely replace branch bricks. As is often the case, clicks and bricks is the best solution.

Now at Work

e-cash for m-commerce

The Mondex electronic purse

When your daughter calls from her mobile phone late at night to say she's low on petrol and hasn't got any money, it would be really handy just to transfer ten pounds over the phone connection from your purse to hers. You may soon be able to do just that – Mondex (a subsidiary of Mastercard International) has already developed the technology. The Mondex smart card, the size of a credit card, is a purse for electronic cash. Mobile phones with a slot for a Mondex card for transactions are available now: for buying cinema tickets, topping up your e-purse – or giving your daughter some petrol money. But most phone networks, cinemas and banks are not quite ready for that just yet.

There are sound reasons for using e-cash. Banks would save money: in the UK it costs around £4 billion each year just to handle and maintain the bulky coins and notes we all carry around for casual spending. There are advantages for consumers, too: e-cash is less bulky, never requires change, and can be used for on-line transactions. Mondex card transactions are much simpler than credit cards – no creditworthiness to check, no maintaining of card accounts and no subsequent billing and receiving of payments. As with hard cash, the whole transaction is completed instantly at the point of sale, and it can all be anonymous. Despite these advantages, adoption is slow. It may take a 'killer application' – a new and exciting commercial use to boost Mondex in the same way that VisiCalc, the first spreadsheet program, boosted the Apple personal computer. The appeal of e-cash should be strong in the youth market and those without bank accounts, so could on-line gambling or gaming be the killer application, with the purse used for payment for games and receipt of winnings? Adoption so far has been in homogeneous communities: a University campus, or a big company or city area where many people make similar small purchases. For instance in Sherbrooke, a region of Quebec, 600 local merchants and 700 vending machines, parking meters and photocopiers accept Mondex e-cash. Around the world there are now millions of Mondex cards, with strong uptake in 18 Asia Pacific countries including Japan, Australia, China, Hong Kong, Indonesia and Malaysia.

Let's hope hard cash doesn't disappear completely, because you can't spin your Mondex card to see who serves first at tennis, or play shove ha'penny with it in the pub.

Cheap, fast messaging

To get things done at work, people must communicate in various ways. For meetings, people have to be together – same time, same place – and we all know how difficult that can be to arrange. It's expensive, when you add the cost of the participants' time. Phone conversations can be expensive too. Both parties have to be free but not together – same time, different place – and playing telephone tag can waste a lot of time.

For some purposes, real-time conversation by one of these two methods is essential, but for many other purposes, sending a message is sufficient – different time, different place – and that is easy now. Not long ago we had to make do with faxes, memos and letters, which incurred secretarial and delivery costs, and involved a delay. All difficulties and delays to a message add to the overall 'transaction cost' – the cost of delivering the message. Now, we have instantaneous message delivery by voice mail, email and SMS texting. You can even reach people in meetings, if they have their cell phone set to silent. The transaction cost is close to zero, enabling faster decisions, and thus faster response to customers – always a significant competitive advantage.

Fast, accurate messaging between organizations is also an advantage. Since the 1970s, some large organizations that place regular orders, such as manufacturers, supermarkets, and the National Health Service, have been able to exchange purchasing and delivery information through a private network linking the computers of purchasers and suppliers. It automates the procurement cycle, resulting in fewer errors and lower costs. The system is called Electronic Data Interchange (EDI). Each industry (automotive, chemical, etc.) has its own network specially configured by the network supplier to suit all the trading partners, who usually had different incompatible computer systems. It was very expensive to set up, and only big companies could afford to join, but it was worth it for the savings in time, clerical and stationery costs.

The Internet has changed all that: Internet protocols and computer languages have solved most incompatibility problems, and it is cheap and easy for computers to talk to each other. Some big organizations with mission-critical supply chains have stuck with their private networks, but many companies now regularly exchange commercial information with their suppliers and customers over the Internet. It is EDI by another name, e-commerce, but some of the old EDI standards for message formats are still found to be useful.

The advantages are obvious: the whole process of inviting tenders, receiving quotations, placing orders, receiving the invoices and paying – that took weeks using the postal service – can now be completed the same day if necessary. The money comes back to the seller more quickly, the buyer needs lower stocks to support a given level of trading, and planning is much easier for both. In fact it makes the whole process easier, and as we shall see later, collaboration along the supply chain fosters trust, which in turn can bring closer co-operation in other areas. For instance, some companies involve their suppliers

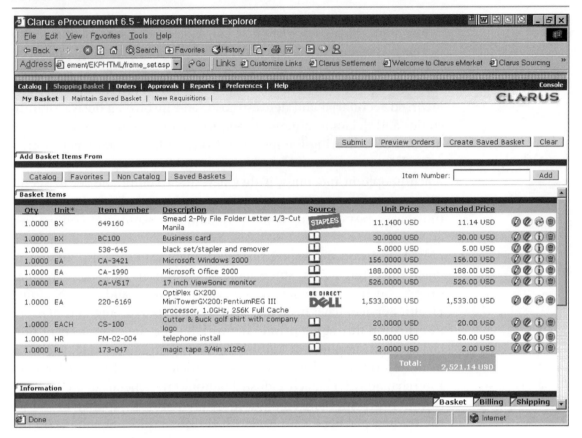

Figure 1.2
Clarus Electronic procurement user interface

in new product designs and sales forecasts, to avoid future production and supply problems.

The net result of faster response in the supply chain is of course lower costs that can be passed on to the customer. And that brings competitive advantage – a mutual benefit for all.

Cheap, accessible filing

The third reason why computers are sure to take over in more and more areas of organizational life is that they can make any information already collected for one purpose instantly available to be used for many other secondary purposes. This has opened up totally new ways of using information. Let us take for example the way information about groceries bought by customers can be used in a retail outlet. In corner shops the proprietor often operates the till and once the customer has paid for his or her purchases the only record of the transactions is on the till roll – to all intents and purposes inaccessible. It is of little consequence though because the proprietor is close enough to the action for decision-making and knows roughly what the day's takings are, how many customers have been served, and whether there has been a run on a particular item.

In the supermarket, however, there may be 30 checkout operators and 10,000 or more different lines stocked. At peak times, purchases may be leaving the supermarket at a rate of 40,000 items per hour. Stocks of each line must be reordered to arrive at the rate of consumption, or changing demand for particular lines caused by promotional activity or food scares could easily lead to empty shelves or overstocking. The supermarket therefore cannot afford to throw away 'till roll' data collected for the primary purpose of calculating how much to charge the customer. Once collected it must be used again for stock control, a secondary use. And that's not the end of the story: information is expensive to collect, but once held in digital form it costs next to nothing to store and so can be freely used over and over again for a variety of secondary purposes. For instance, till roll data collected over a period of months or years can be analysed for long-term trends and presented graphically to aid in forecasting and strategic planning. Till roll data becomes valuable for direct marketing when linked to particular customers who present a loyalty card. Customers who buy cat food may be interested in special offers on cat litter, and those who buy diapers may try a new range of baby foods. Their addresses are known, so they can be targeted for mail shots customized to their life-styles and preferences.

Fast, excellent team results

Before the 1980s, those halcyon days of limited competition and mostly under-supplied markets, big companies employed corporate planners to examine trends, make forecasts and prepare five-year plans for a future that was assumed to be predictable. They had to believe it, because their supertanker organizations took forever to change direction. But with competition increasing, it was not long before the forecasts were 50% wrong, 100% wrong, or predicted the opposite of what actually happened. Soon, big business sacked its corporate planners and looked for ways to be more agile. Then, instead of trying to control the future, they could turn on a sixpence and grab opportunities or avoid threats as they arose.

It was not just their size that made them inflexible, though that didn't help in those days before email and computer conferencing. The fault lay in their hierarchical management structure. When an opportunity or threat arose, it was often the troops in the front line that spotted it first. They would pass the message up through the management levels, delayed in in-trays at each level, until it reached someone near the top who could decide what should be done. Then the decision would be passed down the tree again. In tall hierarchies decisions just took too long, and by the 1980s and early 1990s, after missing opportunities and colliding with threats, businesses discovered that workers are quite capable of taking middle management decisions for their selves. They were quickly empowered to do that, and a raft of middle managers were 'let go'. It was a stark choice: go bust – or 'downsize' and re-invent as a flatter organization. At a stroke, flexibility increased and payroll costs decreased. However, empowering workers is not just a question of writing new job descriptions. New power means new decisions, and that calls for new access to information.

INFORMATION OVERLOAD

We all know there is more information of every type available now than ever before. How often are you 'personally selected' at home, and at work, for the chance of receiving a fabulous holiday – and some information? Most of it is junk information – junk mail, e-mail, and junk faxes that you file straight away in the waste paper bin – and guess who personally selected you? A computer, of course. They are great for sending out information: more computers are used for word-processing than for any other task. Computers are amazingly fast at processing some types of data, in particular financial and numerical data once it has been converted into electronic digital signals. There are even programs for filtering out, or redirecting, certain classes of email, but computers cannot yet open the morning postbag, sift out the junk and bin it.

So history is repeating itself: the invention of the typewriter with its high output of thirty or forty words per minute did not lead us to employ fewer scribes to write letters and other documents. Instead we employed more people to produce much more written work and now the word processor is having the same effect. The net result is more people with keyboard skills than ever before, and far more information on every conceivable subject, competing for our attention – and often failing to get it.

It seems the computers that help us manage information by processing data faster, far from solving our problems, actually create new problems by adding to the volume, variety and complexity of information available. Nevertheless some organizations thrive in this new environment; they use computers and modern information systems to make better decisions more quickly, allowing them to respond faster to customer requirements, which in markets today brings significant competitive advantage.

RESPONSIVENESS TO CUSTOMER NEEDS

Nobody likes being kept waiting, and often we will pay to avoid it. When you get back from your holidays you can post off your snaps to a cut-price processor – or get them processed at Boots and pay a premium to have them back within the hour.

Business customers don't like to be kept waiting either; it can actually cost them money, and so suppliers who deliver promptly have a significant edge on their competitors. To be able to deliver standard items fast, suppliers need only hold stocks, but for services and products designed specially to the customer's requirements, stock holding is not possible. The ability to deliver promptly then depends upon how well the organization can marshal its resources to make and deliver to meet the customer's order. And that involves fast, efficient handling of information – about what to do and how to do it.

Now at Work

Mazak wins markets, with factory automation

Yamazaki Mazak, the Japanese machine-tool manufacturer, has a factory in Worcester, close to Coventry where British manufacturers once made and supplied machine tools around the world. Opened in 1987 the Mazak automated factory does not manufacture for stock, but can deliver to their customers' specifications within one or two months. This is amazingly fast when you consider that other manufacturers typically quote a six month delivery. Mazak never make batches of product, as used to be the custom in Coventry. In this way they keep each of the stages in the manufacturing process free of the logjams and queues that develop with batch production. Thus they can speed their customers' special requirements through the factory without delay. The Mazak factory can produce 100 machines a month, in a range of 55 different models. Each model has optional features and so they seldom produce the same product twice running. Each order requires a different set of manufacturing instructions.

How do they handle this factory information? A paperwork system just would not be fast enough. So, customer orders and specifications are processed on the screens of CAD (Computer aided design) workstations. Then this design information is transferred electronically to the screens of process planners who work at CAM (Computer aided manufacture) workstations. Here the design information is converted into CNC (Computer numerical control) programs that are used to control the automatic machine-tool processes used in the factory. All the computers and machine-tool processes are linked up together through a computer network, and the whole production process is scheduled and co-ordinated by a supervisory computer to form an advanced example of CIM (Computer integrated manufacture).

And what does this all mean to the customer? It means taking delivery of an individually designed, high quality product only two months after placing the order instead of six months – bringing forward the pay-back period and break-even point by a massive four months. No wonder that Yamazaki Mazak is the world's biggest producer of CNC lathes, machining centres and manufacturing systems. Mazak are truly world-class performers. www.mazak.com

WORLD MARKETS

The Mazak factory in Worcester is not a curious phenomenon that managers can afford to ignore; it is becoming the norm in manufacturing. For instance, some car makers will soon achieve the '14-day car' capability, allowing customers to specify their own car and have it ready for collection within fourteen days.

Multinationals operate around the world and countries no longer have cosy, protected home markets. The world is a global market place in which only the world-class players thrive. This is great for consumers because it means we can choose from the best value products and services available in the world. But as managers of organizations it means we face increasingly intense competition.

WORLD-CLASS PERFORMANCE

World class is a term coined by Dick Schonberger, consultant and author of *Building a Chain of Customers*, to describe any organization which is consistently held in the highest regard by its customers, and can therefore compete successfully in world markets. Tom Peters, another American, author of *In Search of Excellence*, *Liberation Management* and *Beyond Hierarchy*, describes these organizations as excellent. They both agree that somehow, these organizations are consistently able to meet and often exceed their customers' expectations.

This kind of exceptional performance cannot happen by chance: it must be made to happen by getting everyone in the organization to work constantly towards that goal. Why? Because customer expectations are constantly rising. What we as consumers are delighted with today, we come to expect tomorrow, and so any organization that stands still on quality and customer service will soon fall behind.

Unfortunately, however, until recently most western organizations were saddled with a crippling handicap that had to be unburdened before they could hope to achieve excellence. This handicap was an all-pervading heritage familiar to everyone at work. It had always been there, we could not imagine life without it, and it was seldom questioned. It was of course the 'command and control' system with those near the top of the tree making the decisions for the rest lower down.

It's incredible to think that towards the end of the twentieth century, most people at work in organizations of any size still found themselves constrained by a structure first adopted thousands of years ago. It was appropriate for the Roman army, and for businesses during the reign of Queen Victoria, because then, populations consisted mostly of uneducated masses, with only a small, educated elite equipped to take charge of them. But that changed half a century ago, with an educated majority in developed nations. What a waste of potential: all those educated people in the lower half of the tree with ideas about their jobs and no opportunity to use them.

A REVOLUTION

However, two developments in the 1970s signalled change that would place much higher value on ideas and creativity. First, thirty years without a world war had allowed nations to rebuild their industries, which were now competing instead of armies, to conquer the world. Japan, whose industrial base was completely destroyed at the end of World War 2, had built new factories and developed new management systems that were clearly superior to those in the west. American, British and European motorcycle, automotive and electronic industries were beginning to feel the heat. World trade and competition was picking up, and western factories were closing because customers preferred the better design and superior quality of Japanese products. In the west, Japan was accused of copying western products, but eventually western companies had to copy the Japanese methods of just-in-time production and kaizen quality assurance. Global competition was too hot, and western companies couldn't beat the Japanese methods, so they had to copy them. Ironically it was two American quality experts, W. E. Deming and J. Juran, who in the 1950s taught the Japanese how to do kaizen.

The second sign of change in the 1970s was that more companies were bringing computers out of the research labs and using them for business purposes. Initially there were big savings to be made by automating the jobs of comptometer operators and copy typists. Later, networks of computers would speed up the business cycle, allow better use of resources, and make possible new ways of co-ordinating and running an organization.

This period of unprecedented competition, coupled with revolutionary change, saw the death of the industrial age and the birth of the information age. Millions of manual workers and the craft skills of the industrial age were replaced by machine minders and programmers who wrote that hard-won craft skill into programs for computer-controlled production machinery. Computers and machines now do most of the repetitive stuff, leaving people to do just the awkward knowledge work that requires information and creativity. Competitiveness now depends on knowledge workers – in every area, from initial concept through to after-sales support. They are the people who have ideas, and know how to make them work.

THE INFORMATION AGE

Managing a command-and-control organization depends on telling the workers what to do, then seeing that they do it. It was easy to measure output and quality with a tangible product. Easy also to see if a manual worker was working hard or slacking. But how do you supervise knowledge workers? If a designer or programmer is staring into space is he or she thinking about a work problem – or planning a holiday? How do you even measure the output or quality of the work as it is being done? So, if you cannot control knowledge workers, can you command them? Perhaps, but only in broad terms, because the knowledge worker will be closer to the action and therefore often knows better than the supervisor what needs doing.

Knowledge workers cannot perform well in the secrecy and mistrust of a traditional command-and-control environment. They are best motivated by being given the problem and trusted with all the available information, then left to find a solution. Instead of trying to command and control them, it is better to make sure you hire the right people, then inform and entrust them. This is not an easy message to sell to chief executives, many of whom feel they are paid to call the shots, and there are still plenty of organizations with scope for better management of their knowledge workers. However, there is also a growing band of new style organizations that have abandoned the command-and-control model and the multi-layer hierarchy. You can read about one of them – Semco – in the box below.

Now at Work

Hierarchy abandoned at Semco – prototype for success in a changing world

Ricardo Semler became CEO of Semco, Brazil, when his father Curt passed control to him in 1980. It was a traditional engineering company with 12 layers of management and $2 million annual revenue. Ricardo started by scrapping the 12 layers and firing 60 per cent of the managers. He replaced the layers with three concentric rings: six Counsellors at the centre, surrounded by ten Partners, in turn surrounded by everyone else in a large circle of Associates. In the large outer circle, people are arranged in teams of five to twenty, each with an elected Co-ordinator.

Worker teams at Semco set and monitor their own production goals, and decide when they start and finish work each day. They also help redesign products, formulate marketing plans, hire new colleagues, and appraise their bosses twice a year. The financial books are open to them, and they are encouraged to take classes on how to read balance sheets and other financial statements. Executives set their own salaries and 23 per cent of all profits are distributed as bonus equally amongst all workers. All workers are expected to use their brains and so naturally Semco does not give prizes for employee suggestions.

Twelve years later in 1992 Semco was six times bigger, productivity was up sevenfold, profits up fivefold and there were periods of 14 months when not one worker left the company. There was a backlog of 2000 job applications and in a poll of Brazilian college graduates, 25 per cent of the men and 13 per cent of the women voted Semco as the company they most wanted to work for.

More recently in a September–October 2000 Harvard Business Review paper, Semco is reported to have added a $30 million commercial property management business, and in turn that led to the creation, with Semco's support, of an on-line exchange to facilitate the management of commercial construction projects. The exchange was so successful that it has become a springboard for further Web initiatives such as virtual trade shows.

References

Semler, R. (1993). *Maverick! The Success Story behind the World's Most Unusual Workplace.* Century.
Internet search, using key words *Semco Brazil*.

Towards the end of the twentieth century, many organizations realized that the old ways of organizing were no longer appropriate. Few, however, were able to make the leap that Semco made. At the time it wasn't exactly clear what to do, so various approaches were tried. Since the mid 1980s the most significant developments were:

- Total Quality Management.
- Human Resource Management.
- The Flatter Organization.
- The Learning Organization.
- Business Process Re-engineering.

All these approaches helped organizations adjust to the new imperatives of the information age, but none of them provided a complete solution. Their contributions were as follows.

TOTAL QUALITY MANAGEMENT

TQM was proposed as a way of improving quality and productivity, at a time when Japan was winning markets from British and American manufacturers. Managers thought: here is a set of techniques that will solve our problems. But TQM called for more than techniques: it called for groups of workers to form quality circles that would study quality and production problems, and recommend solutions. Now at the time, this required a radical shift in thinking. These quality circles were expected to gather data, analyse it and make decisions – in other words, do the middle manager's job. The idea of workers actually thinking about their jobs and deciding how to do them didn't fit in with the style of management that prevailed then, and middle managers felt threatened. In consequence TQM programmes often failed to fulfil expectations. However, an important bridgehead had been established: in many organizations this was the first time that workers had been authorized to collect data, encouraged to learn how to analyse it, and empowered to act on the results.

The three cornerstones of TQM are:

■ an obsession with quality – as defined by the customer;
■ a scientific approach – changing things, then measuring to check for improvement;
■ all one team – working together in an atmosphere of openness and trust.

Clearly these depend on data, information, and knowledge, supported by free and open communications – all of which can be enhanced by appropriate information systems.

HUMAN RESOURCE MANAGEMENT

The personnel function is being re-invented as Human Resource Management to suit the new requirements of knowledge workers in the information age. Remember Douglas McGregor's Theory X? People in command-and-control organizations behaved in a passive, lazy, unimaginative way that would be entirely unsuitable for an inform-and-entrust organization. We need just the reverse of that behaviour today: people who are pro-active, energetic and creative. In other words Theory Y behaviour, how those same Theory X people behaved as soon as they got clear of the organization at the end of each day. Fortunately, people tend to behave how they are expected to behave. Tell people what to do and they will wait to be told, but expect people to do what is necessary and they will get on and do it.

The 'law of the situation', as described by Mary Parker Follett in her 1925 paper, makes commands unnecessary. Inform people of the situation, and they will do what any sensible person would agree is required.

One objective of HRM is to foster an organizational culture in which people are regarded as the most valuable asset, not like other resources that are exploited and cast aside when no longer needed. People are where the knowledge and skills reside, those assets that are so important to the organization, and that are lost when people leave the organization. Another role of HRM is to recruit suitable people, then retain and develop them to maximize their value to the organization, rather than seek to minimize the cost, as usual with other resources. HRM planning becomes long-term, pro-active and strategic, rather than short-term, reacting ad hoc to situations as they arise. In the HRM environment, people are expected to commit to self-set goals, and manage themselves in the achievement of those goals, instead of simply complying with imposed goals and controls. Instead of having narrowly defined specialist responsibilities, people today are being asked to work in ambiguous and changing roles, with multiple skills and broad job responsibility. And as they know their own weaknesses better than anyone, they are encouraged to take responsibility for their own training and development.

THE FLATTER ORGANIZATION

This goal had immediate appeal to chief executives: here was a way to make quick savings that didn't appear as a crude cost-cutting exercise. The declared objective was to make bureaucratic organizations more responsive by taking out the middle managers. There are two immediate effects: with fewer levels the chain of command is shorter, and at each level the span of control is wider. Fewer levels allow decisions to pass through quicker, and with wider spans of control, managers have more subordinates who, being less closely supervised, are forced to take more decisions for themselves. Commands and controls are dramatically reduced: there is less buck-passing, and more decisions are made closer to the action.

Whatever the motive, it reduced the hierarchy that 'is a means of executing the wishes of the people at its head, and so other people's views become irrelevant' (Fairtlough, 1994). At about the same time, Peter Drucker (1993) commented that 'Knowledge is the only meaningful resource today. The traditional factors of production ... have become secondary. They can be obtained ... easily, provided there is knowledge.' Clearly a structure that neutralizes knowledge at all levels below the top is entirely unsuited to the needs of the information age. In 1991 IBM had 14 layers in their world-wide hierarchy. By 1994 they had abandoned hierarchy in the UK (except in the factory) in favour of a federation of 32 small self-managing businesses, free to act however they wish, but accountable to a UK board.

Restructuring of this magnitude came at a time when business information systems paralleled the structures they served, and were difficult to change. Thus a command and control hierarchy would have an information system based around a central mainframe database at the top, and a tree-like network stretching out to people in the hierarchy below, with access to information restricted just to that which each person needed to know for their particular job.

Fortunately the general move towards flatter structures came at about the time the Internet was opening up to business. The Internet protocols made it easy to construct networks where everyone's computer is connected to everyone else's, so that whatever new form the organization takes, the information systems can be adjusted to accommodate it. Previously most information system traffic consisted of highly structured formal business data, such as budgets, sales forecasts, orders and production figures. The new private business networks that use Internet protocols and software are called Intranets. The volume of traffic carried by Intranets is far greater than that carried by the old mainframe systems, and the bulk of the extra traffic is informal, unstructured multimedia communications and files being shared between managers and teams in these flatter, more fluid organization structures.

THE LEARNING ORGANIZATION

This was MIT Professor Peter Senge's (1990) slant on how to get an organization to respond quickly to opportunities and threats. His book gave perhaps the most complete practical guide to managers on how to create an organization responsive to the shifting needs of the new era. He covered most of the new themes in the box below, but there was one important omission. Although he recognized that hierarchy posed a threat to his proposals, he never suggested replacing it. His radical proposals were hard enough to swallow; to suggest to big company clients like Ford and Royal Dutch Shell that they should scrap hierarchy could perhaps have been a bridge too far. They might have rejected the whole deal as unworkable.

If the goal of learning is knowledge, there were other authors thinking along similar lines: Ikujiro Nonaka and Hirotaka Takeuchi (1995) proposed the knowledge-creating company, and Tom Peters (1992) writes about knowledge management structures, and the 'new organizing logic'. Peter Drucker (1993) explains why the productivity of knowledge and service workers will demand fundamental changes in the structure of organizations, and totally new organizations. But despite the logic of all these authors, it is unlikely that many companies would ever scrap the hierarchy like Semco did, unless the payoff was bigger, more quantifiable and more certain, and that's just what was promised by the last approach in our list.

BUSINESS PROCESS RE-ENGINEERING

In the same year that Senge's book was published, Mike Hammer (1990) published a paper in the *Harvard Business Review*, titled 'Re-engineering work: don't automate, obliterate'. Instead of using computers to automate the business functions performed in separate departments, Hammer advocated starting from scratch, re-designing organizations around business processes that previously spanned several departments. This, he promised, could reduce costs, and response time – not by ten per cent but to a tenth of what they were. At a stroke, Hammer's paper legitimized and provided the motive for designing the totally new organizational structures that Peter Drucker (1989) said would be needed in knowledge and service work. However, in practice, changing the computer systems proved easier than changing people's deeply held beliefs and prejudices about how work should be organized. Hammer (1993) later admitted that 70 per cent of BPR projects failed to fulfil the promised benefits.

We will return to BPR in later chapters. It is still an important consideration in the design of information systems. More and more people will work in team-based structures, with teams responsible for business processes and projects. Organizations will change organically, as teams dissolve and reform when some projects are completed and others are launched. At any point in time, people will probably be working on several different project teams. Even the armed forces are now less command and control oriented. In knowledge and service work, command and control cannot survive.

Now at Work

New themes for new organizations

Knowledge and service work in the information age requires new types of organization, with new structures, values, methods and objectives. From the written theories, and from the practical examples of early adopters, we can derive some common themes:

- Market competition.
- Non-hierarchical, fluid organization structures.
- Openness, freedom of information, self-management.
- Networks and excellent communications.
- Teams, mutuality, alliances and co-operation.
- Leadership, coaching and co-ordination.
- Shared visions and values, metaphors and ambiguity.
- Knowledge, learning, understanding.
- People orientation, respect for the individual, ethics.
- Commitment, involvement, responsibility, trust.
- Enthusiasm, fun, fulfilment, personal growth.
- Truth, facts, methods, techniques.
- Value and quality determined by the customer.
- Organizational learning and continual improvement of product and service.
- Broader, more complex, more worthy goals.

THE CHALLENGE

The information age is under way. At the start of the industrial age steam was the primary power source, but that soon yielded to the internal combustion engine, and then electric power. We should expect new developments in the information age too. Already we have seen a shift of emphasis from communications to information, and to knowledge. Another shift has been from the individual manager and worker divided and ruled from the top, to teams of workers co-operating and managing themselves. The pace of development shows little sign of slowing, and without doubt new developments will continue. The challenge you face as a manager is how to keep up with developments, and how to pick up on trends that may affect your business. So keep in mind the big picture. When a new development comes along, look at it against the background of other developments. From time to time a development will be a jigsaw piece for your big picture. Don't miss it.

Before moving on to the next chapter, you might find it useful to jot down your answers to the questions below.

REVIEW AND RELATE

These questions may help you review topics in this chapter, and to relate them to your own experience at work.

1 List the three main ways you use IT at work. (Photocopying your bum at the office party doesn't count.) How else could IT help you at work? List three new ways, and the reasons stopping you.

2 How have computers changed your job, and your organization? How might they change your job and organization in the next few years?

3 How far has your organization travelled along a scale from 0 to 10, with command and control at 0 and inform and entrust at 10? Score 10 if your organization conforms to many of the themes in the 'New themes for new organizations' box. Score 0 if you have detailed job descriptions, more than five levels in the hierarchy, poor standards of quality and service, culture of secrecy and mistrust, etc.

4 What IT skills would you like to acquire? How could they help you in your present job and in your career? What first step should you take in acquiring the skills?

5 List the teams that you lead or contribute to in your organization. Include project teams, quality groups, etc. What computer support do teams have? What support would they like to have?

6 How long does it take for your organization to respond to customer enquiries, orders and complaints? How could information technology help?

7 What topic or topics did you find most interesting in this chapter? What books or Web sources might you refer to, for more information? Write the topics on a Post-It memo and stick it on your PC screen.

REFERENCES AND FURTHER READING

Buyers guide – new car prices and specifications, *What Car?*, Dec. 2001, Haymarket Motoring Publications Ltd.

Deming, W. E. (1988). *Out of the Crisis.* Cambridge University Press.

Drucker, P. (1989). *The New Realities.* Heinemann.

Drucker, P. (1993). *Post Capitalist Society.* Heinemann.

Fairtlough, G. (1994). *Creative Compartments – A Design for Future Organization.* Adamantine Press.

Follett, M. P. (1941). *Dynamic Administration.*

Hammer, M. (1990). 'Re-engineering work: don't automate, obliterate.' *Harvard Business Review*, July/August.

Hammer, M. and Champy, J. (1993). *Re-engineering the Corporation. A Manifesto for Business Revolution.* Nicholas Brealey.

McGregor, D. (1960). *The Human Side of Enterprise.* McGraw-Hill.

Nonaka, I. and Takeuchi, H. (1995). *The Knowledge-Creating Company.* Oxford University Press.

Peters, T. (1992). *Liberation Management. Necessary Disorganization for the Nanosecond Nineties.* Macmillan.

Schonberger, R. J. (1990). *Building a Chain of Customers.* Hutchinson.

Semler, R. (1993). *Maverick! The Success Story behind the World's Most Unusual Workplace.* Century.

Senge, P. M. (1990). *The Fifth Discipline. The Art & Practice of the Learning Organization.* Century.

Simon, H. A. (1977). *The New Science of Management Decisions.* Prentice-Hall.

CHAPTER 2

How organizations handle information

Our little systems have their day;
They have their day and cease to be.

'In Memoriam' (1850), Alfred, Lord Tennyson

IN THIS CHAPTER...

- How information is delivered to users in old and new style organizations.
- How to perform and excel in the new, flatter organizations of the information age.
- Some principles and practices to help understand the information needs of individuals and groups.
- Categories and characteristics of information for decision-making, planning and control.
- How control systems work, the different elements in a control system, and how this applies to the design of information systems.
- Computer systems for controlling production and projects.
- Computer systems for the re-engineered, extended enterprise.

INFORMATION AND RESPONSIBILITY

How would it make you feel at work if you were suddenly given access to a stack of sensitive corporate information you didn't need for your job? Probably as nervous as carrying a Tesco bag of banknotes up the High Street to the bank – unless you expect a directorship. Otherwise you'd not want the responsibility, though you'd probably be flattered for being trusted with it.

In the command-and-control organization, everything is predictable and planned in advance. Everyone has watertight job descriptions that don't overlap with anyone else's, and the job descriptions determine the information each person needs. The structure of the information system mirrors the tree-like reporting structure of the organization chart, and access to information is only assigned on a 'need-to-know' basis. This is because if people lower down were trusted to know as much as those higher up, the status and power of those in the upper levels would be undermined, threatening the whole structure. Information means power and influence; at all levels, managers only release it when it benefits them to do so.

OK, this is a stereotype, overstated to make a point. But everyone knows what it feels like to work in that environment, because we all experienced it as children. At home and school, parents and teachers had absolute power and knew everything, while we were powerless and supposed to know only what we were taught. The world is changing fast, but organizations very similar to this stereotype still survive today. Working for them is not all bad: life is simple. You are not responsible for anything outside your job description for a number of hours each month, and in return you get paid a fixed salary.

In the new organization (sorry, here comes another stereotype) people have to grow up quickly. Nothing can be predicted far in advance, there are no detailed job descriptions and no organization chart. People are expected to use a range of skills, and take responsibility for a number of tasks in collaboration with several self-managing work teams. The structure of the information system is a web-like network of links that allows information to be accessed from whoever has it, to whoever might need it, and most information held is freely available to all. Trust and influence is not given by status or position, but earned by the quality and reliability of a person's contributions to team results. Life is complex: you negotiate your roles on teams, share responsibility for everything, and in return you get paid a salary and possibly share a profit-related bonus equally with team members. Exciting but scary.

Enough to make anyone feel nervous initially.

MEETING INFORMATION NEEDS

Working in a command-and-control organization you are told your job, and what information you need for it, and then given only that information. But in inform-and-entrust organizations there is no central planning of information flows. You decide what information you need, and get most of it for yourself by requesting it, or finding it via the 'enterprise portal' – a kind of Intranet home page. That's because your information needs are changing all the time, depending on which teams you are working with, and what roles you are fulfilling.

The system can only work if everyone makes available any information they have that may be useful to others. You have a duty to share it

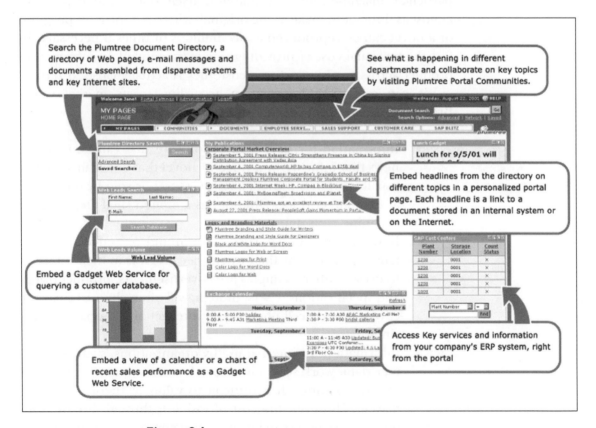

Figure 2.1
Corporate Portal, design by Plumtree. www.plumtree.com

– so easy on the Intranet – so that anyone can access it if they need it. This free, open, broadcast communication is the norm for people who have learned to operate efficiently as a team. It is what Gerard Fairtlough (1994), ex-CEO of Shell Chemicals UK, and founder CEO of Celltech, calls 'communicative competence'.

INFORMATION AS A RESOURCE

Information is a corporate resource, like other resources such as capital equipment, raw materials, or finance. In law, information, such as product designs, best sellers and computer programs, is classed as intellectual property. It requires effort and expense to produce, and has value because copies of it can be sold. The courts recognize the rights of ownership and are prepared to protect them.

But information is different from, say, capital equipment because a particular machine can only manifest itself once, and copies are almost as difficult to make as the original, whereas a software program or a novel can be reproduced easily, millions of times if necessary. In fact the marginal cost of providing one extra copy of an information product across the Internet to a customer is actually close to zero.

We can categorize information according to its market value. Broadly there are three types of information:

- Information for sale, such as software that can be used, or news that informs, or a video or novel that entertains. This is usually privately owned, and access to it is sold by the owner at the market price. Often it has a limited shelf-life, its value declining with time.
- Information for free, such as train and passenger jet timetables, provided by the owners, because it is in their interests to do so. Other examples are advertisements, product prices and specifications. Users, though, will often choose to pay for easy access via cell phones, the Internet and specialist magazines.
- Information for internal use by organizations, such as customer data, work schedules, sales forecasts, budgets and minutes of meetings. It is difficult to value, as there is no legal market. However, the cost of losing it through fire or computer catastrophe can be fatal: most companies never recover from a major loss, and close within two years.

INFORMATION FOR ENTERPRISES

Management information is mostly for internal use of course, but that means internal to a single enterprise, not necessarily just one company. When separate, often competing organizations co-operate in a joint enterprise, defining what is internal can be difficult. The distinction between internal and external is even more difficult to define for the pure 'virtual organization' – that loose, semi-permanent network of designers, manufacturers, marketers and distributors linked through the Internet, but with no premises of its own. In all these examples, information is essential for controlling the inputs and outputs of the enterprise. The products and services offered must be delivered on time, in the requested quantities and to the agreed quality. Progress in achieving these targets must be monitored, so that actual performance can be compared with planned performance, and in the event of a difference, appropriate action taken.

We are talking here about operational information. It is the essential, basic information for running the business, for which the first management information systems were designed. It originally consisted only of alphanumeric characters – letters and numbers – to represent the plans and performance of the business. Now, graphs and charts may be used, but the information still remains highly structured – presented in a simple, consistent format, easy to interpret and free from ambiguity.

For the user to value operational information, it must be:

- relevant – applicable to the user's needs,
- complete – no missing data,
- accurate – a true representation of the circumstances,
- clear – presented in a way that is easy to interpret, and
- timely – up to date, and available promptly

– because these factors enhance its usefulness in decision-making.

On top of this relatively narrow stream of structured operational information, today's information systems carry two-way torrents of highly unstructured, informal, often incomplete and ambiguous multimedia communications. It represents the daily babble of conversation as managers try to make sense of the information they receive from hundreds of digital and non-digital sources – the neurones firing in the 'organization as brain' as it decides what to do.

There is far more information available than can be handled either by the network or by the users, so instead of information being pushed to the users, the new rule is to expect users to pull the information from the system when they need it. It is difficult to categorize this information as it can be almost anything. It includes:

- e-mail, voicemail, computer conferencing;
- searching, updating and analysing data in remote databases;
- joint authors sharing the editing of the same document, same time from different places;
- surveys, multimedia bulletins, computer-aided learning;
- Internet and Intranet searches for information.

The value of operational information is obvious, but the content of informal e-mails and multimedia traffic is so diverse that it is difficult to evaluate individual exchanges. Information systems are open to abuse, in the same way that the plain old telephone was. Of course it is wrong to spend hours at work just chatting to a friend or booking your holidays via the phone or Internet. However, informal social exchanges with workmates, customers, suppliers and alliance partners are essential for getting to know and trust the people you work with. There has to be trust for people to work together. Without it, teams don't perform and alliances don't succeed. Smiles and handshakes are best for building trust, but phone and e-mail chats can sustain it between face to face meetings. It's also important for those in charge of the information system to trust the users. If old command-and-control habits kick in, and they monitor and question the purpose of individual messages, social exchanges will dry up, trust will decline, co-operation will be less efficient and the whole enterprise will suffer. Trust is critical for virtual organizations and especially for alliances of competing organizations. Fortunately, using Internet technology, enterprise Intranets – 'Extranets' delivered via virtual private networks (VPNs) – are easy to set up.

INFORMATION TO AID DECISION-MAKING

A key role of information systems has always been to deliver the information needed for making decisions. Until the 1990s, nearly all enterprises had hierarchical organization structures, so naturally the reporting structures and the information systems had the same tree-like design. But now there are enterprises that have abandoned hierarchy in favour of flatter, team-based structures. They operate with reporting structures and information systems that look more like nets than trees. Thus after a decade of moving to flatter structures and re-engineering around business processes and teams, some organizations are still tall and hierarchical, some are flat and networked, but most are still somewhere in between.

Now at Work

How self-managing work teams at Aughinish Alumina Ltd have achieved the impossible

According to traditional received wisdom, Aughinish Alumina Ltd (AAL) is a strategic impossibility. AAL is a continuous-process plant on an island in the Shannon estuary in Ireland, importing expensive bauxite from Guinea and using standard rate electric power to refine it into alumina. They are selling in over-supplied world markets in competition with low-cost producers in Australia, Brazil and Jamaica, who sit on top of bauxite mines and use cheap electric power and cheaper labour. In 1992, their owners Alcan (Canada) had over-capacity and were selling alumina cheaper than it was being produced by AAL, with little prospect of the market improving. So how come the plant isn't derelict and quietly rusting away in the mists and rain that sweep in from the North Atlantic?

In 1992 AAL was a traditional command-and-control hierarchy, with five levels from Managing Director to front line workforce, reduced from eight levels in 1988. Industrial relations were bad: there were 43 unresolved grievances lodged against the company. Two years later in 1994, using only leaderless teams, 25 per cent fewer people ran the plant to produce 20 per cent more alumina, and AAL were on course to achieve by 1995 their survival target of a $25 per tonne cost reduction on 1992 prices.

How?

In late 1992, a strategy team was formed with the aim of a 20 per cent reduction in controllable costs through –

■ technology gains: stretching plant productivity and efficiency, and,
■ people gains: harnessing the discretionary (knowledge) capability of the workforce.

By November 1993 new values and vision based on openness, trust and self-management had been hammered out in discussion with the workforce, and a team-based organization structure was in place at AAL. The new structure – if that is the right word to describe it – consists of three groupings: the Managing Director and three senior managers; twelve co-ordinator/facilitators; and then the rest – a workforce of around 430 people organized as self-managing teams.

There is a high level of communicative competence and capacity for critical debate throughout the plant, and time and place is made available for this to continue. Individual and organizational learning was the driver for change, and gradually trust was built, as process teams tried out their new empowerment and discovered its reality. Within less than a year, universal scepticism was replaced by virtually total acceptance of the effectiveness of the new organization to deliver the business outcomes. Teams now report a widely-held feeling of common sense about the new way of working. It is not empowerment they experience, more the removal of barriers to sensible working.

By Spring 2000, AAL, now owned by Swiss group Glencore, was producing 1.4 million tons of Alumina per year, up from a previous maximum of 0.8 million tons. Grievances had fallen to about two per year, and the Human Resources Department were selling courses to other enterprises on 'Staff Development for Flat Organizations'.

Sweeney *et al.* (1994).

The way decisions are made depends on the structure, so once again let's look at the two stereotypes – the classical command and control hierarchy and the new inform and entrust flatter organization. Then you may be in a position to gauge for yourself what happens in organizations in between.

DECISIONS IN HIERARCHIES

Managers make their decisions in support of the objectives of their organization. But the types of decision taken – and the information needs – are different at different levels in the organization. According to R. N. Anthony (1990) of Harvard:

■ Senior managers must carry out the strategic planning. They develop overall goals and methods of achieving them.

- Middle managers have the job of management control. They apply and monitor the methods to ensure the goals are achieved effectively and efficiently.
- Junior managers are responsible for task or operational control. They must ensure specific tasks are carried out effectively and efficiently.

The overall picture is that while top managers do more planning, middle and lower managers spend more time controlling to those plans. Of course all managers do some planning and some controlling: it is the proportions that vary at different levels in the organization. The whole picture is summarized in Figure 2.2.

This may seem too theoretical, so let's take an example of a large manufacturing organization that has headquarters staff, and several factories. If we were to look at three managers at senior, middle and junior levels and the decisions they have to take, we might find the pattern to be like that shown in Figure 2.3.

DECISIONS IN FLATTER ORGANIZATIONS

The same types of decision still need making, but are shared more uniformly by all, instead of the important, interesting decisions going to the people at the top, and only the boring repetitive decisions to the people at the bottom. A common format for flatter organizations

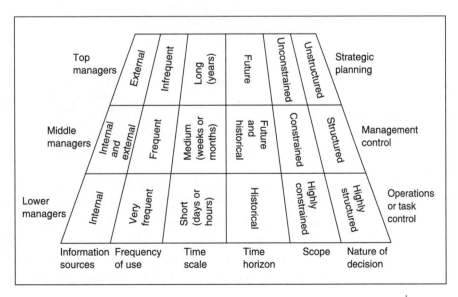

Figure 2.2
Top managers plan; lower managers control

	Top managers (Strategic planning)	Middle managers (Management control)	Lower managers (Operations/Task control)
Job title	Operations director	Factory manager	Production manager
Typical decision	Planning new factories and new products	To find the best way to make new products. To budget for existing products	To work to sales targets. To achieve production targets
Information sources	External: sites, markets, economic and social trends	External: raw materials, new machines and labour. Internal: stocks and production	Internal: orders outstanding, resource availability and deployment
Frequency of decision	Infrequent and irregular	Every quarter, or every month perhaps for budgets	By the hour, or daily
Time scale	New factories, new products take a year or more to come on stream	Budgets are quarterly. New production lines take months to install	Production supervised hourly, monitored daily
Time horizon	Forward looking to steer the organization	Future planning and historical monitoring	Mostly historical, comparing achieved output against targets
Scope	Unconstrained. Searching for the right questions as well as the right answers. What else could or should be planned instead of new factory?	Constrained to meet the plans of top managers	Highly constrained, to meet budgets, targets, forecasts
Nature of decision	Unstructured. Often no clear precedents to follow in decision making	Semi-structured. Many decisions and plans have precedents and methodology, e.g. network analysis, budgeting	Highly structured. Well developed routines and procedures for production and operations management

Figure 2.3
The decisions managers make

is to have three levels of seniority: a few Counsellors responsible for strategy, a few Partners, responsible for the major business units of the organization, then everyone else – Associates – working in teams, primarily responsible for running the day-to-day operations, but with a say in strategy too. In the absence of commonly accepted titles, I have adopted those used at Semco, as described in Chapter 1.

- The Counsellors (directors) are leaders, not dictators. They are responsible for the structure and culture of the organization. They determine the purpose of the organization, engage everyone in an ongoing debate on strategy and adjust it as appropriate.
- The Partners (senior managers), one at the head of each business unit, are accountable to the Counsellors for the performance of the business units, gauged on their contribution to the purpose of the organization, and shareholder value.
- The Associates (other managers, that is, everyone else) operate in self-managing teams. Each team has an elected co-ordinator and is responsible for a permanent business process of the organization, such as Order Fulfilment – from order to payment – or for a temporary development project, such as the launch and handover of a new service facility.

Now at Work

British Petroleum has gone flat

BP Amoco is amazingly flat and lean for a $200bn corporation with 105,000 employees, and 154 business units that span the globe. There is nobody between the general managers of the business units and the small group of operating executives who oversee the businesses with Chief Executive Lord Browne. The way Browne sees it, the people in the business unit – those closest to BP's assets and customers – should run their businesses. But the leaders of this flat decentralized global corporation remain deeply engaged in helping to shape the strategy and drive the performance of the businesses.

How is this possible? It is achieved though BP's Virtual Team Network, and their Intranet. The Virtual Team Network comprises of a growing number of special PCs set up for running groupware, videoconferencing, electronic chalkboards, scanning and faxing. The Intranet has over 40,000 home pages. The General Managers of business units use home pages to list current projects and performance targets. Functional specialists use them to describe the experiences and expertise they have to offer. Every technology discipline has its own site.

All staff are encouraged to list their own expertise in Connect, the name for BP's knowledge and expertise directory. Connect allows staff to contact people with specific expertise who, in a ten-minute phone call, can often help with a problem. The principle is that the most valuable knowledge is stored in people's heads, and the most efficient way of accessing it is via conversation.

The Virtual Team Network started in 1995 as a $13 million pilot project in BP Exploration. It was not led by an IT specialist, but by Kent Greenes from Human Resources. A third of the money went on behavioural scientists who helped people to learn how to work in a virtual environment. It was crucial that people learned to be open and to trust and co-operate, rather than be possessive about information. The project made savings of at least $30 million in the first year alone. It links teams in the Gulf of Mexico with teams off the Shetland Islands and teams in Indonesia, and now it is being extended beyond the organization to contractors working in the North Sea.

INFORMATION TO SUPPORT TEAMS

Hierarchies use teams, though in that environment sometimes teams don't work as well as they might. Project team members are often drawn from existing employees in different departments. For the duration of the project, they are expected to split their time between their permanent role and the project team. Team members are then accountable to two bosses – their department manager and their project manager, thus breaking a basic tenet of the classical organization and creating potential for dispute over priorities.

Network organizations, as noted earlier, use teams extensively. The network organization is a team of teams. Different members serve in several different teams all the time, but it doesn't cause a problem. Usually the teams and the members all belong to the same business unit, and therefore all come under the same boss – but that is largely irrelevant anyway, because the business unit manager neither has time nor inclination to sort out priorities between people who should be managing their own priorities anyway.

Teams cannot function without free and open communications between their members. Without communication there can be no team, only individuals, each doing their own thing. What is needed to ensure good communications between team members? There are only two essentials:

■ channels, or means of communicating, and
■ motivation, or desire to communicate

– and though one can compensate for the other to some extent, both must be adequate. If for instance you know from experience that a colleague is difficult to get hold of on the phone, but you have a strong desire to speak to them, you will persist. If, however, the personal cost in terms of trying unsuccessfully to get through becomes too high, you will probably give up and the communication will fail. There will be longer-term effects too: in future you may not even attempt to communicate because you expect it to be too much effort, and teamwork then becomes seriously weakened.

Now suppose the channels are adequate; you know that with portable phones, voice-mail and e-mail, one way or another you will get through. But let's suppose that in the past you have found communicating with your colleague to be unsatisfactory for one reason or another, then even though the channels are adequate, you probably won't communicate. You have to believe that your colleague will respect your views, value your comments and co-operate. If you know from experience that the most likely response will be stonewalling: 'I can't do anything about that' – or buck passing: 'You'll have to speak to Chris' – or just plain rejection: 'That's your problem, not mine' – then are you going to bother communicating?

So the free flow of information within an organization doesn't just depend on the channels, the systems and the technology; it also depends on the culture, the willingness to work as a team, and the level of respect and trust we have for our colleagues.

INFORMATION FOR CONTROL

Control is essential throughout every type of organization, tall or flat.

Control system concepts

We need to define a few terms first. In control theory, we assume there is a 'system' that has a 'boundary'. 'Inputs' flow into a 'process' which changes them in some way and converts them into 'outputs' that flow out of the system.

A control system has another element, and that is something called 'feedback', where the output of the system is compared with some desired standard and, if there is a difference, the input or the process is adjusted in some way to bring the output back into line.

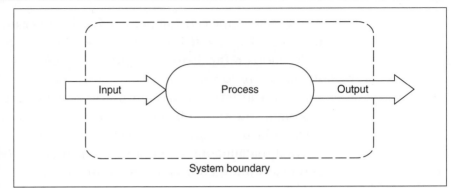

Figure 2.4
Block diagram for
a simple system

We will touch upon systems again later. The concept of a system is important, so here is a familiar example to illustrate the concept. When you take a shower at home, do you have a hot and cold tap that you have to adjust to get the right temperature, or do you have a thermostatically controlled unit?

A simple tap-controlled shower is a system for producing a flow of warm water by mixing inputs of hot and cold water. It can deliver warm water at the temperature you require, but it is not an automatic control system. If someone turns on a hot tap somewhere else in the house, thus reducing the pressure of the hot water input to your shower, the output of warm water goes cold and you have to adjust the shower taps to bring the temperature back within acceptable limits.

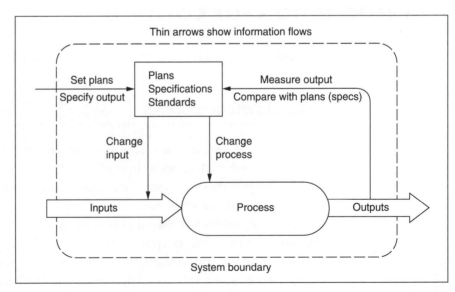

Figure 2.5
Block diagram for
a control system

A thermostatically controlled shower is an automatic control system. Before you step under the shower you provide an information input by means of setting the control knob to the value, or standard, required. Then, the hot and cold inputs can change, but providing they remain within the design limits, the thermostat will automatically compensate for changes in the inputs, to provide a reasonably constant output temperature. If the temperature or pressure of the hot water input falls, the temperature of the output will begin to fall. But as soon as it does, the unit detects that there is a difference between actual output and planned output, increases the proportion of hot water in the input to compensate, and brings the output back in line with the standard.

To summarize, a simple control system has the following elements:

- Input.
- A process for modifying the input in some way.
- Output.
- A standard to which the output should conform.
- Measurement of the output.
- Comparison of the output with the standard.
- Feedback.

Strictly speaking we should refer to this as negative feedback, because the adjustment to be made to the output is always in the opposite direction to the error, and in proportion to the size of the error. For instance, if the shower water is too hot, the mixture is made cooler, and if it is very much too hot it is made very much cooler.

Management control systems work in just the same way in principle. In production control, for instance, if we have to produce 40,000

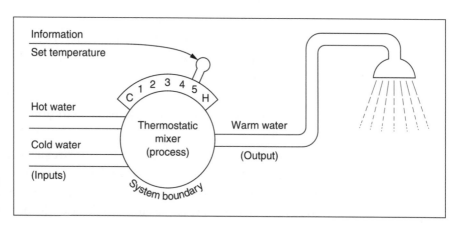

Figure 2.6
Control system
for a shower

units in one month, and by the end of the first week we have produced 8000, we know that we are 2000 behind schedule because the plan requires 10,000 per week for 4 weeks. Negative feedback suggests that we should turn up the wick a bit – increase production because of the shortfall of actual production compared to the plan – by working overtime, or whatever means. Without early monitoring in this way, the error may get even worse and perhaps become irretrievable within the time remaining until the due date.

Computers are ideal for the routine collection of production information and comparing it against the plan. Production planning and control was one of the first business functions to be computerized, after the accounting and payroll functions, nearly thirty years ago.

PRODUCTION CONTROL: MATERIALS REQUIREMENT PLANNING (MRP)

Controlling the production of cars, or mobile phones, or microwave ovens, involves more than just counting the number of finished items each week and then working some overtime if the number is less than planned. To put together a complex assembly of parts regularly and in large quantities involves detailed logistics to ensure the right quantities of components are available when required, and the right amounts of raw materials are available to make those components.

Materials Requirement Planning software has three main inputs:

- The MPS or Master Production Schedule. This is a schedule of the quantities of a finished product to be delivered each week for several weeks ahead.
- The BOM or Bill of Materials. This is the parts list for a finished assembly, arranged in the order in which they are required during manufacture.
- The current inventory or level of stocks of finished products, and parts, and their delivery lead-times.

Remember, the purpose of MRP software is to achieve the Master Production Schedule (the planned future output per week), but at the same time to control levels of raw materials and work-in-progress (WIP) so that overstocking and stock outs do not occur.

The print-outs consist of:

- Reports to production, telling what should be produced and when.
- Reports to purchasing, telling what to buy and when.

It works like this. The MPS (master production schedule) is determined by sales and marketing, partly from forecasted sales, and partly from orders received. It consists of a schedule of numbers of finished assemblies to be produced each week:

On-hand inventory at end of August = 100

Month		September				October				November	
Week No.		37	38	39	40	41	42	43	44	45	46
Forecast demand (gross requirements)		150	150	160	160	150	140	140	140	120	
Projected on-hand inventory (gross availability)		200	50	140	230	80	190	50	160	40	
Production planned (receipts) MPS		250		250	250		250		250		

To find projected on-hand inventory, add on-hand inventory for the preceding week to production planned for the current week. Then subtract forecast demand.

Figure 2.7
Master production schedule for a table lamp

The BOM (bill of materials) for a product is a structured parts list, in the form of a hierarchy, with the top level, level 0, being the finished assembly. The next level down, level 1, consists of the major sub-assemblies from which the final assembly is put together. Level 2 shows the parts from which the sub-assemblies are made, and level 3 may be materials from which the parts are made. For instance a table lamp might have a BOM looking like Figure 2.8.

You can see that the BOM contains information on how the product is actually made. There are sometimes choices as to how the product is assembled and this will affect the BOM. For instance, should the plug be put on the flex before the flex is put on the lamp, or afterwards? Also, the greater the complexity of the final assembly, and the more operations there are to be performed, the greater the number of levels in the BOM. For instance, if our table lamp manufacturer just puts together parts and sub-assemblies made by outside contractors, the BOM may only have three or four levels.

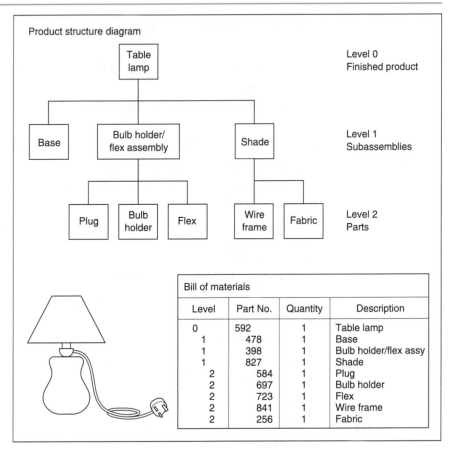

Product structure diagram

| | | Level 0 Finished product |

Table lamp — Level 0 Finished product

Base | Bulb holder/ flex assembly | Shade — Level 1 Subassemblies

Plug | Bulb holder | Flex | Wire frame | Fabric — Level 2 Parts

Bill of materials

Level	Part No.	Quantity	Description
0	592	1	Table lamp
1	478	1	Base
1	398	1	Bulb holder/flex assy
1	827	1	Shade
2	584	1	Plug
2	697	1	Bulb holder
2	723	1	Flex
2	841	1	Wire frame
2	256	1	Fabric

Figure 2.8
Bill of materials
(BOM) for a table
lamp

If, however, the company makes the parts in several stages from raw materials, builds them into sub-sub-assemblies, then sub-assemblies and final assemblies, then the BOM may have twice as many levels.

The third input to the MRP system is the Inventory file, which keeps a tally of raw materials and work-in-progress, together with the lead-times for replenishment, either by making or buying from outside. The lead-times for manufacturing are of course influenced by the size of batch ordered. The software assumes a batch size that strikes a balance between the high cost of holding large batches in stock, and the high cost of lost production when resetting machines if many small batches are planned.

When the MRP system is run, it works backwards from the amounts required each week in the master production schedule to produce a time-phased assembly schedule. It takes into account the lead-times to find out when the sub-assemblies must be started if they are to be ready in time for final assembly. Then working backwards in time again, the software computes when the parts must be started if they are to be ready for making into sub-assemblies. And of course the materials must be ordered soon enough for them to arrive in time to be made into parts.

By chaining back through the stages of production like this, the software works out when to release Purchase Orders to suppliers, and send Works Orders to the shop floor for manufacture, taking into account the delivery times and manufacturing lead times.

In fact, with just a simple product like a table lamp, a production assistant could probably keep tabs on the logistics. But in a manufacturing plant with a range of complex products, each with its own Master Production Schedule and Bill of Materials, and several products perhaps using the same sub-assemblies, the calculations rapidly become unmanageable without a computer.

Some disadvantages of MRP

MRP has been around since the 1970s. It was the only way we knew of handling the logistics for complex products without carrying huge buffer stocks of work in progress at every stage of production. However, MRP requires very heavy investment in hardware, software, maintenance and training. Typically it would take a million pounds to install, and a year for an average size company to get up and running with MRP.

There are many different proprietary brands of MRP but most of them work in time units (called time buckets) of one week, and assume batch production. Taken together, these two factors mean that even though levels of inventory and work-in-progress are 'controlled', there must still be batches of WIP at each stage for the system to function. So a company that installs MRP may be committing itself for the life of the system to working with substantial amounts of WIP. It may be possible to work with smaller rather than larger batch sizes, but even that is far from ideal when competitors are working with just-in-time (JIT) production systems using batch sizes of one unit.

Working with a high level of WIP has several serious disadvantages:

- It ties up capital.
- It makes design changes difficult.
- It makes it difficult to adjust the throughput rate to match sudden changes in demand.

■ It tolerates poor quality manufacture, whereas JIT will not. With JIT, the whole factory stops when a faulty part is produced – a strong incentive to produce zero defects.

PROJECT CONTROL: CRITICAL PATH METHOD

In manufacturing, controlling the flow of products is all-important. In the service sector it is teams and activities that must be co-ordinated and controlled. In both, however, there are due-dates to be met. In manufacturing, MRP is used to work back from the due-date to find out when to start work on products, and in the service sector a similar technique is used to work back to find out when project activities should start and finish. The technique is called network analysis or critical path analysis. The technique originated in the manufacturing sector, but it is even more useful in the service sector. Have you ever started a project with lots of different things to be done before the due-date deadline? If so, you will surely understand the basic principles upon which critical path analysis is based – which are scheduling forward from the present, and scheduling back from the due-date, to see if everything can be fitted into the time available.

Critical path analysis dates back to the 1950s when after World War II several very large projects were under way in the United States, and these were presenting new problems of co-ordination and planning. It is in the nature of projects that they last only for a period of time, during which many different teams and types of activity have to be co-ordinated and brought to a successful conclusion by the due-date. Two groups of researchers were addressing these problems and they came up with variants of essentially the same technique: CPM (Critical Path Method) and PERT (Program Evaluation and Review Technique). PERT was used to control the US Navy's Polaris Missile development programme and was credited with bringing forward the completion date by two whole years.

Few managers get involved with projects as big as Polaris, but PERT can be just as effective in controlling smaller projects such as launching a new service or product, installing a computer system and training staff to use it, or launching a sales training programme.

Here's a simple example to illustrate how it works. Suppose you are in charge of a team responsible for arranging a sales training programme for your organization. You have listed all the components of the project. These are the things or 'activities' that members of your team must do, and the times needed for doing them – the activity 'durations' in days:

List locations	2
Select locations	4
Plan topics	3
Get speakers	7
Arrange speaker travel plans	5
Design and print brochure	14
Final check on travel plans	8
Take reservations	6
Run training programme	10

The technique has three phases:

- The planning phase when you decided what activities will make up the project.
- The analysis phase when you use the computer to schedule the activities.
- The control phase when you monitor the project, and hold it to plan.

Planning

In our example, the planning phase is complete, and the results are shown in the table above.

Analysis

During the analysis phase, we must show if some activities are dependent on other activities being completed first. For instance, in building a house, you cannot plaster the walls until the walls are built, so plastering must be scheduled to follow on, in series, after wall-building. However, there will be other independent activities as well. For instance, once the walls are built the plumber and electrician need not work in any special order. Either can do their part first before the other, or they can both work at the same time in parallel.

Returning now to our sales training programme, clearly the speaker travel plans cannot be arranged until the locations have been finalized. This is a dependent relationship. However, it is OK for the speaker travel plans to be arranged at the same time as the brochure is being prepared, because these activities are independent.

Project managers used to sort out all these logical relationships by drawing arrows on paper to represent activities, with the dependent arrows chaining across the page one after the other, and the independent activities shown in parallel. This created a kind of network effect, with the arrows fanning out from the start point on the left of the page, and then converging onto the finish point on the right-hand side.

Before the PC, the network was the main analytical device for determining the critical path – the longest chain of activities through the network. The longest chain is the shortest time in which the whole project can be completed. The network was the main device for scheduling the activities, but it was a poor device for communicating the schedule to those who were responsible for performing the activities, and so the results were usually displayed in the form of a Gantt chart (horizontal bar-chart).

Until PC programs were available, you needed expert draughting skills and a degree in logic to draw up a network – as you can see from Figure 2.9, an old example for a chemical plant construction project.

Now, however, computers do it all, rescuing thousands of business students and project managers from ever again having to draw up a network chart. All that's necessary is for you to enter the list of component activities along with their durations, and then link together any dependent activities in the appropriate order. Then at the click of a mouse, you can display or print out the schedule either as a PERT network or as a Gantt chart (see Figures 2.10 and 2.11).

And what is more, you can plan several different projects and enter the human resources assigned to all activities on all the different projects. The computer can then check through all the projects and flag clashes where the same resource is being called for by several activities at the same time. Then you can let the computer reschedule to avoid clashes, or you can do it manually yourself. However, if you work in a team-of-teams organization you might think this is taking central planning a stage too far. Resources are resourceful: people are good at working round conflicts.

It's up to you how you use it. The computer has converted what used to be a somewhat limited and laborious technique into a simple, powerful tool for supporting many aspects of a project manager's routine.

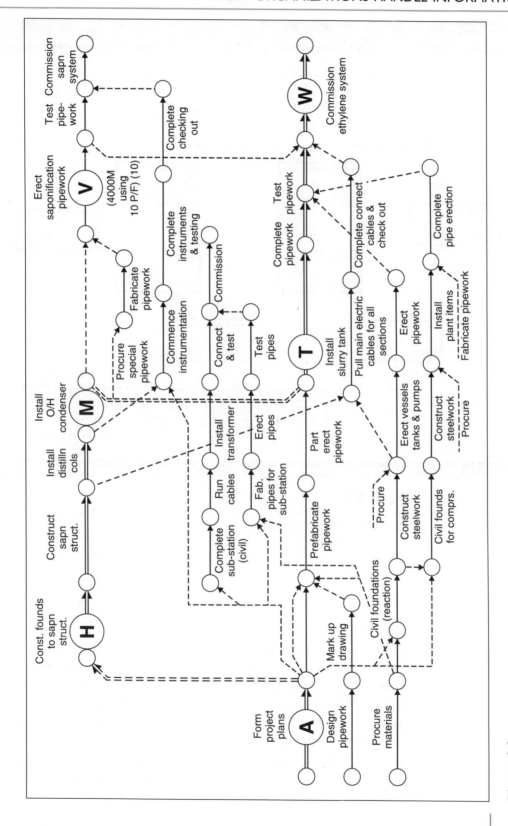

Figure 2.9
Network of activities for a plant construction project. Can you spot the critical path?

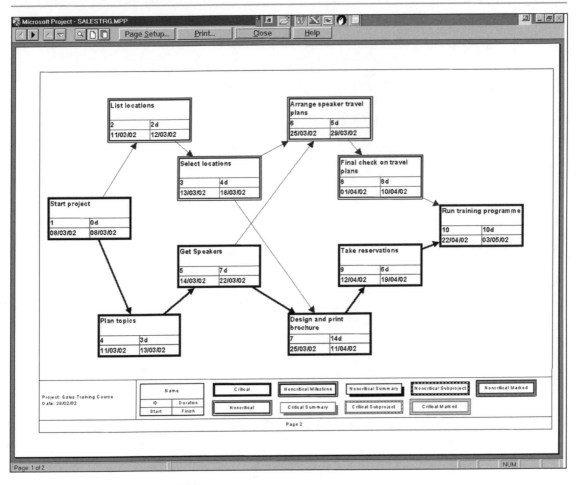

Figure 2.10
Network for arranging a sales training programme (prepared using
Microsoft Project software)

Control

If a critical activity (one lying on the critical path) is delayed by so
much as a day, the whole project will be delayed by the same amount.
The critical path is just one of many chains of activities that run from
start to finish through the network – but it is the longest one. It
therefore determines the shortest time in which the project can be
completed. All the other shorter chains through the network have
more time available than is strictly necessary for their completion,
so it probably won't matter if they over-run by a day or two, so long
as they don't grow to be longer than the critical path. Typically per-

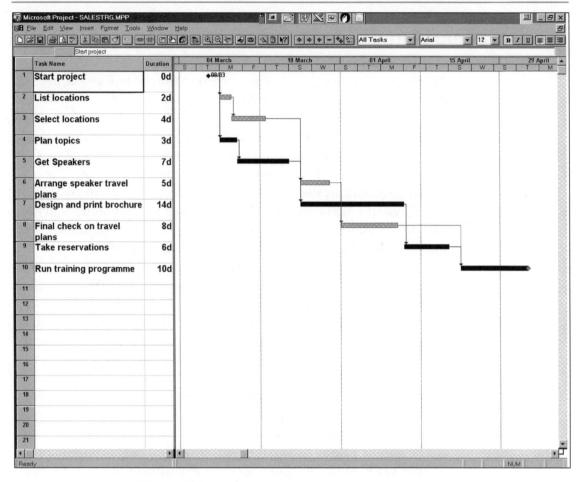

Figure 2.11
Gantt chart for arranging the sales training programme (prepared using
Microsoft Project software)

haps less than a quarter of all the activities in a project may turn out to
be on the critical path, and that is what makes this technique so
popular with managers. It allows you to focus on those few critical
activities where your attention will be most effective.

During this control phase it is important to make sure everyone
knows when they are working on critical activities, and the importance of sticking to schedule.

Microsoft Project is one of the best-known examples of project
planning software. Most suppliers of management information systems offer their own proprietary versions, bundled with other modules in an information system package.

ENTERPRISE RESOURCE PLANNING

The word 'enterprise' can mean 'a corporation or business firm', and it can also mean 'a bold and difficult undertaking', perhaps conducted jointly by more than one firm. Enterprise Resource Planning (ERP) is therefore the perfect title for a solution that integrates all the computing needs of a corporation into one package, and also supports co-operation with suppliers, partners and customers.

ERP was born in the 1990s. It is the direct descendant of MRP in the 1970s and MRP2 in the 1980s, each generation adding functionality to the functions inherited from the previous generation. MRP was only for planning materials requirements, but MRP2 could also plan other resources such as machines, operators and finance, as well as materials – but only in the Production Department. This was still in the days when functions and departments ran from top to bottom of many organizations, like silos or stovepipes. Operations and Finance Departments were run separately and had their own systems. Communications between them were few, and often adversarial rather than co-operative. Thus it seemed natural for payrolls and accounting to run on a separate computer system from that used by production and stock keeping, even though both departments used the same basic data on quantities and costs of production.

The aim of ERP is to integrate all the computing requirements of an enterprise, so that only one up-to-date version of basic data is held, and is available to everyone who needs it. The business case for ERP was that the IT assets of organizations had been built up over many years, and were poorly structured for the new competitive markets. Businesses were trying to re-engineer around business processes that spanned several different departments, and the separate computer systems in different departments could not support these new business processes. For example, when a sales enquiry was received, it was not possible over the phone in real time to check stocks, give a price, quote delivery, reserve an item and quote an order number. Too many separate incompatible systems were involved.

In theory there are two different approaches to enterprise computing. The one-stop-shop approach is to ask an ERP vendor to install an integrated suite of programs to replace many of the old applications packages. Enterprise Applications Integration (EAI) is the other approach, where you install 'middleware' at the hub of a set of links, like spokes, to each of the legacy applications that you want to keep. You can then add further modules to enable transactions with suppliers, partners and customers. The middleware acts as interpreter, translating messages flowing between the incompatible systems. In practice, many enterprise projects are achieved through a mixture of these methods. Leading suppliers of ERP solutions include SAP, the German company with its R/3 software, and American companies PeopleSoft and Oracle.

All enterprise solutions are extremely complex projects, and managers tend to underestimate the problems and changes that staff must make to their work practices. At the same time as learning how to operate the new information system and follow new work procedures, staff must adjust to a new organization structure and culture. Many employees feel the influence of the customer for the first time. They have to take on new decision-making responsibilities, perform several different roles, and handle much more information. And on top of all that, the business cycle speeds up, the new processes taking minutes or hours to complete instead of days or weeks.

So much is different after ERP: for employees it is like working for a new company, and for the company it is like having every employee starting on their first day with the company. Business performance will inevitably follow a J-curve before the benefits kick in. Here is what Steve Baldwin of Deloitte Consulting said in February 1999, after interviewing 62 US businesses that had implemented ERP packages from SAP, Oracle, PeopleSoft or Baan: 'When we interviewed businesses, four out of five said implementing ERP software hurt the business in the first sixteen months.'

ERP was supposed to be the final down-payment for a sustainable future, but in IT there's always something new just around the corner, as we shall see shortly.

I hope Chapters 1 and 2 have helped explain the revolutionary changes occurring in the world of work caused by information technology. We will return to some of the topics in more detail later, but now it's time to get personal. In the next two chapters, there are opportunities for you to fill in any gaps in IT and communications skills you may need to help manage your work, your team and your business.

REVIEW AND RELATE

Here again, some questions to help you review this chapter, and relate it to your experience at work.

1 Do you work, or have you worked, in a self-managing team, or have you contributed to a project? Did your team communicate outside of face to face meetings? How well were communications between team members supported? What IT support would you like to have, next time you work with a team or on a project?

2 Estimate the percentages of your time at work that you spend on each of the following activities: strategic planning, management control, and operational control. From this analysis, would R. N. Anthony classify you as a junior, a middle or a senior manager?

3 Give an example of a decision you often have to make at work with inadequate information. What extra information would make the decision easier or safer next time? What IT or other infrastructure could deliver the information you need?

4 Who inside your organization receives the results of your work? Do you regard them as your customers? If you were to ask them how you could improve the quality of service or product that you deliver to them, how would they answer? Do you fear that if you asked them, they would gain at a cost to you? If you were part of a process team including people upstream and downstream from you, could discussions lead to everyone gaining?

5 Are you required to operate to an annual budget? Do you have regular monthly or quarterly budget reviews? If so, use control system terms (input, standard, feedback, etc.) to describe the review as a financial control system.

6 The table below lists in the first column the seven activities making up a complete project. In the second column are the activities that immediately precede each activity, and in the third column are the durations of each activity in weeks.

Activity ref.	Depends on	Duration
A	–	2
B	–	5
C	–	1
D	B	10
E	A, D	3
F	C	6
G	E, F	8

(a) By hand, draw the network for these activities. (You don't need the durations for this.) Now label each arrow with its activity letter, and its duration. At this stage, leave the event circles empty. Make sure all the arrows point forwards to the right.

(b) Divide each event circle with a vertical line. Now do a forward pass through the network, starting at the first event on the left and working to the right. In the left half of each event circle, put in the earliest time each event can occur. Remember that an event cannot occur until all routes through to that event have been completed. Thus the earliest event time for each event is equal to the length of the longest route through to that event.

(c) What is the shortest time that the project can be completed in? It is the same as the earliest event time for the last event on the right.

(d) Now fill in the latest event times by doing a backward pass, starting at the last event on the right and working back towards the left. Put the latest event times in the right half of each event circle. The final event on the right will have a latest event time equal to its earliest event time if the project is to be completed in the shortest possible period. The penultimate event(s) will have a latest event time equal to the latest event time of the final event less the duration of the activity in between. If there is more than one path leading back to an earlier event, it is the longest path that should be used to find its latest event time.

(f) Mark up the critical path. It is easily recognized as the sequence of activities linking all the events which have their earliest event time equal to their latest event time.

7 A promoter wishes to present a summer concert in the gardens of a mansion near Oxford. She decides to use PERT to help manage the project, and the time estimates for the activities are as follows:

Activity reference	Description	Immediate predecessor	Time estimate
A	Select musicians	–	5
B	Contracts with agents	A	10
C	Arrange travel & accommodation	B	14

D	Radio, adverts, promotion	B	7
E	Print tickets, programmes	B	6
F	Sell tickets	D, E	21
G	Confirm travel & accommodation	C	11
H	Hire ticket sellers	C	16
J	Rehearsals	H	2
K	Present concert	G, F, J	3

(a) Draw the network for the project and indicate which activities are on the critical path.

(b) What is the shortest time that the project can be completed in? How might knowing this be useful to the organizer?

(c) If the project is delayed, it may be necessary to reduce the project duration by shortening an activity. One such proposal is to contract out the ticket selling so that activity H takes only 1 day. What effect would this have on the expected project duration?

8 Prepare a critical path network for the following activities involved in the preparation of a cheese and pickle sandwich. Assume you have as many helpers as necessary. Determine the critical path, and calculate what the shortest 'project' time will be. Of all the activities originating from the first event in the network, which one could have the latest starting time? How late could it start?

Activity	Duration (seconds)
Get bread from bin	60
Unwrap and cut two slices of bread	50
Get cheese from shopping bag	40
Cut one slice of cheese	50
Get pickle from cupboard	240
Put pickle in assembled sandwich	40
Get butter from refrigerator	80
Put butter on two slices of bread	70
Assemble two buttered slices and cheese	40
Cut sandwich in two and serve	40

9 A manufacturer of consumer electronics, in conjunction with an advertising agency, is planning an advertising project to launch a new personal computer. The project will involve newspaper and television advertising and will conclude with a press conference. The project activities are as follows:

Activity reference	Description	Timw (weeks)	Depends on
A	Plan campaign	2	–
B	Contracts with newspapers	3	A
C	Write text	3	A
D	Take photographs	4	C
E	Prepare artwork	2	D
F	Artwork to newspapers	1	B, E
G	Contract with film maker	3	A
H	Contracts with TV companies	3	A
J	Write film script	4	A
K	Make film	6	J, G
L	Film to TV company	1	H, K
M	Arrange press conference	2	F, L

Draw a network for the advertising project. Show which activities are critical. What is the total project duration?

The agency wishes to shorten the overall project time, and is considering the following ideas:

(a) the photographs for the newspaper advertisements can be taken while the accompanying text is being written.
(b) by allocating extra resources, the duration for agreeing the film contract can be shortened.
(c) by allocating extra resources, the duration for making the film can be shortened.

Which one of these should the agency choose in order to shorten the project? How many weeks can be saved?

REFERENCES AND FURTHER READING

Anthony, R. N, Dearden, J. and Bedford, N. M. (1990). *Management Control Systems* (5th edition). Richard D. Irwin Inc.

Curwin, J. and Slater, R. (1996). *Quantitative Methods for Business Decisions* (4th edition). International Thomson Business Press.

Fairtlough, G. (1994). *Creative Compartments – A Design for Future Organization.* Adamantine Press.

Sweeny, P. and Taylor, J. (1994). 'A case study of transition in a continuous process company towards empowerment using self-managed work teams.' Paper at HRM Conference. Nottingham Business School, 14–15 December.

CHAPTER 3

Information and personal effectiveness

> 'I wonder if anyone is born to obey,' said Isobel. 'That may be why people command rather badly, that they have no suitable material to work on.'
>
> 'Parents and Children' (1941), Ivy Compton-Burnett.

IN THIS CHAPTER...

- Tips on how to influence people.
- How to analyse, understand and explain information.
- How to make numbers more comprehensible.
- How to structure a brilliant presentation.
- Using statistics to save money and be fair to customers.

BETTER COMMUNICATORS MAKE BETTER MANAGERS

Do you know Aida? Aida guides me when I have something important to say. You might spot that when I introduce you later, if you haven't already met. In this chapter you can pick up some tips and skills to enhance your individual effectiveness at work. These same skills may also improve your team's communicative competence, the group skill rated highly by Fairtlough that we touched upon in the previous chapter.

To be effective at work it helps to be a good communicator, and that does not mean sending lots of people lots of information. We are opening a real can of worms: human communication is a huge subject, involving sociology and psychology as well as personal, practical and technical skills. The focus of course will be on computer skills, but set in the context of human communications generally. We will visit the following topics:

- Cultural environment.
- Push and pull.
- Message structure and content.
- Personal and technical skills.

Cultural environment

The most important environmental factor affecting human communications at work is the culture of the organization. The culture is a set of values, norms and expectations that people hold. Is there a culture of individualism, or team work? Are people generally supportive and trusting of each other, or competitive? Are people open, honest and truthful about what they believe, or does a blame culture make people secretive, devious and careful about what they say?

Teams of knowledge workers cannot perform without norms of truthfulness, openness and trust. Such teams can only perform in hierarchies if they insulate themselves from the prevailing organizational culture. Teams must form, storm, norm, and then perform. At the storming stage, members must learn to be open and truthful about what they believe. Of course this exposes differences of opinion that must be resolved, often heatedly. When the storming is over, the group accepts norms of behaviour for resolving differences. This done, the groundwork is laid for the good, open communications that are essential for the team to perform. For teams in a command-and-control culture, it is a kind of micro co-opetition in which members agree not to compete but to co-operate while in the temporary alliance of the team.

Why are truth, openness and trust so important for team members? Because without these values, no joint development of ideas can occur. In strict command-and-control hierarchies, for instance, there are always more senior people around, who have the power to promote or fire you. This has two obvious effects: you won't disagree with your boss's ideas; and you won't contribute to a colleague's ideas, because you will benefit more if your own idea prevails. This kills any possibility of dialogue taking place. Dialogue is a constructive exchange that builds on a good idea to a new, better idea. Dialogue never gets beyond the first rung when participants don't contribute, or remain locked in a destructive battle for their own idea. It is why, as Senge (1990) explains, 'a team of committed managers with individual IQs of above 120 can have a collective IQ of 63'.

In the short term there is little you can do if the environment is hostile to good communications – other than try to promote a friendly micro environment for your team.

Push and pull

The enterprise Intranet allows information to be posted on pages that are accessible to all who might need it. The enterprise portal is the one-stop self-service shop for information. It has directories and search engines to make it easy to find and pull off the information you want. It is now a pointless waste of everyone's time to push routine reports onto a long circulation list of often reluctant readers. Circulation lists usually exclude more people than they include, and so they are not the most appropriate mechanism to foster openness and trust. If you really must draw the attention of people to the new information on one of your web pages, send them an e-mail but make it brief. Put the main message in the subject line: 'July Sales up 5 per cent' – for instance. Then put only your web page address in the body of the message. When double-clicked, it will take the reader straight to the page.

We must all take joint responsibility for communicative competence, the ultimate achievement of which is when, on hearing the briefest of verbal prompts from a member, a team knows instantly what the member is thinking. It works on the football field and it can work for business teams too. This allows fast and efficient communication, the equivalent of quick thinking in the 'organization as brain' analogy.

The paradox to resolve is how to be open and free with information, without clogging the channels with information. The politics of command and control made it important to be heard saying the right things, but in today's team-based organizations it is important to be seen doing the right things. So, only use e-mails for short, urgent messages, or to be blunt, stop being so pushy.

Message structure and content

A technical model of communication is often portrayed as in Figure 3.1:

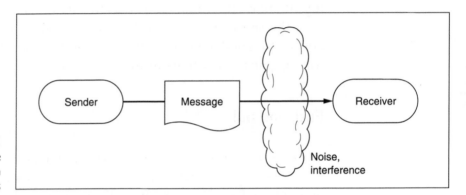

Figure 3.1
A model of the communication process

It has three stages:

- A sender prepares and transmits ...
- A message via some medium to ...
- A receiver who receives and understands the message, thus completing the communication process.

Or does it? A managerial model of communication should have a fourth stage: action. The essence of management is getting results through people. It is not enough, therefore, if the receivers of your message just receive and understand it. They must behave differently in some desired way from how they would otherwise have behaved. That is the ultimate test of effectiveness. So how can you improve your chances of securing action? Remember Aida. The letters stand for:

Attention.
Interest.
Desire.
Action.

– the milestones past which a salesperson must lead a prospect on the rocky road to Action: reaching for cheque book or credit card.

Not many people can get away with an autocratic management style these days, so if you want action, you must sell your message. The best sales people can get inside their prospect and see things from their perspective. You should try to do this too. If you are about to send a message to your boss, or your team, what have they been banging on about recently? Is it reducing costs, or increasing market share? Whatever it is, try to get their attention by relating your message to their interests. For an e-mail, use words in the subject line that relate to their interests. That will get their attention (step one) before the message is opened, and increase the chance that it will be opened sooner rather than later. For a PowerPoint presentation, don't waste the potential of the title page – think carefully about how to grab attention, and start to develop interest (step two).

To develop interest, stay inside your prospect. Often at work you may need to include technical material in a message, but unless you are addressing engineers, your audience may find little intrinsic interest in technicalities. So, in the words of R. O. Kap, who advised on writing technical reports, 'consider the needs of your reader'. The first need of your reader (or audience) is to see the relevance of the message. If it is not seen as relevant, it will be skim-read at best, then binned, deleted, forgotten . . .

Your audience may also need some ancillary knowledge in order to understand the main message. Ask yourself: 'If I were my reader, what would I need to know in order to understand this message?' If you don't know your audience well enough to answer this question, keep the main message uncluttered, and put explanations in a glossary or footnotes.

By now your prospect has seen the relevance and understood the message, but will not yet have bought in to it. Time now to be open about the advantages, risks, costs and benefits. If you are sold on the idea, there's a good chance you will be able to create desire (step three) in your audience. Once they have bought it – made it their own – they will be committed to action (step four). But remember, to buy something, there is always a personal cost. To buy a new idea may require dumping commitment to some old favourites, so try not to price yourself out of the market. Allow time, and don't ask for too much, too soon. Describe how good it will be in the new scenario: sell (that old chestnut) the sizzle, not the steak.

Personal and technical skills

Good salespeople are probably born, not made, but innate personal skills are not the only requirement. Selling also requires the ability to refine and simplify the message, especially when selling complex ideas. This is especially the case where numbers are involved, in presentations and reports for instance. Remember, consider the needs of your reader – and that means don't expect your reader to work hard to understand what you are trying to say. Do the work for your reader – refine and simplify. Numbers presented as a table make most people's eyes glaze over, but when totals, sub-totals and averages are displayed as charts, their significance is instantly obvious.

Why are figures difficult to understand? Because they are in code, an abstraction that we have no innate ability to handle. Numeracy has to be learned. So too does literacy, but words are more natural, and easier to learn.

We could construct a scale of abstraction, for ease of understanding, for different types of message. If you hear a scream, instantly you are alert, heart pounding. Nothing abstract about a scream – even your cat understands it. If you encounter a dog, you can see instantly whether it is friendly or not – and again, so could your cat, because both cats and humans can process images and recognize shapes and patterns almost instantly. Moving up the scale from these primal messages, the simplest level of abstraction is a picture, then the spoken word, usually learned by humans before the age of one year old. Next come written words, and then numbers.

So, in considering the needs of your readers, save them from having to work hard to understand the numbers in your presentation. Convert the numbers to shapes and images. By using charts and graphs you move the message down the scale of abstraction and make it easier to understand. Make no mistake: this is the right approach. It is not pandering to the lowest ability, or treating adults like children. It is doing all you can to ensure your message is received loud and clear – and understood.

Before we leave this topic, I have some anecdotal evidence that supports the argument for making numbers simple to understand. For many years I have taught quantitative methods to young managers on Masters courses, and the range of abilities on entering the courses has always been very wide. Some managers dropped mathematics at school at the age of 14 years. This does not make them bad managers; we all have ways of hiding our weaknesses and compensating for them. So when you see someone nodding sagely while viewing your figures, don't just assume they understand them as fully as you do.

FINDING AND SHOWING THE MESSAGE IN THE NUMBERS

All enterprises generate a torrent of figures, recording sales revenues, stocks held, quality levels, production volumes, customer complaints, advertising expenditure, to name just a few. This river of data carries dispersed within it valuable infoormation that the enterprise needs to succeed in global markets.

Competitive advantage depends on continual improvement, and knowing how to achieve it. Advantage is gained by having sufficient people with the skills to analyse the growing flood of data, to present it convincingly and achieve the necessary improvements. Computers can help by doing the spade work, but they cannot ask the questions that might lead to insights on how to add value and delight customers.

You can probably see where this argument is heading: as a knowledge worker you need some basic analytical skills to help manage a business today.

In Chapter 1 you read how Total Quality Management was an important step in the transition from hierarchical to team-based organization. TQM requires teams to work obsessively on improving the quality of processes. Get the process right, and you won't need to waste money inspecting the output for conformance. For instance, if you manufacture in batches, when a faulty part is made, often the fault is not discovered until later, and by then it is difficult to trace what went wrong and put it right. If you manufacture without batches, one at a time just-in-time (JIT), faults will be discovered instantly, because the part cannot be hidden in a batch and passed down the line to the next stage. If one machine stops, the whole line stops, so mistakes cannot be covered up. An investigation can discover what went wrong, and the process can be adjusted to avoid that particular error ever occurring again. Thus each new error forces a new improvement in the process.

In the 1970s when in the West we were installing MRP computer systems to plan and control production in batches, in Japan they were perfecting their kanban system of producing just one item at a time, using nothing more technical than a white square painted on the floor between each stage of production, just big enough to hold one item of work in progress. Whereas we had an army of workers paid only to follow instructions issued by computer, and an army of middle managers, quality controllers and programmers to keep the whole system running, in Japan teams of production workers were meeting after work in 'quality circles' to analyse results and improve the process. They were expected to acquire the necessary analytical skills, and in companies like Nissan, in Sunderland, every employee is given their own Kaizen manual (kaizen means 'continual improvement'), showing how to use Kaizen tools – mostly basic statistics – to analyse problems. No prizes for guessing if it was kanban or MRP that produced superior quality and productivity that won markets all around the world.

A scientific approach

TQM is the western version of Kaizen. Both are founded on the requirement for everyone to use a scientific approach to find ways of improving things at work.

The Scientific Method was first described by Francis Bacon, Lord Chancellor to King James I, and a founder member of the Royal Society. Bacon, who was a contemporary of Sir Francis Drake and Sir Walter Raleigh, proposed the method in his book *The Advancement of Learning* (1605) as a basis for adding to knowledge and enabling understanding.

The method has four steps:

1 Observe some effect or phenomenon, and define it precisely.
2 Hypothesize, or guess its cause.
3 Experiment by running a test, in order to ...
4 Prove a relationship, and thereby construct a theory relating cause and effect.

This method has formed the basis for advancing our understanding in every scientific field of study.

There are critics who feel that for busy managers it all sounds a bit too academic. That's why quality guru the late Dr Deming proposed the PDCA or Plan–Do–Check–Amend cycle that has been taken to heart and used to such effect in Japan, and why IBM used a similar 4-step cycle, Analyse–Solve–Implement–Maintain, as part of their Market Driven Quality programme. These cycles and the one used by 'learning organizations', Question–Theory–Test–Reflection, are all loosely based on Bacon's original supposition, and they all require evidence to be analysed and small experiments or tests to be carried out, to discover how to improve. This is what the Kaizen tools are for.

THE KAIZEN TOOLS

We will examine the more important of these, starting with the simplest, and finishing with tools based on the Normal curve. This is more difficult to understand, but is absolutely fundamental to an understanding of how to achieve consistent quality. Once you grasp its significance it will alter for ever the way you perceive a quality failure.

These are the tools we shall examine:

Pie, bar and scatter diagrams.
Pareto diagrams.
Ishikawa diagrams.
The Normal curve, and standard deviation.
$\bar{X}$ and R charts.

The tools can be drawn on a marker board or on paper without using a computer. You can read how in the pages that follow, preferably with a pencil and notepad at hand. A fairly accurate, ten second sketch of a chart can add real punch to an ad hoc presentation. For a given set of figures you should know roughly what the chart will look like. Then when you use your PC to prepare charts (as described later), you can check the output and spot any mistakes.

First, a brief description of each of these tools.

Pie, bar and scatter diagrams

You must be familiar with pie and bar diagrams. They are widely used in newspapers and magazines – media that are dedicated to good communication. The power of these diagrams lies in their simplicity. They make figures less abstract, easy to understand and imbued with significance. Diagrams are brilliant because they analyse as well as communicate. They are widely used by teams to analyse evidence and gain insight into problems.

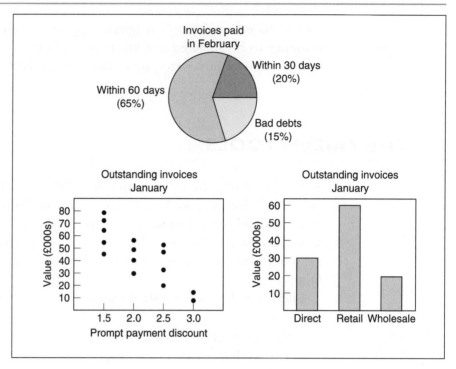

Figure 3.2
Pie, bar and
scatter diagrams

The scatter diagram is another simple chart, not quite so familiar perhaps, used for showing whether there is a connection between two variables. Do sales increase when spending on advertising is increased? By charting sales against spending, the relationship, if any, is revealed.

Pareto diagrams

These diagrams are used for 80/20 analysis. A century ago, the Italian economist Vilfredo Pareto showed that it was common in most nations for about 20 per cent of the population to own about 80 per cent of the wealth of the nation. These same proportions crop up in many business circumstances. For instance, 20 per cent of items in a warehouse commonly account for 80 per cent of the value of all items in the warehouse. The ability to separate the vital few from amongst the many less important items is a powerful aid to focus your attention where it can be most effective.

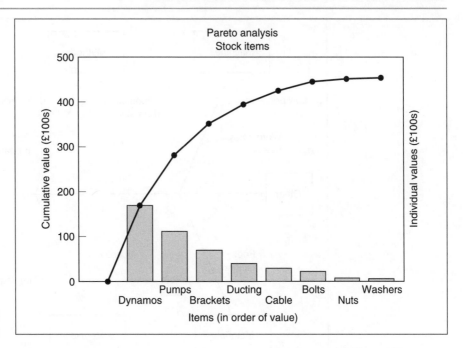

Figure 3.3
Pareto diagram

Ishikawa diagram

The Japanese professor Kaoru Ishikawa invented this cause–effect, or fishbone, diagram. He designed it for teams to use when analysing problems. It is less useful for communication purposes. Its purpose is to help a team develop a comprehensive view of all the factors that might influence a problem. It was intended for use by quality circles – groups of about ten people – in a room with a marker board.

Normal curve and standard deviation

These are fundamental to the study of variation. If you are serious about improving quality, there is no alternative – you must get familiar with the Normal curve and its standard deviation. Why? Because top quality is impossible where there is significant variation, and to reduce variation is the same as to improve quality. High variation means low predictability. If a product or service varies each time you supply it, your customers can't know what to expect, and quality assurance is all about meeting and exceeding your customers' expectations. For instance, in a supermarket, shopping can take just 20 minutes – or as much as an hour if long queues form. This is high variation and low predictability that most customers will seek to avoid.

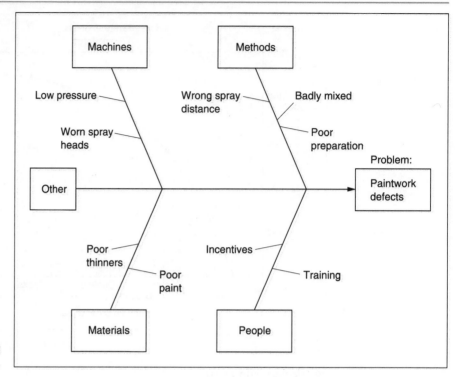

Figure 3.4
Ishikawa diagram

Some will shop elsewhere to avoid the risk of an hour-long ordeal, even when shopping elsewhere takes longer on average.

Variation can be of two types: that due to a special, assignable cause, and that due to many common, unassignable causes that mostly cancel each other out but occasionally stack up one way or the other.

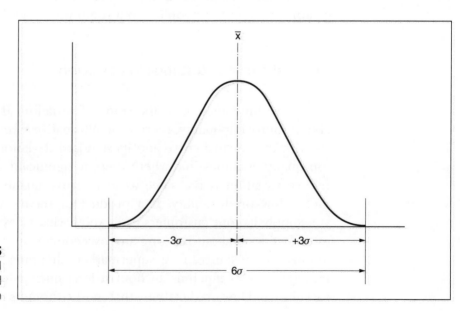

Figure 3.5
Normal
distribution and
standard deviation

Unfortunately in practice it is difficult to tell the two apart, and if you treat a chance stacking up of common causes believing it to be a special cause – or vice versa – you will actually increase the amount of variation and make the situation worse! For example, suppose you are in a rifle target shooting competition and you want to maximize your score with five shots. If you were to fire all five shots without adjusting the sights you wouldn't expect all the shots to go through the same hole in the target; there will be some natural variation due to common causes, and the shots will form a group of five holes – not too far apart, one hopes. Now suppose you start the competition knowing that your sights are reasonably well but perhaps not perfectly adjusted, and the first shot falls a little to the left of the bulls-eye. You could adjust the sights to compensate before firing the next shot, and continue like that each time compensating for the error of the previous shot. Or, you could fire all five shots without adjusting the sights, and in fact this will result in a tighter grouping and a higher score.

Treating common-causes variation as if it were a special cause is what Dr Deming refers to as tampering with the process. In business a manager who makes an immediate adjustment to procedures, because a single customer has complained, is tampering. The knee-jerk reaction of the macho manager usually does more harm than good in the long run. Many UK managers don't understand these statistical concepts: all Nissan employees are encouraged to learn about them.

X̄ and R charts

These can be used for monitoring our processes for supplying services and products. The average and range for samples of five are charted, making it possible to distinguish between common and special causes, and detect even slight changes in a process before it results in out-of-spec output. The charts are simple to use, but do require some statistical knowledge to set up. You may hear the term 'six-sigma' bandied about by employees from IBM, Motorola and other quality conscious companies. What they are referring to is the expected range of common cause variation that is controlled by using $\bar{X}$ and R charts.

These then are some of the kaizen tools needed to support the myriad of small experiments that should be going on at all levels

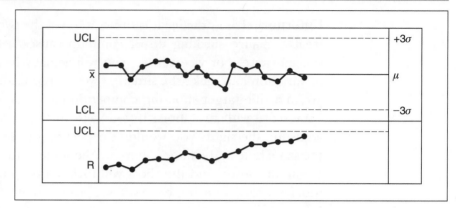

Figure 3.6
$\overline{X}$ and R charts

everywhere in your organization if it is to keep up with rising customer expectations. The organizational culture should encourage everyone to make small experiments, and recognize that many of these will fail. Then, people will be prepared to take small risks and not be afraid of the errors that come with trial and error. 'Practise walking on water on shallow ponds.' That was Sir Colin Marshall's slogan when, as CEO of British Airways, he took the company from losing £200 per minute in 1981 to become 'The World's Favourite Airline'.

USING THE KAIZEN TOOLS

Like any skill, practice makes perfect, and doing something for the first time is always difficult. Remember when you first learned to ride a bike? Now you know you can ride one anytime, even after years of not riding. Probably you learned to ride watching someone else first, then having a go yourself. So in that tradition, here are some examples of how to use the Kaizen tools, with lots of help and detailed guidance each step of the way. In the 'Review and relate' section at the end of this chapter you will find exercises with less help, for you to test your understanding.

If you are unfamiliar with PCs and spreadsheets, do the exercises manually and read Chapter 4 before trying to follow the computer instructions in this chapter.

How to draw a pie chart

The pie chart is ideal for breaking down a grand total into its components to show their relative sizes. For instance:

- Total sales, made up from Northern, Midlands, Southern, and Export divisions.
- Total Council spending, on Education, Social Services, Highways etc.
- Total costs, on labour, materials, transport, overheads etc.

You should restrict yourself to four or five slices at most, or the chart will get cluttered with detail and lose impact. If you must include the detail, put it in a table later on for those who are interested.

Manually

To prepare a pie chart manually is awkward, because you need drawing instruments, and the final result will depend upon your drawing skills. You need a pencil, a ruler, a pair of compasses, and a protractor. (You may have to raid your daughter's or son's pencil case!) A calculator would be useful too. The steps are as follows:

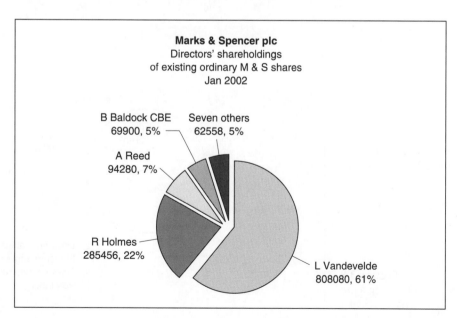

Marks & Spencer plc
Directors' shareholdings
of existing ordinary M & S shares
Jan 2002

B Baldock CBE
69900, 5%

Seven others
62558, 5%

A Reed
94280, 7%

R Holmes
285456, 22%

L Vandevelde
808080, 61%

Figure 3.7
A pie chart

1 Draw a circle.
2 Calculate the angle for the first slice. To do this you calculate the proportion of the total that the first component represents, then work out this proportion of 360 degrees. For instance, suppose you have the following figures:

Fixed costs	250
Variable costs	270
Overheads	230
Total	750

The whole pie represents the 750, and each slice must be sized in proportion. The first slice is the fixed costs of 250. These are one third of the total 750, and so you need to draw a slice which is one third of the whole pie circle – in other words, one third of 360 degrees, which is 120 degrees.

3 Now draw the slice for these fixed costs, by first drawing a radius from the centre of the circle to the right until it touches the outside of the circle. Now use your protractor to measure 120 degrees round the circle from this radius and draw a second radius. Label this slice 'Fixed costs'.
4 Next calculate the size of the second slice, as follows:

$$(270/750) \times 360 = 129.6$$

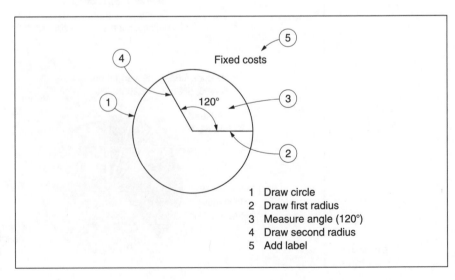

1 Draw circle
2 Draw first radius
3 Measure angle (120°)
4 Draw second radius
5 Add label

Figure 3.8
Drawing a pie chart, stage 1

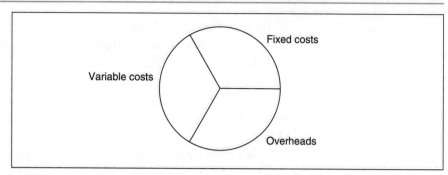

Figure 3.9
Drawing a pie
chart, stage 2

The second slice should be 129.6 degrees, but 130 degrees is perfectly close enough. Again, measure 130 degrees round the pie from your second radius and draw in the third radius. Label this slice 'Variable costs', and the remainder of the pie 'Overheads'.

And that's it; the pie chart is finished. You can jazz it up a bit to make it more visually interesting by adding a title and colouring it in if you wish, but don't make it too complicated. The essence of good communication is to keep things simple.

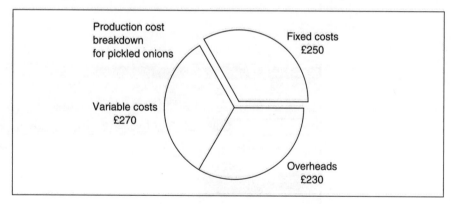

Figure 3.10
Drawing a pie
chart, stage 3

By computer

A more satisfactory way is to use a PC with spreadsheet software. With Microsoft Excel, for instance, all you need do is list on the spreadsheet grid the component names and their values in two adjacent columns. Then tell the computer how you want the information displayed. The way to do this varies according to the software you are using, but if you use the Chart Wizard in Excel, for instance, it's a breeze. For the same figures we used in the manual exercise, the steps are as follows.

First, type the cost categories and values into two adjacent columns in the spreadsheet, and select both columns by clicking and dragging from the top left of the table down and across to the bottom right of the table.

Then click the Chart Wizard button, and make choices in the series of dialogue boxes that follow, and presto! There's your pie-chart.

Now if you want to change something, just double-click on the chart to edit it, then click on the detail you want to change, and you can customize it. You can add some embellishments: a two-line title, and choose different cross-hatching, or colours, for the slices. You can even pull out slightly, one or more slices of the pie, to add impact.

Without doubt, charts are the most powerful way of presenting numerical information in your reports. The best way of transferring graphs from Excel into Word (or other Windows word processor) is by copying your graph to the clipboard as a 'picture', and then pasting it in at the desired position. This will ensure it looks just as you expect it to do, and will also produce the highest print quality.

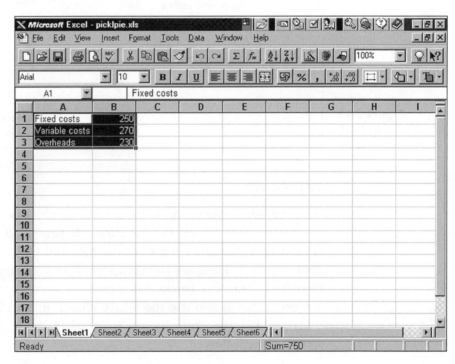

Figure 3.11
The cost categories typed into Microsoft Excel

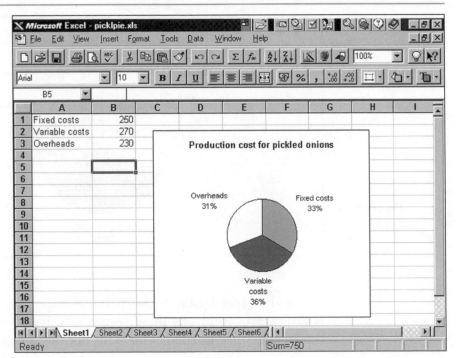

Figure 3.12
The basic chart
produced by
Excel's Chart
Wizard

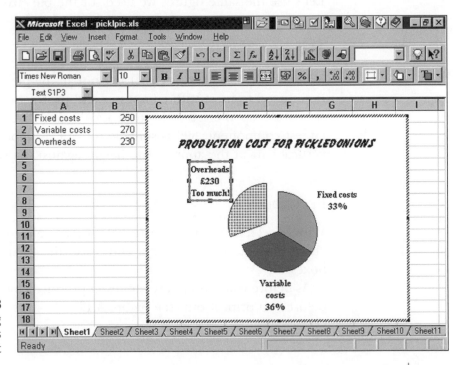

Figure 3.13
Modifying
selected elements
of the basic chart

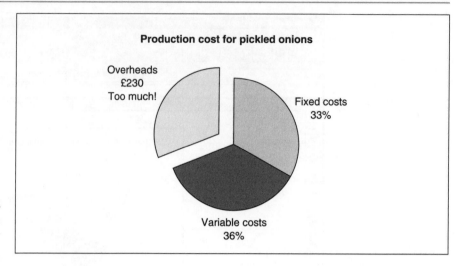

Figure 3.14
The finished pie
chart, after
printing

Use the Help facility to learn the specific mouse clicks and keyboard presses to invoke these commands. It is not difficult and like the bicycle, once learned, your skills become almost instinctive.

How to draw a bar chart

Let's use the same figures we used for the pie chart.

Manually

Manually the bar chart is easier to do than the pie chart, because you don't need to mess with compasses and protractors. You need a vertical scale up the left side, to a nice round figure larger than the largest component. 300 is suitable for our example. Then, just draw vertical bars at the appropriate height against the scale.

By computer

With Excel it is still much easier. The steps are the same as for the pie chart, but you make different choices in the Chart Wizard dialogue boxes.

As before you can modify the result produced by the Chart Wizard, before you print it out (see Figure 3.17).

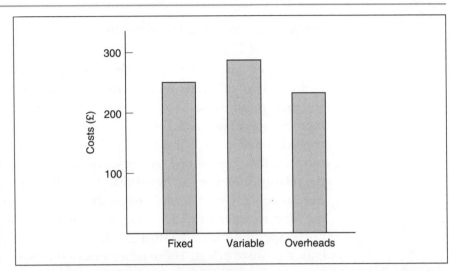

Figure 3.15
Drawing a bar
chart

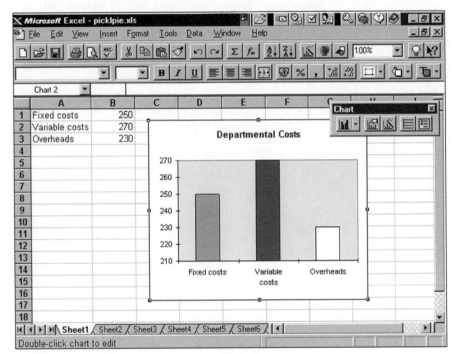

Figure 3.16
The bar chart
produced by
Excel's Chart
Wizard

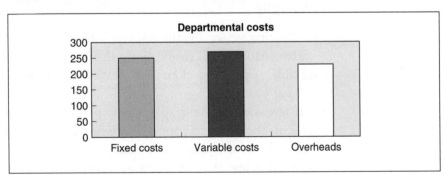

Figure 3.17
The modified bar
chart, as printed

How to draw a scatter diagram

The scatter diagram is great for seeing if there is a relationship between two different measurements. Suppose you want to check whether monthly sales tend to increase when you increase your monthly spend on advertising. You should expect some kind of positive relationship. (Positive means when one increases, the other does too. Negative means one decreases as the other increases.) However, the relationship may not necessarily be perfectly clear, as other factors can influence your sales as well as the money you spend on advertising. Bad weather can have a negative effect and so can your competitors' spending on advertising, whereas a fall in interest rates may have a positive effect. These other external influences – uncontrolled variables – tend to obscure the effect of your advertising and sometimes it is only by charting sales against advertising that you can see the trend.

In this example, the spending on advertising and the corresponding sales for the last nine months were as follows:

Month	Advertising (£)	Sales (£000s)
Jan	5000	80
Feb	6500	42
Mar	1900	52
Apr	3000	51
May	7800	69
June	9000	90
July	3500	55
Aug	6000	60
Sept	7900	120

Manually

In charting generally, the convention is to put the controlled variable – advertising in this case – along the bottom, or x-axis. The dependent variable, sales, will then rise or fall by amounts measured on the vertical y-axis.

It is easier to use graph paper. Just draw the axes and mark off a scale up the left, to a round figure not less than the largest sales figure – say 120 in this case. Now mark off a scale along the bottom, to a figure not less than the largest advertising figure – say 9000 in this

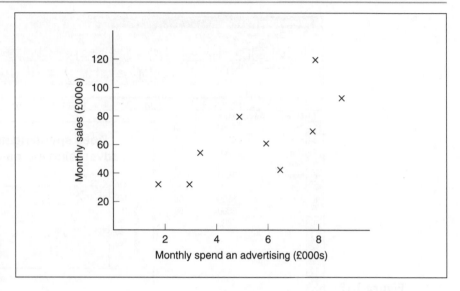

Figure 3.18
Drawing a scatter
diagram

case. Then you just chart the points on the graph by hand. It takes a little time, but it is easy. The quality of the results depends on your skill and patience.

Remember it doesn't matter in what order you plot the points so long as you don't forget any of them. All you are trying to show is that higher values of sales are associated with higher values of advertising, month by month, whenever they occur. The cloud of points should drift upwards and to the right.

By computer

By now you can probably guess how to set about this task with your PC and spreadsheet software. The steps are:

1 Type the months (just for reference), advertising spend, and sales into three adjacent columns on your spreadsheet.
2 Now set the range of values in the Advertising column as the *x*-range. These values will then appear along the bottom of the chart, and we would expect the monthly sales to go up as we move along the bottom axis from the lower values on the left to the higher ones on the right.
3 Similarly, set the range of values in the Sales column as the *y*-range. With Chart Wizard in Excel it is just a matter of responding appropriately in the dialogue boxes.
4 The scatter graph is done, and there is a weak, positive relationship, the scatter of points revealing a trend upwards and

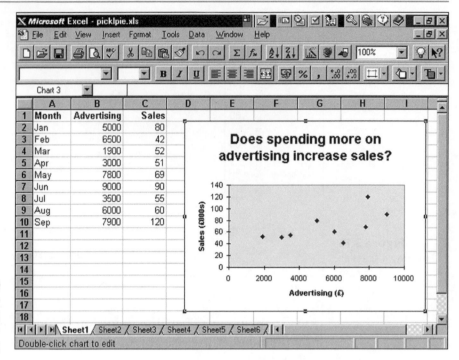

Figure 3.19
The scatter
diagram produced
using Excel, ready
for printing

to the right. Higher values of sales seem to be associated with higher values of advertising. The little black squares on the border of the chart tell you that it is selected, ready for printing, or copying and pasting into a word processed report, for instance.

How to draw a Pareto diagram

This is a really simple technique. It identifies the few critical factors amongst the many other less important ones. There are basically three simple steps:

- Rank the items in order of value.
- Work out their proportions of the total (just as you did for the pie chart).
- Plot a running total.

And if that is too difficult you can even get away with just ranking the items in order of value and plotting them as a bar chart.

Once again, the PC and spreadsheet make the task easy, at least to produce a passable likeness to a Pareto diagram. But first, the background: let's see where the technique came from.

Vilfredo Pareto was an Italian economist who in 1896 attempted to show that income is not randomly distributed in any society, but that the bulk of all income is concentrated in the hands of a fairly small proportion of receivers. A century later and nothing has changed.

When he plotted the percentage of income against the percentage of the population receiving the income, he came up with a curve of characteristic shape that, as is the case with the Normal Distribution curve, has since been found to crop up in a variety of different situations. The curve looks like Figure 3.20, and is variously known as a Pareto curve, a Lorenz curve, 80/20 analysis, and ABC analysis.

The object of the analysis is to isolate the 'vital few' from the 'less important many'. In the field of stock control, for instance, most factories hold a large number of small value items and a small number of large value items. A simplified picture looks like Figure 3.21, in which 80 per cent of the money spent goes on only 20 per cent of the orders placed, the rest of the orders account for only 20 per cent of the expenditure. It is easy to overlook this fact, and there is a natural tendency to spend almost as much administrative effort on small purchase orders as on large ones. Adopting one standard form and procedure for every purchase amounts to administrative overkill on cheap items, while falling short on the largest non-repeating orders.

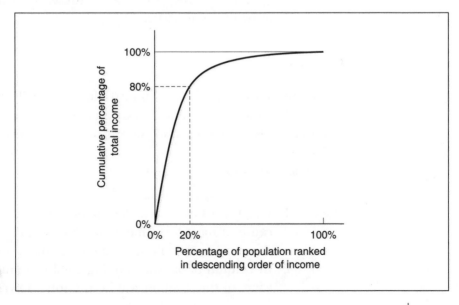

Figure 3.20
The Pareto curve

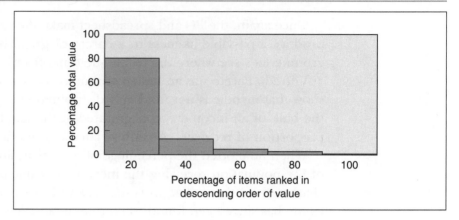

Figure 3.21
Pareto analysis
simplified

Pareto analysis can be used in any situation where you want to focus in on the few key factors. Here are some situations where Pareto may be useful:

- Cost analysis – to pick out the highest cost items, or operations, or processes, or elements.
- Time analysis – to pick out the few most time consuming operations, or processes.
- Scrap or wastage analysis – to pick out the main causes for high scrap rates.
- Breakdown analysis – to discover the main causes for machine breakdowns.
- Quality failures – to analyse these and find where or how most of them occur.

Manually

Here is an example to show how to do it manually. Suppose you wish to analyse the causes of downtime on a production line. We know the minutes lost due to each of the various causes. They are as shown in Figure 3.22.

The procedure is as follows:

1   List the causes in order of importance, starting with the cause of most lost time, in a table with column 1 containing the causes and column 2 showing the minutes lost.
2   In column 3, list the running total of minutes lost. The last value in this column will be the total downtime.

Reasons for down time	Minutes lost
Tool breakages	1
Repairs	10
Operator absent	2
Low air pressure	3
Fire alarm	6
Mechanical faults	34
Electrical faults	82
Interlock open	1
Parts shortages	18
Accidents	4

Figure 3.22
Pareto example:
causes of down
time and time lost

3 In column 4, take each running total in column 3 and express it as a percentage of the total downtime.

4 Now chart the running total of percentages against the reasons listed along the bottom axis ranked in order of largest first.

5 By looking at the curve, you can now split it into two sections: the first 20 per cent of reasons (about three, Electrical Mechanical and Parts in this case) account for a little over 80 per cent of the total minutes lost. The remaining 80 per cent of reasons together only account for about 20 per cent of the total. If you wish, you can split the range into three sections, A, B and C. The A reasons are the most important, lying on the steep part of the curve, and the C reasons the least important, on the flat part at the top. The B reasons as you

Cause	Minutes lost	Running total	Cum. % of total
Electrical faults	82	82	51
Mechanical faults	34	116	72
Parts shortages	18	134	83
Repairs	10	144	89
Fire alarm	6	150	93
Accidents	4	154	96
Low air pressure	3	157	97
Operator absent	2	159	98
Tool breakages	1	160	99
Interlock open	1	161	100
Total minutes lost	161		

Figure 3.23
Pareto example:
ranking and
summing the
values

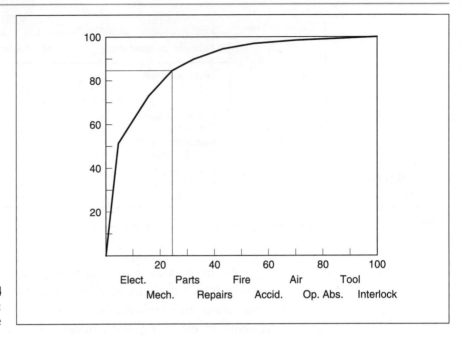

Figure 3.24
Pareto example:
drawing the curve

might expect are the ones in the transitional range in between.

We now know that electrical faults are the main cause of lost time, even though it may turn out that they don't occur very often. If this is the case and we want to improve efficiency, we know where to start: by preventing even a small percentage of electrical faults we can make a big reduction in downtime.

By computer

The Excel Chart Wizard does not offer Pareto analysis, but it can be done by other means as follows:

1 List your reasons for down time in the first column of your spreadsheet.
2 Put the corresponding minutes lost in the second column.
3 Rank the items in order of descending value – in other words, largest minutes lost first, then next largest and so on. Excel will do this for you in a flash: just use the pull-down Data menu, click on Sort, and enter the appropriate responses in the dialogue box that appears. Click on the Help button (or press the F1 key near the top left of your keyboard) for a more detailed explanation.

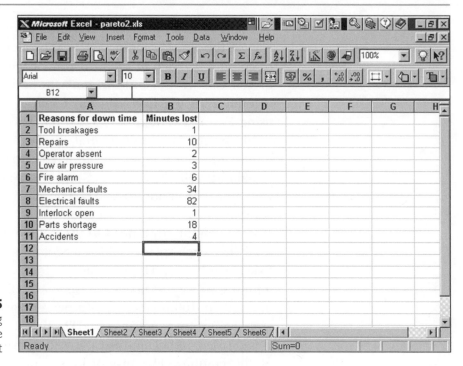

Figure 3.25
The Excel listing
of causes and time
lost

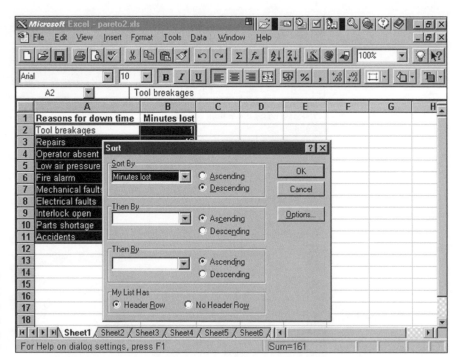

Figure 3.26
Selecting Sort
from the Data
menu to rank the
causes in
descending order

4   We now want to produce the running totals, so in the first row of the third column, repeat the value in the same row of column 2. Then in the next row of the third column, i.e. in cell C3, write a little formula to add the next value in column 2 to the first value in column 3. In our example using Excel, it should be = C2 + B3. This will then automatically bring the running total into cell C3. Then in one mouse operation, you can copy this formula into all the remaining cells in column 3 and the running total values will appear instantly. (Excel's Help facility explains how to copy formulae.)

5   Now in column 4 we need to display the proportions of the total that each of the values in column 3 represent. With Excel that's easy. The total at the foot of column 3 is 161 minutes, so we just take each value and divide it by 161 and multiply by 100 to show it as a percentage. In practice, one way is to put into cell D2 the following formula: = C2/161 × 100. Then just copy this formula into the rest of the column. The proportions – percentages actually – appear instantly.

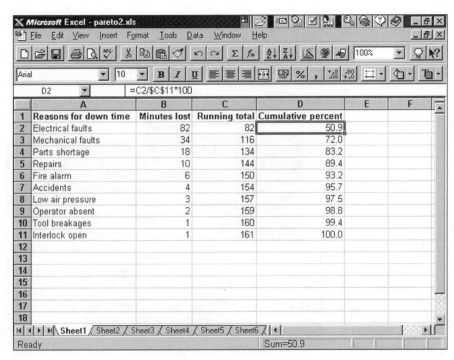

Figure 3.27
The table of data ready for charting

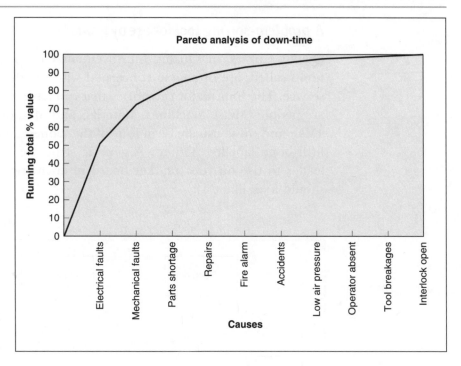

Figure 3.28
The finished
Pareto curve

6 The final step is to display the information graphically. Use Excel's Chart Wizard to produce the appropriate combination graph. Then copy it as a picture into your word processed report and print it out.

How to draw an Ishikawa diagram

Here's another simple technique with a fancy name. In fact it is so simple you might question whether it can really be of any value. Simple it may be, but it is also powerful.

The Ishikawa diagram is named after its originator Dr Kaoru Ishikawa, a Japanese professor who, along with Deming and Juran, was in at the beginning of Japan's quality revolution during the 1950s. He suggested that groups called quality circles should use this diagram, also called a fishbone or cause–effect diagram, for problem solving, and identifying cause and effect relationships.

The diagram is different from some of the other techniques because it is not much use in reports, and the like, for communicating information. It is more of an informal tool to provide a focus for the group, in producing a comprehensive review of all possible causes of some observed effect. It is a useful tool for a group leader working on a marker board to collect and categorize ideas.

A problem-solving tool for use by groups

Quality Circles, or Quality Improvement Groups as they are sometimes called, are of course concerned with the quality of product or
service. The four major categories that can have an impact on quality
are people (Men), Machines, Materials and Methods – known as the
4Ms – and these usually form four of the 'bones' along with a catch-all
fifth bone labelled 'Other'. A generic structure for you as a group
leader to use on your marker board in analysing a quality problem
should look like this:

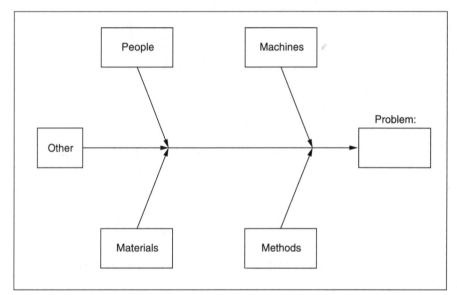

Figure 3.29
Starting an
Ishikawa diagram

You then add little bones to these five main bones for subsidiary
causes under each of the five categories.

A PC is not ideal for preparing Ishikawa diagrams, and it is difficult
even to suggest a rigid procedure for using this informal tool.
Another example might help, however; Figure 3.30 shows an
Ishikawa diagram produced by a Quality Circle while they were discussing a problem of customers in a restaurant complaining that food
was cold.

The Ishikawa diagram can be used by any problem-solving group
interested in determining causes and effects. It should not be
reserved just for quality problems, and the main bones need not
necessarily be just the 4Ms. It can be used as an informal, flexible
tool wherever appropriate.

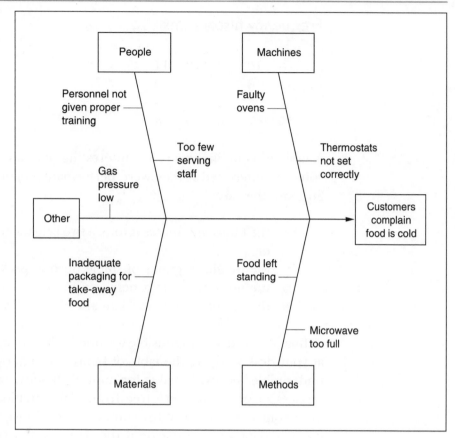

Figure 3.30
Using the
Ishikawa diagram:
reviewing causes
of complaint

THE NORMAL DISTRIBUTION AND STANDARD DEVIATION

In contrast to the earlier techniques, to get the most from this subject you need to know some elementary statistics. Let's review the main properties of the Normal curve and the way it is used.

So what is this curve? It is a bell-shaped distribution that crops up in all sorts of situations wherever variation occurs. It often arises when we plot a frequency histogram of a set of results clustering around some central value. The histogram reveals the pattern, or profile, of the figures, showing how much they cluster together, or how widely they spread out.

Frequency histograms

6	10	9	13	11
12	8	8	1	9
7	3	12	10	9
15	7	10	9	8

A table of data like this is less interesting than a train timetable, but you'd be interested if they were performance figures for your team. Suppose they are:

- the times in minutes it took a fire brigade to arrive at the fire, or
- the weight in grams of single portion packs of jam, or
- the number of rings before a phone was answered, or
- the minutes a bus was late after its scheduled arrival time.

Imagine yourself responsible for one of the situations above, sitting at your desk studying the table of figures. You know that variation is undesirable because it makes for unpredictability, and customers seek services or goods that are free from high variation. You know you must control variation. What you need is to derive information from this raw data, to help decide if the figures are acceptable, or if you should take some kind of action.

There are three types of summarizing measure that you might find useful:

- A single typical value to represent all the values. This is usually the average, or arithmetic mean. You could then compare this directly with the planned schedule or target, or specification. There is usually room for improvement. The average of these figures works out at 8.85.
- A single figure measure of variation, or spread. The simplest measure is the range from the very smallest figure to the very largest figure in the set. It is easy to understand and to calculate – you just subtract the smallest from the largest figure. The range in this case is 14. But the range is not the best measure of spread because it is derived from just two freak figures, and that is not a reliable way to describe a large body of data! As you might expect, statisticians have developed better ways to measure the spread, or variability, of a set of figures. The most important of these is the standard devia-

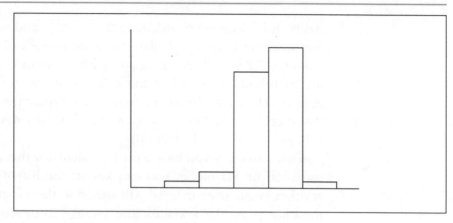

Figure 3.31
Tightly clustered
figures

tion, which we will look at in more detail later. Its value in this case is 3.13. The standard deviation is always smaller than the range – usually between a quarter and a sixth of the range. It is often represented by the Greek symbol sigma, σ.

■ A profile of the spread of figures. Do most of the figures cluster tightly around the average with the numbers tailing off rapidly further away? Or are the figures spread more uniformly across the range?

The figures in our table produce a distribution that is roughly bell-shaped.

Bar charts or histograms of the figures are one way of helping you picture exactly what is going on. The shape can often give important clues on what to do to improve control.

As you know by now, if your data is in digital form on disk, you can use a spreadsheet such as Excel to produce bar charts quickly and

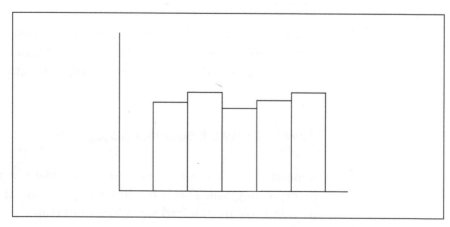

Figure 3.32
Uniformly spread
figures

easily. It is also easy to calculate the average and standard deviation. Suppose you want to calculate them for a block of figures extending from cell A2 to cell E6 on the spreadsheet. With Excel the commands are as follows. First select the cell where you want the average to appear. Then type in the command to display the average, which is =average(A2:E6). And to display the standard deviation in another cell, just type in =stdev(A2:E6).

Alternatively, if you have a pocket calculator that can be switched to statistical or SD mode, you can key in the list of figures one after another (your user manual will describe the exact procedure), and then just press the x̄ key for the average to be displayed, and the σ key for the standard deviation to be displayed.

For decision-making, many managers feel more comfortable with just a graphical presentation, from which they can get a feel for the most commonly occurring figure, the amount and the type of spread of the figures. The table of figures we started with makes much more sense to most managers when displayed like this:

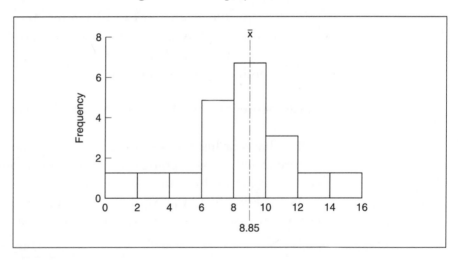

Figure 3.33
Histogram of figures

However, the single figure measures of average and standard deviation are still useful because they are more suitable for monitoring over time, to see if trends are in the right direction.

How to draw a frequency histogram

Some detail is lost when you summarize data in the form of a frequency histogram. This is because we group together values of about the same size in standard sized 'class intervals', and count how many readings there are in each class. This is how we get the bell-shaped profile with a well-defined peak showing that most values lie close to the average. If we counted the original values, it could quite easily happen that every value would be different. There could be no bell shape then, just a region on the *x*-axis where individual values would be more densely packed.

To get a meaningful histogram, it is important that you choose the most appropriate size for the class interval. Choose intervals that are too many and too small, and you get a histogram with lots of superfluous peaks and troughs – misleading because they are the product of random chance and unlikely to have any meaning. But choose too few and too large a class interval, and although you can still see the main features of the distribution, you lose too much detail and will be in danger of missing real secondary features.

As a general rule, choose a class interval that will result in a total of between 4 and 10 classes across the full range of values. For instance, this table shows the mileages claimed by sales representatives over a period of weeks:

552	747	478	602	404	581	744	567
612	559	541	648	707	599	622	720
460	644	523	625	633	606	530	658
655	645	508	666	648	637	460	540
493	642	690	555	667	525	456	493
795	705	608	480	592	651	655	610
523	548	555	495	532	567	689	591
577	412	590	712	520	578	522	678

The steps for constructing a frequency histogram are:

1 Search the table for the largest and smallest values. They are 404 and 795. The range is therefore 391 and this may be split into about 8 classes, that will therefore have a width of $391/8 =$ about 49. A suitable class interval to try would be 50. Our *x*-axis should therefore extend from 401 to 800, divided up as follows: 401 to 450; 451 to 500; 501 to 550 and so on.

2 The next step is to count the number of values that fall into each of these classes. The easiest way to do this is to write down the class intervals and then, taking the readings from the table one by one, mark a tally against the appropriate class interval:

Class	Tally
401–450	//
451–500	//// //
501–550	//// //// /
551–600	//// //// ///
601–650	//// //// ////
651–700	//// ////
701–750	//// /
751–800	//

3 Now count the tallies, write down the frequency for each class, and check that the total of frequencies matches the total number of values in the table. You should note that the shape of the tallies actually gives you a clue as to what the histogram will actually turn out to look like – it is like a histogram turned on its side.

Class	Tally	Frequency
401–450	//	2
451–500	//// //	7
501–550	//// //// /	11
551–600	//// //// ///	13
601–650	//// //// ////	14
651–700	//// ////	9
701–750	//// /	6
751–800	//	2
Total		64

4 Now just draw the histogram or bar chart as shown in Figure 3.34.

You can judge the average value near enough for decision-making: it is the value of the peak of the histogram – about 600. If you work it out using your calculator and the original data the average comes to 596 to the nearest whole number.

Also the range is $800 - 400 = 400$. A quarter of this is 100, and a sixth of this is 67, so we would expect the standard deviation to lie between these values. In fact working it out with your calculator it comes to 86 to the nearest whole number. But what is the standard deviation, and why is it superior to the range as a measure of scatter?

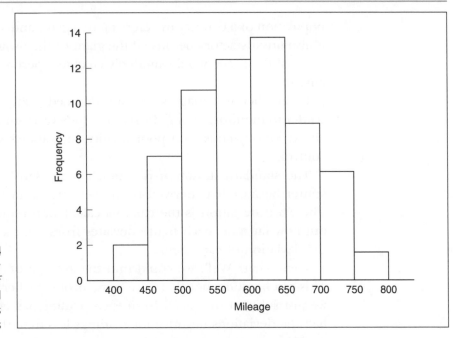

Figure 3.34
Frequency
histogram of
mileages travelled
by sales
representatives

WHAT IS THE STANDARD DEVIATION?

Like the range, it is a measure of the amount of scatter in a set of numbers. It is often represented by the Greek letter sigma, which looks like a number 6 that has fallen flat on its face, σ.

In any set of figures, it is quite common for most numbers to cluster around some value near the centre. However, we also expect some numbers to be further away from the centre. We put this down to natural variation caused by many tiny influences, some negative and some positive, that on average tend to cancel each other out but occasionally stack up to produce a value further from the centre.

This effect results in the histogram having a bell shape, but if we only know the mean of a set of figures, we have no way of knowing whether the bell is low and wide, or high and narrow. For instance you must have seen boxes of matches with the label 'Average contents 48 matches'. This could be true if half the boxes were empty and half had 96 matches in. In fact most boxes contain 48 and nearly all boxes have between 47 and 49 matches, but we have to take that on trust; the average figure on its own tells us nothing about how widely spread the distribution might be.

The range is unsatisfactory for describing the spread of a whole population of figures because it is derived from just two freak figures that in themselves are far from typical. It is a bit like typifying the population of a country by referring to a giant and a dwarf. The range is also unsatisfactory because if the giant or the dwarf died or left, the value of the range would suddenly change – perhaps by quite a large amount.

Remember as managers we really do need a satisfactory measure of scatter to monitor, in our efforts to reduce variation. High variation is always synonymous with poor quality, and always suggests a lack of control.

The standard deviation is a much more satisfactory measure of scatter because it is derived from every figure in the set of figures. The word deviation is the clue: its calculation requires that we find out how far away each figure deviates from the mean. This is called the deviation of each figure.

Then what? Well, we could find the average of all the deviations. This can be done, but there are some problems here. For instance, if we just subtract the mean from each reading, we end up with about half the deviations negative for readings less than the mean, and half positive, for those greater than the mean. These then cancel each other out when we work out the average deviation; the answer always comes to zero, which is not much help.

Mathematically there are two ways round this problem. One is we could ignore the positive and negative signs and just work out the average size of the deviations. This is sometimes done and is called the Mean Absolute Deviation (MAD), but there is a better way.

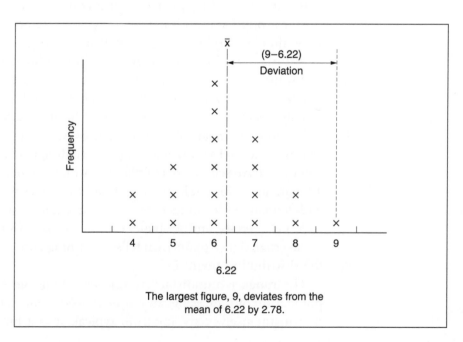

Figure 3.35
Deviation

The largest figure, 9, deviates from the
mean of 6.22 by 2.78.

You may remember from school that multiplying two negatives produces a positive. Well suppose we 'square' each of the positive and negative deviations – that is, multiply each by itself. We will then have a set of positive values for which we can calculate the average.

This Mean Squared Deviation is more commonly known as the variance of the set of figures. But it too is not used much, mainly because it is so big and cannot be compared directly with the individual values from which it was derived. It is big because all the deviations were squared – remember? So what should we do? Unsquare it of course – that is, find the square root of the variance, or Mean Squared Deviation. And that is exactly what the Standard Deviation is: the root of the mean squared deviations.

So now you know – and if you think the calculations sound tedious they certainly used to be before the calculator and the PC came galloping to the rescue. But it has always been valued because it plays a fundamental role in statistics. It is the foundation for statistical process control (SPC), and the use of $\bar{X}$ charts and R charts, which we will examine shortly, but first a few more words on the Normal distribution.

WHAT IS A NORMAL DISTRIBUTION?

The Normal distribution is a particular bell-shaped distribution, similar in shape to the frequency distribution we produced earlier from the table of mileages claimed by sales representatives. If in that example we had charted each value with a single point on the graph instead of a histogram bar, we could have drawn a curve through the points. It would have a similar bell shape to the one shown in Figure 3.36, and we could say it approximated to the Normal distribution.

In fact the Normal curve has a formula defining the shape precisely, dependent on the mean and the standard deviation. Thus for a true Normal curve, if we know the mean and the standard deviation, we know everything about that distribution. We know for instance that 95.45 per cent of all readings will lie within two standard deviations' distance either side of the mean.

This is very useful because if we have a process that we know produces a distribution approximately Normal in shape, we can predict that about 95 per cent – that is about 19 in every 20 – of all readings in the future will lie within plus and minus two sigma of

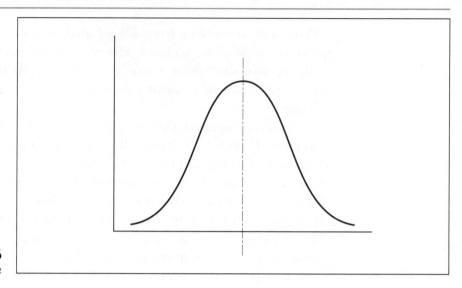

Figure 3.36
The Normal curve

the mean, so long as the process remains stable. Therefore if we get a reading outside these limits it is a warning sign. We should begin to suspect something might have gone wrong with our process. Such a large deviation should only occur in about one in twenty readings. It is sufficiently unusual from natural variation or common causes for us to start thinking that perhaps there might be a single special cause that has upset the stability of the process.

We also know that 99.8 per cent of all readings will lie within three standard deviations either side of the mean. These are the six-sigma limits used by IBM, Motorola and others.

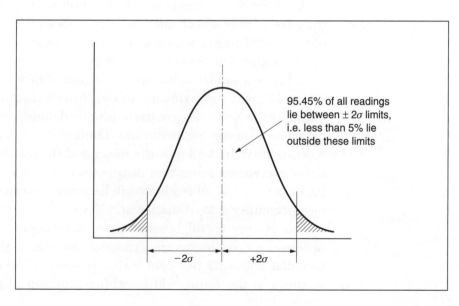

95.45% of all readings lie between ± 2σ limits, i.e. less than 5% lie outside these limits

Figure 3.37
The 4σ limits

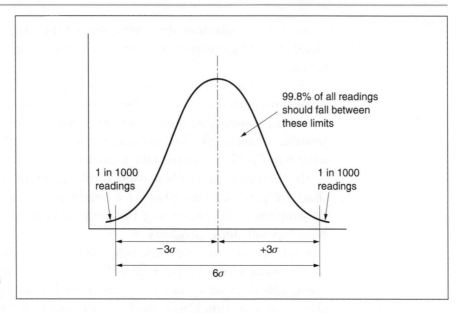

99.8% of all readings
should fall between
these limits

1 in 1000
readings

1 in 1000
readings

−3σ   +3σ

6σ

Figure 3.38
The 6σ limits

Again they use them to help distinguish between common and special causes of variation. They are triggers for action because 998 in 1000 readings should lie within these limits. For a stable process the chances of a reading falling outside these limits due to expected or common cause variation is about 1 in 1000 above, and 1 in 1000 below.

In other words, any reading outside the 6σ limits is almost certainly due to a special cause. The process should be stopped and the cause discovered and eliminated to bring it back in control again.

So, with the Normal distribution and the standard deviation, we have the makings of a system for monitoring processes to ensure that they continue to produce within specified limits, or at least to the best the process is capable of. Let us now examine how such a system can work.

X̄ and R charts

These are a proven method of monitoring and controlling a manufacturing process without the need for 100 per cent inspection.

Statistical process control has been around for 50 years or more. It was during the 1940s that Walter Shewhart, an American statistician, developed the control charts that are still in use today. We can only guess how his thought processes evolved as he developed his charts, but his thinking probably went through the following phases.

To start with, he was obviously aware of the Normal distribution, its standard deviation and the chances of values lying outside the 4σ and 6σ limits.

He also knew that inspection was expensive, and 100 per cent inspection adds quite a lot to the cost of each product without adding any extra value. And also as a statistician he would know that it is possible to infer conclusions about a whole population based upon what you find in a sample taken from that population.

He therefore probably started thinking about the process rather than the product, and whether it might be possible to control that by sampling rather than using 100 per cent inspection to weed out the out-of-specification products.

But he must also have been aware of a major difficulty, namely this. A process producing 5 per cent defective items is quite unacceptable, but is still difficult to detect by checking samples of one item. The chance of detecting it will also be 5 per cent or a 1 in 20 chance each time. In fact we can work out that on average you would have to take about fifteen samples before you would have an evens chance of picking up a defective item.

On the credit side, however, he would know that trends are useful in detecting and predicting change, and probably used a 'run chart' to show the output in comparison with the specification limits, and reveal trends as a sign of change in a process.

A run chart is just a continuous graph for monitoring samples of one item taken from the output of the process. If there is any drift or

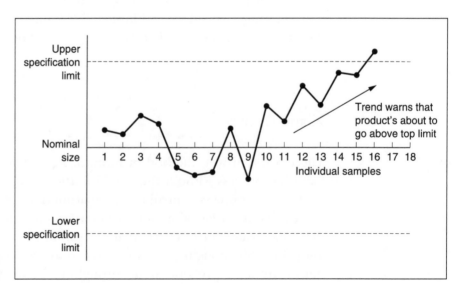

Figure 3.39
The run chart

gradual change taking place then this will eventually begin to show up as a trend on the graph.

But the masterstroke was when he tried taking small samples of five items and averaging the readings, then charting the averages on a continuous graph, instead of the individual values. The sensitivity of the technique was amplified at least twenty-fold, making it very likely that an output containing only 5 per cent defective items would be detected with the very first sample of five items.

So how does it work? Well, there are two effects of averaging. One effect is that random variations in the process are smoothed out by the averaging. For instance, any much larger value will be averaged along with four other less extreme values. Smoothing the results like this will reveal any underlying trends that might otherwise be obscured by the variation.

Another effect is that a distribution of the averages will be a Normal distribution with very steep sides as shown in Figure 3.41. If we draw in the 4σ limits for the average, we can see that only a very small shift in the average, $\bar{X}$, will carry the majority of the distribution outside the limit, indicating a very good chance that the first sample of five will have an average outside the limits, flagging a probable disturbance to the process. These 4σ limits for the average, $\bar{X}$, are called control limits, and are distinct from the specification limits that will be more widely set.

Don't worry if this short explanation goes over your head. The important thing to remember is that averaging samples of five and using control limits instead of specification limits amplifies the sensitivity of the monitoring process by at least twenty-fold. This makes the $\bar{X}$ chart very likely to detect an out-of-spec process at the first sample, even if the process is only producing 5 per cent defective items.

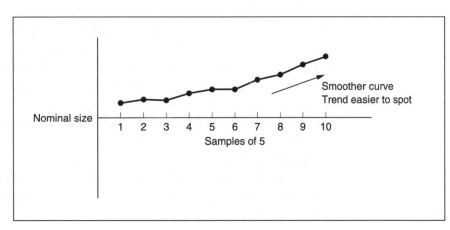

Figure 3.40
Charting averages
of samples of five

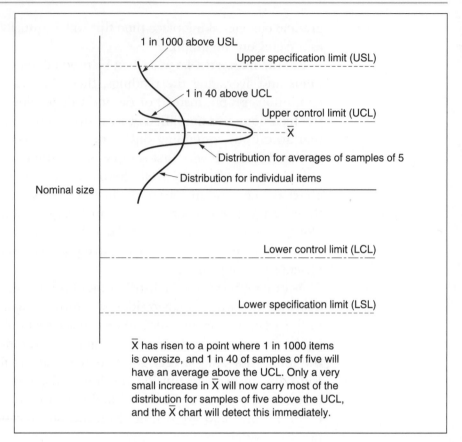

Figure 3.41
Control limits and
the X̄ chart

Before we leave the theory to see how these charts work in practice, there is a last point to cover. By averaging samples of five, we have introduced a new problem. There is a chance that our process may be disturbed in such a way that it produces a wider scatter of results, either side of the same average figure. For instance, if we are monitoring a filling process for filling jars to a certain weight, the process could become more erratic, producing some jars very much overweight and some very much underweight, but in a balanced way such that the average is not affected. Our X̄ chart will not pick this up of course, because it is only sensitive to changes in the average.

However, it is a simple matter to guard against this possibility. We produce a second chart called an R chart for monitoring sample range. So on taking a sample of five, we must calculate the sample average X̄, and plot it on the X̄ chart, and at the same time we must calculate the sample range R, and plot it on the R chart. The R chart has a control limit marked on it that is separate from and smaller than the overall allowable range in the whole output of the process. You would probably expect this to be the case, because the range within a sample will be smaller than the range within the overall output. After all, it would be extremely unlikely that the overall largest and overall smallest items should both be picked up within the same small sample of five.

The method of establishing the positions of the control limits on the control charts is beyond the scope of this introduction. It is however perfectly straightforward, and tables of factors are available to avoid the need to work out the values from first principles each time.

So let's now see how the charts are used in practice.

HOW TO SAVE MONEY WITH $\bar{X}$ CHARTS

Let us take a look at the economics of these charts, to see if it is worth messing with statistics. I hope by now you are convinced of how important it is to reduce variation, even though the customer benefits are difficult to cost-justify. But there can be very large and immediate direct savings to be made, by cutting down on waste.

Some time ago I worked as a packaging engineer for General Foods in Banbury, an American company now known as Kraft Foods UK. One of their lines was Maxwell House instant coffee that they packed in 100 gram jars on automatic filling lines running at 400 jars per minute. They employed an operator who took five jars from the line every so often, weighed the contents and plotted the results on $\bar{X}$ and R charts. We can do a few rough calculations now, using estimated figures to see if it was worth it.

How much does a 100 gram jar of instant coffee retail for? The price has been around £1.50 for the last five years, so let's say the coffee retails at 1.5 pence per gram.

Now Kraft must be sure of putting at least 100 grams of coffee in each jar, or they will get on the wrong side of the Weights and Measures people, so they set their filling machines to an average fill weight of slightly greater than 100 grams. Then, there will be very little chance of any underfilling due to the natural variation in fill weight produced by the filler. Ideally the filler should be set to fill at an average fill weight of just 3σ above the nominal fill weight (Figure 3.42).

In theory this will result in about one jar in a thousand being very slightly underfilled which in practice is as good as can be expected. To

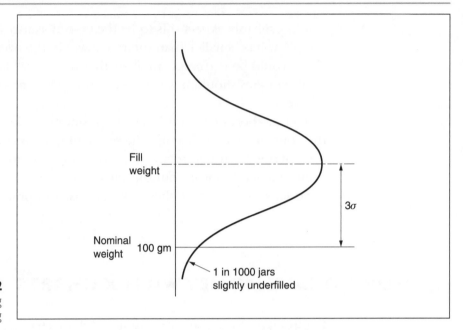

Figure 3.42
Avoiding
underfilling

achieve a consistent average fill weight at this setting, however, requires constant monitoring using control charts as outlined above.

Now suppose this approach saves on average just one gram of instant coffee per jar – less than a teaspoon full. How much money will be saved in a year?

400 jars per minute over an 8 hour shift is $400 \times 60 \times 8 = 192,000$ jars.

Over five days a week for a year this grows to $192,000 \times 5 \times 50 = 48$ million jars.

The retail value in pounds of one gram from each jar is $48,000,000 \times 1.5/100 = £720,000$.

Now let us take just one tenth part of this as the true figure, to take account of the retail mark-up, and lost production due to breakdowns and market restrictions. £72,000 would be enough to pay for the running of the control charts and still leave a saving of £1000 per week. Not bad, eh? It's amazing how those few grains from each jar add up, isn't it? – and that's just on one of many packing lines in one factory. Kraft is the second largest food company in the world, with revenues of $34 billion. World wide their savings from statistical process control must be worth millions of dollars.

The charts have to be set up in advance by someone with the know-how to do it. Then anyone can fill in the charts and know what to do if the charts flag a warning. These are the steps:

1 Run the process for a while until it settles down. Then take about ten samples of five, making fifty in all. Calculate the averages and ranges of these samples and then look up in the appropriate tables for the positions of the control limits to set on the charts.

2 Now give the charts to the operators and tell them how often to take samples. This will depend on the value of the product, the rate of production, and the costs of sampling. If a sample shows the process has gone out of control, then all the output since the previous sample may have to be re-processed. The sampling should therefore be fairly frequent. But if the sampling involves the destruction of the product, then sampling should not be too frequent.

3 The operators should then take samples at the recommended intervals and if the $\bar{X}$ and the R plot satisfactorily within the control limits, they should allow the process to continue without adjustment.

4 If however an $\bar{X}$ value falls outside the 2σ limits, this is a warning that the process may have gone out of control or is on the point of going out of control. However, even when the process is in control, about one in every twenty readings will fall just outside the 2σ limits – one in forty above the upper limit, and one in forty below the lower one. Therefore if there is no trend leading up to the out-of-limit value, the process should be allowed to continue without adjustment, but another sample of five should be taken immediately.

5 If this too falls outside the limit, the process should be stopped and reset, because with the process still in control, the chance of two out-of-limit values occurring consecutively is $1/40 \times 1/40$ or one in 1600. This is such a remote chance that we must conclude that normal variation is not the cause and there is some other special cause for the two out-of-limit values. The cause must be determined and eliminated to bring the process back into control.

I hope you can see now that control charts are a very powerful way of distinguishing between common and special causes of variation. If you are ever in charge of a process that you think may benefit from their application, you can find out more from the references that follow shortly.

REVIEW AND RELATE

This chapter has been less descriptive, more practical in content. We touched on a variety of different techniques – all of immediate relevance to managing business processes. I hope you found it easy enough reading, but it is not until you try using the techniques that you discover whether you fully understand them.

If there are some techniques you would like to practise, select from the following exercises. You can do them manually or using a PC, whichever you prefer. Either way, it can only add to your confidence and repertoire of management skills.

Pie charts and bar charts

1 Draw a pie chart to represent the data below, derived from the 2001 Annual Report for British Sky Broadcasting Group plc.

Breakdown of Shareholders, as at 30 June 2001

Type of Shareholder	Percentage
Fund Management Groups	47
Insurance Companies	18
Miscellaneous Banks	10
Pension Funds	6
Other	19
	100

2 Recent mortality statistics produced for Oxfordshire Health Authority analysed causes of death under 90 different headings. In summary, there were 4681 deaths, of which 1255 were caused by neoplasm; 2134 were caused by circulation diseases; and the rest by a variety of other causes. Show this data as a pie chart, and add a suitable title.

3 In February 2000 a survey of on-line retailers produced the following estimate of quarterly market size for products bought over the Internet in Europe:

Product Sector	£ (millions)
Computer equipment	222.3
Travel/Holidays	178.1
Groceries	80.2
Books	44.3
Music and Video	32.1
Other	46.5
Total	603.5

Represent this data as a bar chart, suitably annotated and titled.

4 In 2001 a survey of more than 600 US companies found that, on average, the IT budget was being spent as follows:

Company	Per cent
Enterprise Resource Planning	31
Customer Relationship Management	21
E-commerce	15
Supply Chain Management	14
Other	19

Show this as a bar chart. Show it also as a pie chart. Which do you think is the most effective as a communication?

Scatter diagrams

5 Plot a scatter diagram for the following small (too small to be representative) sample, to see if there is any relationship between price and maximum speed in small cars. The data has been derived from *What Car?* magazine, December, 2001.

Model	Price (£)	Max Speed (mph)
Alfa Romeo 147, 1.6	13,175	119
Audi A2 1.4 SE	14,945	107
BMW 316 ti Compact	16,265	122
Daewoo Lanos 1.4 S	7,980	98
Fiat Seicento	5,940	93
Ford Focus 1.6 Zetec	11,480	115

Mercedes A-class 140 Classic	13,025	106
Nissan Micra 1.0 S	7,250	93
Renault Clio 1.2 Authentique	7,495	100
Toyota Yaris 1.0 16v	6,995	96

Number the cars 1 to 10 and mark each point on the graph with the appropriate reference number.

6 Texmills DIY wants to see if sales are boosted by newspaper advertising. The level of advertising and the volume of sales for each of seven months are as follows:

Month	Advertising spend (£)	Sales volume (£)
June	8,630	102,430
July	4,480	103,720
August	19,110	151,220
September	12,160	148,990
October	3,910	53,100
November	8,470	68,800
December	17,140	118,750

Chart this data as a scatter diagram. What does it indicate?

Pareto analysis

7 The stores in a hospital department hold just ten items in stock. The usage and values of the items are shown in the table:

Item	Annual usage (items)	Unit value (£)
1	244	68.10
2	585	58.30
3	76	76.35
4	74	52.64
5	7,413	4.60
6	63,800	3.21
7	2,135	2.95
8	558	4.30
9	424	9.20
10	468	13.45

Calculate the value of annual usage for each item. Rank them in descending order, and plot them as a Pareto curve.

Which approximately 20 per cent of the items form approximately 80 per cent of the annual usage value?

Which items would you classify as A, B and C items?

8 There are ten products in the range offered by a marketing company. The sales revenue attributable to each product is shown below:

Product ref.	Sales revenue (£000)
1	310
2	140
3	44
4	180
5	86
6	1,067
7	116
8	96
9	68
10	720

Set these products on a Pareto curve, and thus identify the few vital products from amongst the many other important products.

Cause–effect diagrams

9 An airline operating out of Heathrow has a problem of late flight departures. A quality group is convened to uncover the causes of late departure. During a meeting of the group, the main reasons suggested by members were as follows:

- Aircraft arrival delayed.
- Cockpit crew late or unavailable.
- Aircraft problem requiring maintenance.
- Late on-board catering supplies.
- Slow security clearance procedures.
- Pushback tug unavailable when required.
- Baggage handlers late to aircraft.
- Fuel late to aircraft.
- Air traffic control delays.

■ Cabin cleaners late.
■ Delays due to bad weather.
■ Flight weight and balance sheet late.
■ Delay for late passengers.
■ Cabin crews late.

Prepare a cause–effect (Ishikawa) diagram with bones for the 4Ms and 'Other' causes. Fill in the effect on the right hand side, then attach the causes listed above to the appropriate bones.

10 Write down in two or three words a problem or undesirable effect you are aware of at work. Construct a fishbone diagram consisting of the 4Ms and any other bones necessary, and then attach possible causes to the appropriate bones. If possible, discuss the diagram with someone else familiar with the problem, and see if together you can add to the possible causes.

Histograms

11 A fruit farmer harvests cooking apples. The weight of apples in kilograms yielded by each of thirty trees is shown below:

41.3	52.6	58.9	49.3	53.6
66.8	46.3	51.3	54.4	65.1
45.8	62.3	42.3	46.8	48.8
48.7	51.7	48.3	56.2	53.2
54.1	64.7	63.8	47.2	64.6
46.1	57.5	49.4	65.2	59.3

Produce a frequency histogram of this data, using a class interval of 5 kilograms.

From the histogram, estimate the average weight of apples produced per tree. Compare this value with the true mean of the above figures, computed using your PC or calculator.

Divide the range by 4. This should give you a rough estimate of the standard deviation. Compute the standard deviation using your calculator or PC, from the table of figures above. How does it compare with the estimate?

Would you say the histogram has a shape that approximates to the Normal curve?

12 A company makes drinking chocolate as a powder to be made up with hot milk. The company packs it for sale in containers marked 250 grams. The filler delivers a measured volume of the powder, which because of variations in factors, such as the density of the powder, results in a small amount of variation in fill weight. The contents of one thousand successive packs were weighed, and the results are shown in the table below.

Weight (grams)	Frequency
over 250.0, up to 250.5	5
over 250.5, up to 251.0	17
over 251.0, up to 251.5	44
over 251.5, up to 252.0	92
over 252.0, up to 252.5	150
over 252.5, up to 253.0	192
over 253.0, up to 253.5	192
over 253.5, up to 254.0	150
over 254.0, up to 254.5	92
over 254.5, up to 255.0	44
over 255.0, up to 255.5	17
over 255.5, up to 256.0	5

Produce a frequency histogram of these figures. Draw in the nominal container weight. Estimate the average fill weight being produced by the filler. Should the filler be adjusted to another average fill weight?

Does this histogram approximate in shape to the Normal curve? If so, why might this be worth knowing?

REFERENCES AND FURTHER READING

Caplen, R. H. (1988). *A Practical Approach to Quality Control.* Hutchinson.

Curwin, J. and Slater, R. (1996). *Quantitative Methods for Business Decisions* (4th edition). Chapman and Hall.

Kap, R. O. (1998). *The Presentation of Technical Information* (3rd edition). The Institute of Scientific and Technical Communication.

Computers, programs and communications

Essentially I integrate the current export drive
And basically I'm viable from ten o'clock till five.

'Executive', Sir John Betjeman (1906–84)

IN THIS CHAPTER . . .

- Computer applications packages for business functions (Finance, HRM etc.).
- Computer support for business processes, such as accounts payable.
- How to integrate the functions to support the processes.
- Office automation.
- A summary of common business applications packages: SCM, CRM, etc.

THE COMPUTER: BUSINESS ENGINE FOR THE ENTERPRISE

Simple products can have hard-won knowledge built in, that makes them easy for an unskilled person to use. Take, for example, the twist drill bit you use for drilling 5 mm holes in the wall when you want to put up some coat hooks. Fifty years ago, drill bits were made of carbon steel that snapped easily, and blunted quickly needing regular resharpening. Can you resharpen your own twist drills? Probably not, because you never need to. Carbon steel gave way to high-speed steel, which in turn yielded to tungsten carbide tipped tools that seldom need resharpening. And while drill bit prices have fallen, labour rates have risen, so most people now bin the blunt drill bit and buy a new one. Unless you are one of those people who still darn their socks.

So, the greater the sophistication (knowledge built in) the less skill needed to use the product. It's true of cars with auto gear boxes and ABS braking, and of course it is true of that most sophisticated product, the computer. Yes, the computer. You don't believe it? You can't have used a computer in the 1980s. Then, on switching on, you were presented with just a cursor blinking in the corner of a blank screen. To get the computer to do anything, you had to type in a series of arcane system commands. Today all you need is familiarity with keyboard, mouse and toolbar at the top of the screen. You're just a teensy bit uncertain in spelling and grammar? Not a problem – your PC will correct it.

At work, when purchase orders and sales receipts are prepared, the accounting software is quietly noting the VAT paid on purchases, and payable on sales. Then, no tax accountant is needed to prepare VAT returns for the Inland Revenue at the end of the quarter. The computer can do it automatically.

In the design office, no manual drawing skills are needed – just point-and-click, plus basic keyboard skills. Perfect lines and curves, every time. The designer can concentrate on the design and how best to present it.

In the workshop, computers control the lathes and milling machines that cut to an accuracy of a few microns (thousandths of a millimetre). No highly skilled turners and millers – just a few machine minders here and there, to load and unload the work. The machines can compensate for tool wear, and automatically change tools when necessary. And they don't get hangovers – quality is just as perfect on Monday morning as it is during the rest of the week.

Computers can handle all the routines. They take the graft out of running a business, and remove the need for the armies of clerical and manual workers to do it. It's like fitting a diesel engine to a trireme. You go ten times as fast, and carry ten times the payload, because you don't need all those oarsmen.

THE COMPUTER: SMART MACHINE FOR SMARTER PROCESSES

When the computers for the different functions in a business are connected up, new economies and new ways of working become possible. Information entered at one point in the network for some primary purpose can be used at other points for other purposes.

In the paper by Mike Hammer (1990) on Business Process Re-engineering, he describes how the Ford Motor Company planned to reduce the accounts payable headcount in North America, from 500 to 400. Then they discovered that Mazda's accounts payable organization employed just five people, albeit for a somewhat smaller company. Shocked, Ford re-engineered their own process, and found they only needed about 125 people. In Ford's old paperwork system, the accounting department had to match 14 data items on the purchase order, delivery note and invoice before it could issue payment to the vendor. There were frequent mismatches, delays and investigations. After re-engineering, Ford moved to 'invoiceless processing'. When a purchase order was placed, a copy was stored on-line. When the order was delivered to Ford, the goods receiving clerk would check on-line that the delivery matched the order, and then confirm the delivery. Then the system would automatically generate a cheque for sending to the vendor. The new system required a network spanning the purchasing department, the accounts department and the goods receiving deck at the warehouse – three departments that previously kept separate records. Ford thus required 375 fewer people on the accounts payable process, a process that added no value to Ford's products. When did this happen? Way back in the 1980s.

Hammer explains how businesses operate according to rules, some of them written procedures, and some entirely unarticulated and, thus, seldom questioned. 'These rules of work design are based on assumptions about technology, people, and organizational goals that no longer hold.' Technology has changed, certainly. People have changed, too. Most now are educated, responsible, and seek autonomy. And goals have changed. 'Quality, innovation and service are now more important than cost, growth and control.' Ford's old rules were: forms must be filled in completely and in order; and, we pay when we get the invoice. Now the new rule is: we pay when we get the goods. It sounds common sense, but if you were responsible for accounts payable, how brave would you need to be to propose such an untested change in an organization steeped in the old rules?

The old ways of working are evident in the legacy of separate computer systems used by separate departments of organizations. Now, the new rules of work design are being superimposed on the network of computers serving the whole organization. It is another example of knowledge being built into computers, and illustrates how impossible it is to separate discussion of strategic management from the use of information technology. The risks and rewards are so big. Re-engineering involves pulling apart the business engine, binning some parts, and reconnecting what's left. If it doesn't work properly, you're in serious trouble, as Hammer (1993) later acknowledged. But if it does work, your quality of service is so high, and your costs so low, that competitors must also re-engineer just to stay in the market. Another 1980s case in Hammer's paper describes how the insurance company MBL re-engineered its processing of insurance applications. It foreshadowed the introduction of telephone direct-line insurance, and the effective re-engineering of the retail insurance sector in the western world.

MBL's old process was typical of those used by insurers at the time. Customer applications were handled by a chain gang of 19 people in five different departments. The process employed specialists for credit checking, quoting, rating, underwriting, and so on. Typically it took 22 days to issue a policy, but an application required just 17 minutes' total work on average. Applications spent over three weeks queuing in people's in-trays, just to get those 17 minutes of work done.

In the new process an application faced just one queue and one person. A 'case manager' did everything, supported by network access to remote databases and an expert system to help with difficult decisions. Typical turnaround time dropped to about two to five days, required 100 less office workers, and could handle double the volume of new applications.

Enormous improvements such as these are only possible when we can shed a 'mindset' of beliefs that served us well during the industrial era of tangible products. These beliefs are related to the unwritten rules like those that hampered Ford's accounts payable process before it was re-engineered. The beliefs are held almost at a subconscious level, and so are seldom brought to the surface for examination. Our instincts about work were formed from seeing tangible products being made. Since the pin-makers described by Adam Smith (1776) we have divided work into separate stages and progressed the product through the stages in sequence. The economies are compelling for a tangible product that can only be in one place at a time, but do not apply to an information product. An advertising proposal, for instance, could, if necessary, progress at the same time through six processes in six continents performed by six different team members, all collaborating in parallel.

Concurrent engineering is one example of parallel working. When designers worked with pen and paper, the design of a car engine had to be completed before the engineering drawings could be duplicated and released to the factory. During development there was only one set of paper drawings showing the latest stage reached. The drawings were worked on in the design office, often distant from the manufacturing plant, and so it was impractical to frequently consult the manufacturing staff. No surprise, then, that the design often ended up being unnecessarily difficult to manufacture, and sometimes going back to be redesigned. A change costing £10 at the design stage could cost £10,000 during production, or £10 million for a product recall later. But now, designers prepare their design by computer. Networks make it easy for production planners, factory workers, and even component suppliers to view the design as it takes shape, and to recommend changes. The design process thus extends beyond the design department, to the production department, and beyond the boundaries of the corporation, to include supplier organizations. And that requires a changed mindset and new rules.

INTEGRATING BUSINESS FUNCTIONS AND PROCESSES

We have seen that business processes invariably involve several different business functions, which were traditionally organized in different departments. The process of order fulfilment, for instance, stretches across sales, accounts, stock control, and dispatch, and of course these functions still have to be performed. But the functions don't need to be performed one after the other, by a sales representative, an accounts clerk, a stock keeper and a dispatch clerk. A single customer service manager with access to the computer systems of these four functions can handle the whole process. Then, when a sales enquiry is received, it is possible over the phone, in real time, to check stocks, give a price, quote a delivery, reserve an item and quote an order number.

OK, so what's so difficult about that? Two things: people, and technology. Let's first deal briefly with the people problems, as the

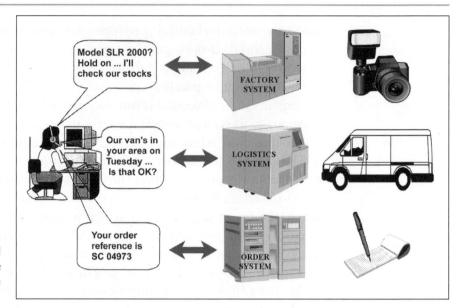

Figure 4.1
An integrated customer service system

achievement of change in organizations is not the primary focus of this book – though even in education it is becoming inappropriate to study management as a set of separate topics in watertight subject areas.

People favour particular jobs because of their background and skills. For instance, accounting appeals to people who are comfortable with numbers and analysis, whereas jobs in sales are attractive to people with well developed personal skills. Perhaps because our education system encourages people to specialize, there are plenty of people with well developed skills in just one discipline, but far fewer with good skills in several disciplines. But re-engineered jobs usually require people with multiple skills. So, do you sack the sales reps, clerks and stock keepers and replace them with a more flexible new employee with multiple skills? Or do you train the sales rep in accounting and stock keeping? Or train the clerk in dealing with customers?

The present job incumbents are not fools, or they would not be running the day-to-day business of the organization. They will certainly see this opportunity for the company as a potential threat to their jobs, yet the change can only be achieved efficiently with their co-operation. Turkeys don't vote for Christmas, so don't make turkeys of employees. Recognize and address their legitimate fears right from the earliest stages of the project. As usual, success depends on teamwork, truth, openness and trust. Generous retraining, redeployment and redundancy may be costly, but not nearly as costly as a project that never achieves the promised benefits, and fails because employees overtly appear to support the project, but covertly fight it every step of the way.

The technological problems are formidable too. It can be expensive and problematic to build a special network to join four separate legacy computer systems, running on hardware supplied by different companies. The applications may be written in different languages (Cobol, C, etc.) for different operating systems (Unix, Windows NT, etc.), hold characters coded using different standards (ASCI, ESBCDIC), and store data in different databases. And even if you manage to do it successfully, what do you end up with? A large, complex system for just one business process, that is difficult to adjust to accommodate other business processes and impossible to fine tune to the business as it develops.

No enterprise saddled with separate departments and separate computing systems for each function can re-engineer their processes without integrating or replacing the old systems. To re-engineer business processes, the enterprise should ideally have a single, integrated suite of programs to perform all the fundamental business functions.

There are four different routes to integration, but in practice organizations often end up with a combination of approaches. These are:

- Enterprise Resource Planning (ERP).
- Enterprise Applications Integration (EAI).

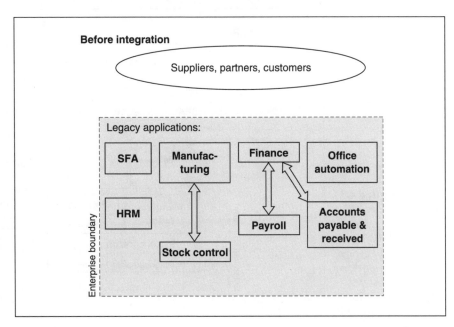

Figure 4.2
Before integration: poor or no integration of applications modules

- Component Based Development (CBD).
- Outsourcing to an Application Service Provider (ASP).

ENTERPRISE RESOURCE PLANNING

ERP offers a one-stop-shop solution, in which an organization can purchase an integrated suite of functions. The three main functions that most software suppliers provide in their ERP packages are Finance, Human Resources and Factory Scheduling. Then there is usually a selection of other functions that can be added. The advantage of going to one supplier is that if anything does not work properly, there is no possibility of buck-passing between different suppliers. However, there is no single ERP supplier that can provide every function a business might need, and usually an organization ends up having to bolt on extra modules, either legacy applications, or applications provided by another supplier. Each module then requires an application interface to be written, to allow it to exchange data with the ERP suite. Because of its manufacturing heritage, ERP solutions tend to be strong on the supply chain side, but weak on the customer demand side. Customer relationship management (CRM) applications are very popular at the time of writing, and ERP suppliers

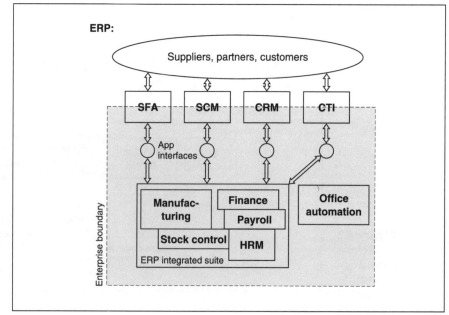

Figure 4.3
After ERP: a well-integrated core of Finance, HRM and Factory application modules, with other applications added as required

are scrambling to form associations with CRM suppliers, or developing their own CRM modules.

ENTERPRISE APPLICATIONS INTEGRATION

This solution allows an organization to choose the best-of-breed in each category of module, and to retain any legacy systems that work well for the organization. At the heart of the new system there is an EAI middleware package with a set of links, like spokes, to each of the new, and legacy, applications. It does not add any extra functionality, but acts as a translator, allowing all the various incompatible modules to exchange data to support the business processes of the organization. The advantages of this approach are that an organization can choose the most appropriate applications for each function, and can add further applications modules later without too much difficulty. The disadvantages are that integrating certain modules can be problematic, and also EAI systems don't respond to requests as quickly as ERP systems, because the EAI module takes time to translate the data flowing between modules.

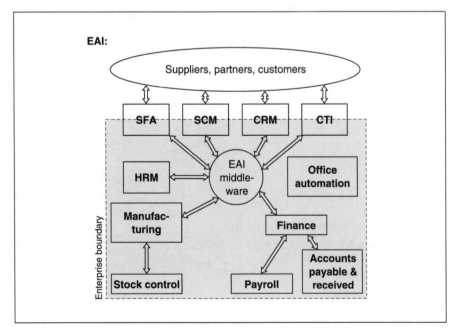

Figure 4.4
After EAI: a middleware hub to translate and deliver inter-module traffic

COMPONENT BASED DEVELOPMENT

This is an alternative method for constructing information systems. Component based systems are potentially much quicker and cheaper to develop, and they are much more flexible and easier to fine tune to shifting business needs in today's changing environment. Instead of building a system by integrating a few large monolithic applications, a system can be built from many smaller modules that are not permanently connected, but communicate with each other when necessary. Thus, components can be removed, modified, replaced, without affecting the integrity of the rest of the system.

Component based systems are radically different from conventional systems. Normally, systems are built from programs coded in procedural languages such as Cobol, or C. Conventional programs are lists of instructions that are followed when called for. Programs and data are stored in separate files, and the programs process the data.

A component, however, is a piece of code written to deliver a particular service or set of services, and wrapped in a defined interface, via which it can communicate with other components. Internally it may be conventional code, or it may be a business object, written in an object-oriented programming language. Object-oriented code is written as sets of rules, such as 'If ... Then ...', that are not executed in any particular order, but execute individually when the defined

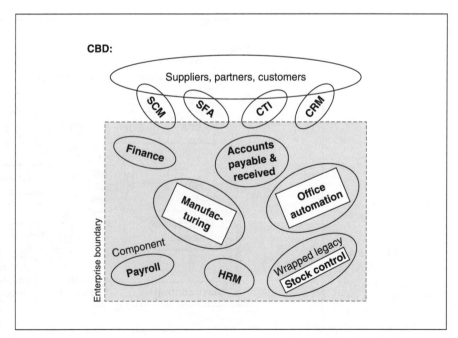

Figure 4.5
After componentizing: wrapped legacies and some new components

conditions arise. Code and data are not held in separate files. Components contain code and data, and represent real-life business entities such as 'customer', 'product' and 'account'. They are placed in a container so that they can interact with each other, just like their real-life counterparts. A component can be removed from the system, modified and replaced, without affecting the rest of the system, thus allowing continual development.

Two features – software re-use and inheritance – make component based systems faster, more accurate and cheaper to develop and maintain. Once the basic components for the business have been written, new systems can be created with very little extra coding. In fact a library of standard components can be built to support re-use, and eliminate the need to write large amounts of new code. Programmer productivity is further enhanced by the ability of components to be linked in parent–child relationships, so that the child component inherits characteristics from the parent component. New types of component can thus be defined in terms of existing ones. For instance, using inheritance, a system for a financial institution might require components for Savings Account, and Current Account, that could both inherit characteristics from a more general Account component, that defines characteristics common to both.

The disadvantage for IT departments in individual companies is the up-front investment needed before the advantages kick in. A new programming environment must be learnt, and it takes time to build a library of components. Also, there are several incompatible object standards battling for supremacy: Microsoft's Common Object Model (COM), Sun's Enterprise JavaBeans (EJB), and the non-proprietary Common Object Request Broker Alliance (CORBA) standards. Which standard should an IT department back?

One way out of this bind is to outsource all or part of the IT function.

OUTSOURCING TO APPLICATION SERVICE PROVIDERS

The Internet protocols TCP/IP allow any computer hardware/software platform to communicate with any other platform. Also, the Java objects and applets can run on any platform, so long as the operating system or browser holds a Java Virtual Machine to interpret the objects. The success of the Internet is due to its interoperability, and this has led to the emergence of organizations specializing in the delivery of IT services via the Internet.

An Application Service Provider (ASP) is an organization whose business is to deliver IT services to user organizations. An ASP can do all that your own internal IT department can do and more – and perhaps better, too. ASPs deliver specific functionality to users via the Internet, in compliance with the terms of a service level agreement (SLA). For a full service, the ASP may install and maintain PCs, plugged into the Internet at the user's site, and deliver a core ERP system consisting of Finance, HRM and Factory Scheduling/Stock Keeping. More modules can be added, as required. On the supply side, supply chain management (SCM) and procurement modules can be chosen. On the demand side, sales force automation (SFA) and customer relationship management (CRM) modules can be added. These modules reach out beyond the organization, upstream to suppliers, and downstream to customers.

Of all the IT assets regularly used by an organization, a large and growing proportion now lies outside its boundaries. Business success now depends less on owning the systems within the boundaries of the organization, and more on how a business uses the systems available, inside and outside the organization. Some users now outsource all their IT needs to an ASP who delivers services via the Internet to the desktop machines the ASP provides at the user's premises. Many organizations, however, operate their own hardware, run their own core ERP systems, and only outsource SCM and CRM – those modules that reach out beyond the organization and are not quite so mission critical.

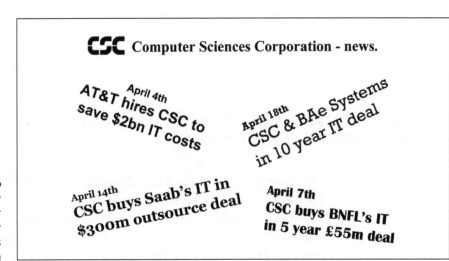

Figure 4.6
April 2000: new clients for Computer Sciences Corporation

You pay per month per seat for the services delivered. The advantages are that you only pay for what you can use, and if business expands or contracts you can change the number of seats you pay for. Also you can update and add to the services you need, without any heavy up-front capital costs. And finally, because ASPs can afford the staff, you can expect better service from your ASP than perhaps you previously got from your own internal IT staff.

Now at Work

Netstore. The Application Service Provider

Netstore and its business partners can host and manage your software applications via the Internet. There are no up-front capital charges – you just pay a predictable per user, per month rate – and for that they will:

■ Host the software.
■ Maintain the servers.
■ Provide data storage.
■ Fix the problems.
■ Provide you with technical expertise.
■ Manage the upgrades.
■ Guarantee availability.

That leaves you free to run your business.

Netstore reported revenues up 50 per cent at year end December 2001. They provide services to 40,000 organizations, including PowerGen and London Borough of Camden. www.netstore.net

COMMON BUSINESS APPLICATIONS PACKAGES

In discussing integration, we have encountered a number of modules that are the building blocks for business processes – the software for specific business functions. Time now for a general introduction to some of these applications packages. Let's start with office automation, as you are most likely to be familiar with these products. In these we can see some general principles that apply to other, less familiar packages in the following areas:

■ Office automation, and business communications.
■ Human resource management.

- Finance, accounting.
- Design and project management.
- Factory and warehouse.
- Supply chain management and procurement.
- Customer relationship management, sales force automation and e-commerce.
- Business intelligence, data warehouses and decision support systems.

It is difficult to avoid using jargon when discussing software. To avoid interrupting the flow with explanations, there is a glossary at the back of this book. Some of the entries cover topics fully enough for them not to need further mention in the body of the book. I hope you find the glossary interesting to browse through.

OFFICE AUTOMATION, AND BUSINESS COMMUNICATIONS

The best way to fill any gaps in your knowledge is to get some hands-on experience. In Chapter 5 you will find exercises to test and extend your knowledge and skills. The main facilities are:

- Word processing.
- Spreadsheets.
- Databases.
- Presentation software.
- Desktop publishing.
- E-mail and groupware.
- Browsers and networks.

Word processing

Microsoft Word is the word processor familiar to most people. It is designed for writing and printing letters and reports. It is optimized to handle text but it can also handle numbers, simple graphics, and you can even prepare and use a simple database using Word. But if you want to work mainly with numbers, graphics, data or web pages or photographs, or a combination of these, there are other packages that are optimized for those situations.

Spreadsheets

Microsoft Excel is optimized for dealing with numbers and graphs. If you want to prepare a balance sheet, analyse sales figures, prepare charts and graphs or generate a budget, then spreadsheet software such as Excel is ideal for those purposes. When you open Excel, you see a grid of columns and rows, with a cell at each intersection, into which you can enter data or a formula. The formula can be written using cell addresses as variables, so that for instance in one cell the spreadsheet can automatically display the total of values in ten or a hundred other cells. Want the arithmetic mean or the standard deviation? A few clicks, a second or two and you've got it. And for charts and graphs there is a wizard to simplify the process.

It is easy to prepare pie charts, sales figures, trend lines, and frequency distributions. In fact, if there is anything you think it would be nice to do with figures, Excel can do it for you.

Databases

Microsoft Access is the database software that comes with Word and Excel in the Microsoft Office suite of programs. It is optimized for preparing and storing records, so they can easily be extracted, edited, sorted and analysed in various ways. For instance, you can use it for

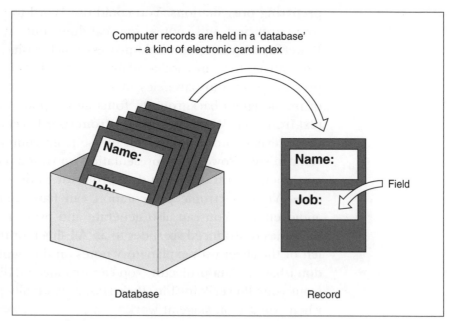

Computer records are held in a 'database'
– a kind of electronic card index

Name:

Job:

Name:

Job:

Field

Database

Record

Figure 4.7
Database, records
and fields

storing customer records. A record is like an electronic card in a card box. The record has fields, like boxed areas on a record card, for containing different types of entry. But a database overcomes the big disadvantage of a card box of customer records stored in alphabetical order, in which you cannot easily find, say, the records of all customers who live in Watford.

For customer records, you need fields for the customer title (Mr, Mrs, etc.), for the first name and for the family name. You could then have a field for the address, or separate fields for each line of the address. How you design the records depends on how you intend to use the database. If, for instance, you anticipate wanting to select all records of customers with a particular postcode, this will be easy if there is a separate postcode field. You can also include fields for dates and values, so that you can search for customers who have made purchases in the last 12 months, or who have placed orders in excess of £2000 for instance. You can also have a field for general notes, or a photograph that can be viewed when the record is extracted, though these cannot be so precisely searched.

Visual presentation software

The Microsoft Office suite also includes PowerPoint, the software for preparing presentations. You could use Word to prepare your OHP transparencies and notes for handing out at a meeting, but PowerPoint makes the whole process much easier, and offers lots of alternatives that are not available in Word. For instance, you can prepare your transparencies in full colour, choosing from a range of pre-designed backgrounds, fonts and clip art. Also, you can copy text from your Word files, graphs from your Excel files, pictures from the Internet, and anything you please from your scanner. Then you can run your PowerPoint presentation on your laptop when visiting a customer, or you can use a data projector to present to a large audience. Your electronic presentation can have animated slides with audio effects. You can also generate and print handout notes, with the slides reproduced six slides to an A4 sheet, or the slides down the left of the sheet with explanatory notes on the right hand side. If you don't have a data projector, you can produce OHPs or 35 mm slides from your PowerPoint file. PowerPoint can really polish up your act when you are on stage at work.

Desktop publishing (DTP)

This is the software for you if you want to combine text and pictures to produce a newsletter or house magazine, or high quality reports and sales literature. In the past the only way was to write the text yourself and then get a typesetter and printer to design the page layout for you and print in the quantities you required. Now, with the right software and a suitable laser printer you can do it all yourself. However, page layout is an art and you need an eye for design to produce really professional results.

Not long ago there was a big difference between WP and DTP. Now the gap has narrowed. Most modern word processors have some graphics capabilities and can set text in multiple columns in different fonts and typeface styles. Desktop publishing though is still much better for preparing artwork for professional printers. You can specify the colours you want using the Pantone range that printers understand, and you can see what line and half-tone pictures will look like when printed at the 150 lpi that the printing press uses.

To get pictures into digital form you may need a scanner or digital camera, and a picture editing package such as Adobe PhotoShop. This will allow you to enhance the picture by adjusting the contrast, brightness, saturation and hue. When you have the pictures how you want them, you can manipulate them just the same as other features to appear on the page: you can enlarge, contract, rotate, reproduce, relocate, and so on.

Messaging

Microsoft offers several packages that facilitate the exchange of information via e-mail. For domestic purposes, Outlook Express is the simplest and easiest to use. At work, however, the bigger Outlook program is a complete desktop information management system. With it you can manage your messages, appointments, contacts, and tasks, as well as track activities, view and open files, and share information with others in your group.

There is a wide choice of e-mail software from sources other than Microsoft. Lotus Notes is worth mentioning because it is designed round a database, specifically to support teamwork and the sharing of knowledge. Lotus is owned by IBM and the menus and options terminology is not quite the same as in Microsoft Windows, so it may take a while for you to get used to it. Its groupware features were unique originally, but since the development of Intranets and Extranets, Lotus Notes has lost some of its appeal. Now, it is possible to set up a database with shared access via a portal and a web browser such as Microsoft's Internet Explorer.

Browsing, surfing and searching

To browse, according to the Oxford English Dictionary, means to read or survey desultorily, and to surf means to be carried over the surf to the shore. Neither of these words does justice to Internet Explorer, Netscape Communicator and other Internet access packages. It would be easy to undervalue these user-friendly packages. They are bundled with other software or given away free to domestic users, but they helped to convert almost overnight a 20 year old network for computer scientists – the Internet – into a consumer product. Explorer is widely used at home by people who have little knowledge of computers, and its ease of use makes it an ideal interface to give access to enterprise Intranets and Extranets. These are private Internet protocol networks that are set up within an organization, and in the case of Extranets, extending beyond the boundaries of the enterprise, to reach suppliers, partners and customers. Browsers give access to information, and can be richly rewarding when used purposefully rather than desultorily.

An Intranet has the capacity to transform internal communications. The first obvious application for it is as a medium for all routine employee communications. It can deliver all the standard information that previously appeared in the employee handbook: guidance on health and safety, disciplinary procedures, the internal telephone directory and so on. It saves a bundle on printing, and need never be more than a day out of date. But that is just the start. Its uses are limited only by the culture that prevails.

One application for the Intranet is employee self-service in Human Resource Management, which neatly leads us into our next topic, software for HRM.

HUMAN RESOURCE MANAGEMENT

We touched on HRM in Chapter 1, showing how important this function is to any organization committed to making best use of its knowledge assets. Traditionally the Personnel Department was responsible for hiring and firing, employment benefits and law, industrial relations, and training and development. These functions remain important, but are no longer the exclusive responsibility of a few staff in a quiet office, cut off from the turbulent mainstream of operations. With the passing of five-year corporate plans, manpower and succession planning are less important, except perhaps for the most senior positions. Choreographing the waltz of a few whiz kids through the organization is not compatible with team building, openness and self-management.

Like the Personnel Department before, the HRM function provides a service to the rest of the organization, but it is delivered in a more helpful and timely manner. When IT and re-engineering eventually tackled the HRM function, first of all the paper files were stored digitally, and then they were networked. This allowed some functions to be opened up to self service, and others to be automated.

Self service can be arranged for employees via any PC connected to the company Intranet. With the files on all employees held digitally, it makes sense for employees themselves to update personal and professional information such as newly acquired skills. IBM's HR Access system allows global, enterprise-wide information access for employee self service on line. Employees can also view job openings, enrol on training programmes, read about corporate policy and consult the employee handbook. Self service lightens the administrative workload, but more importantly, it builds commitment, strengthens teamwork, motivation and satisfaction because employees are more involved and better informed.

Automation of other HRM functions such as training and recruitment further lightens the administrative workload, and can deliver services promptly when and where required. On-line training can be accessed any time the trainee is free. It can adapt to the trainee's rate of learning, and can provide feedback on progress. Recruitment software company Resumix claims their software reduces both the hire cycle time and the cost per hire by about half. The Resumix software allows line managers to create requisitions for job applicants, which can then be posted on dozens of web sites, both internal and externally. The software can accept CVs via the Internet, e-mail, fax or hard copy, and automatically match applicants to jobs. It offers a high level of automation at every stage, from initial requisition to the final hiring process.

FINANCE AND ACCOUNTING SYSTEMS

It was in this area that computers established their first beach head in the business world. Initially, computers were only used by scientists. Businesses did their routine financial calculations with mechanical calculators called comptometers, and big companies employed hundreds of young women as comptometer operators. When the scientists' computers became more reliable, companies started buying time on them to run their payroll calculations. It was much cheaper than employing all those comptometer operators. They lost their jobs – the first casualties of the information revolution.

Financial software packages make it possible to maintain up-to-date records of purchases, sales, stock levels, payrolls and time keeping. The software requires purchase orders, invoices and wage slips to be produced using the system, and in this way the ledgers are all kept up to date automatically by the computer.

Apart from solving many of the filing problems associated with running a business, these packages also save money by automating the production of routine reports, such as quarterly VAT tax returns, and the usual end of year Profit and Loss accounts, and Balance Sheets.

These systems also produce management reports, such as lists of invoices outstanding, and overdue debtors. This support for routine decision-making is essential to the efficiency of any organization. For SMEs, software such as that supplied by Sage is enough. Larger companies will often have ERP software from companies such as SAP, with the finance module at the heart of the system.

COMPUTER-AIDED DESIGN (CAD)

Want to plan a new office layout? Or sketch an idea for a design? Then you'll need a drawing board, a ruler for measuring, compasses, pencils and erasers ... Or you could use a CAD package to develop your design on the screen of your PC before printing it.

CAD packages use just the same processes as your word processor or spreadsheet. Your work will be saved in files, and if you want to produce a design that is similar to something you have done before, you can save time by editing an old file.

Also you can mark a section of a drawing to repeat it or move it or delete it in much the same way as your word processor allows you to electronically cut and paste blocks of text. The only difference is that CAD packages are optimized for manipulating graphics entities – arcs, lines, circles etc. – rather than text or numbers.

CAD packages can be awkward to use if the only input device you have is a keyboard. The keyboard was designed for inputting text and numerals, not graphics entities. For these you really need a mouse – or for finer control, a pen and tablet. Then selecting a graphics entity is easy: you just point and click. Move the mouse or pen, and a pointer on the screen moves with it. You select from a palette of graphics options displayed on the screen by pointing and clicking with the mouse or pen.

If you are thinking of buying a graphics package, there are a number of different types available, some of which make freehand sketching easy, and some that are more suitable for producing line drawings to scale for engineers and architects. AutoCAD is a well-known package for engineers and architects.

PROJECT MANAGEMENT

We discussed project management in Chapter 2. If you are ever put in charge of a project and you can work with a PC, get some project management software. It will pay for itself many times over.

So what kind of work qualifies as project? Here are a few examples:

- Launching a new product or service.
- Overhauling operational equipment.
- Constructing a new building.
- Re-locating an office.
- Installing a computer system.
- Conducting a training programme.

Thus any new work is a project if it lasts for a limited period, involves different groups of workers, and has penalties for late completion. The project manager is responsible for first planning, then controlling the allocation of time, money, people and other resources.

Managing a project is difficult because with new work there are few clear precedents to follow. Also, the people working on the project are often seconded part time and thus have other additional responsibilities and priorities. So all in all, as a project manager you will need all the help you can get.

There are dozens of packages available. Some of the better known ones are Microsoft Project, SuperProject Expert from Computer Associates, MacProject for the Apple Macintosh, and Artemis from Metier. They all require the project to be defined in terms of a list of the component activities which must be carried out, together with activity durations and dependency links.

The software then constructs a critical path network (see Chapter 2) and uses it as the basis for providing decision support for the project manager.

For instance, you can have a print-out of the activities displayed as bars arranged on a Gantt chart, as shown earlier in Figure 2.11. Also, you can enter details of the resources allocated to each activity – the number of hours of each named person's time for instance – and get back a report of exactly when each resource is required.

Most packages can handle several projects all at the same time, and will warn if conflicting demands are made for the same resource. Where conflicts do arise, the software can re-plan the project auto-matically, or allow you to make adjustments according to your own priorities. This is really useful support – information processing at its most meaningful from a management point of view.

FACTORY AND WAREHOUSE

Back in the 1970s most big firms were eventually equipped with sys-tems to handle their financial and accounting needs. The computer industry needed new markets for their products, and so they devel-oped factory scheduling and stock control systems, known as MRP, discussed in Chapter 2. Then in the 1980s MRP was expanded to include Finance and Human Resources, and re-marketed as MRP-2. And then in the 1990s, a third generation of software based on the same foundation of stock control, scheduling, finance and human resources was launched and named ERP, as discussed earlier.

This time round, the human resource component does more than just meet the needs of factory staffing, but is expanded to supply a full service to the HRM function as well. Also the finance module can handle customer orders and supplier accounts. This ERP core is designed for SCM and CRM modules to be easily added, so that an integrated system for the whole enterprise can be built.

Another difference between MRP and ERP is that whereas MRP required the full processing power of the mainframe, and was usually only run once a week during the night shift, ERP can run constantly alongside other processing requirements, providing a view nearer to a real-time picture of the state of play. With an up to date picture of stocks and demand, shortages and surpluses can be avoided, delivery promises to the customer will be more accurate, and costs will be lower.

But the business of promptly delivering products to consumers is not entirely in the control of the manufacturer, who is dependent on suppliers of materials to deliver promptly to them, and transporters and retailers to do their part. For a high quality, low cost service to the customer, a balanced flow of products throughout the supply chain, from primary source to ultimate consumer, must somehow be achieved.

SUPPLY CHAIN MANAGEMENT (SCM)

SCM and CRM are elements of e-commerce that we will visit again in Chapter 7. Here, we have time just to get a feel for the issues at stake.

Managing the supply chain must be a joint responsibility, shared by all links in the chain. There will still be competition on prices along the chain, and there will also be competition between parallel chains. If customers stop buying through a particular chain, all in the chain suffer, so the links in the chain must co-operate to move materials quickly and efficiently along the chain. If I buy five apples at Tesco in Oxford, I want them fresh, not stored for days in various warehouses along the supply chain. Ideally, there should be no storage en route. But to achieve that and keep the pipeline full, when I pick five apples off the shelves in Tesco, someone should simultaneously be picking five apples off a tree at the beginning of the chain, in Devon – or New Zealand perhaps.

How can this kind of response be achieved? For each transfer of product downstream, there must be transfers upstream, back towards the source of supply. Money of course must go back from time to time, but more immediately, information must flow back, to trigger replenishment. Most of these communications are done electronically now, automated such that systems in one organization can exchange information with systems in another organization without human intervention. Electronic Data Interchange (EDI) was invented to do this 30 years ago.

EDI is still used by big organizations in particular industries, to exchange highly structured purchasing and supply messages with the systems of their suppliers. The interchange requires a private network, and an intermediate value-added network (VAN) supplier, who does all the translating to allow messages from one system to be understood by another. The VAN also supplies a hub at the centre of the network, with mailboxes for messages to be posted to by the sending organization, and picked up from by the intended recipient. It can cost £100,000 to set up, and perhaps another £10,000 per month in charges. Communications are absolutely secure, but do not allow real time interactions. Faced with competition from the Internet, EDI in its original format is unlikely to survive, as it is inflexible, only allowing a limited set of pre-structured message types. Also, smaller potential supplier companies cannot afford the entry cost to this rich company's club.

The Internet has already opened up web-enabled EDI to any company. The Internet protocols are like a kind of Esperanto, allowing any computer system to exchange messages with any other computer, so the translating problems are mostly solved. Now, there are market exchanges on the Internet, which operate like the stock market, or the Saturday market in your town square. They are places where buyers and sellers in particular industries can come together, to bargain, to exchange information, to buy and to sell. These exchanges are operated by intermediaries like the old VAN suppliers, but allow faster interchanges of a broader range of communications. This has made possible a series of initiatives.

Now at Work

Exostar takes off

Exostar is a global e-marketplace for the $400 billion aerospace and defence industry. It provides a secure, open service over the Internet, connecting manufacturers, suppliers and customers of all sizes around the world, for trade and collaboration. Although an independent company, it was founded by five of the largest aerospace companies: BAE Systems, Boeing, Lockheed Martin, Raytheon and Rolls-Royce.

Exostar plans to enable 300 procurement systems of the five founders in 20 countries, to connect to 4000 suppliers, and also to interoperate with other industry exchanges. Exostar has already implemented exchange interoperability with

CommerceOne. 'We recognize,' said Exostar's Craig Jeffries in 2001, 'that streamlining the supply chain and standardizing procurement will result in real world gains in productivity, efficiency and cost savings for our member companies.'

Vendor Managed Inventory (VMI) allows a supermarket, for instance, to pass responsibility to the supplier for maintaining adequate stocks of their product at the supermarket. In order to do this, the supplier must have real-time access to real-time stock records at the supermarket. Big companies have had VMI for years, using near-real-time costly EDI systems, but now using the Internet any company can negotiate VMI with any of their suppliers. All that's needed is courage to give the supplier access to the stock records. The purchaser must trust the supplier to maintain stocks at least as well as before, and keep the information secure.

Now at Work

Kimberly-Clark manages the stock levels of its products at big retailers

Kimberly-Clark makes Kleenex, Huggies, Kotex and other well known brands of consumer goods. As long-time e-business practitioners they remain committed to EDI technology, and today the $14 billion company receives 80 per cent of its US orders via EDI.

In March 2001, Terry Assink, CIO at Kimberly-Clark, reports that 40 per cent of its North American consumer revenue comes from managing inventories of its products at big retailers through its Vendor Managed Inventory (VMI) program.

Collaborative Planning, Forecasting and Replenishment (CPFR) takes this a step further. CPFR requires the factory or supermarket to collaborate more equally with suppliers. They work together jointly to develop forecasts and plans for production and sales. Then no one in the supply chain will misinterpret or be taken by surprise by increases in demand caused by promotions and special offers. Sharing sensitive information of this type requires a high level of openness and trust between the collaborators. If competitors found out about a promotion, they might try to avoid losing market share by running parallel promotions, and thus neutralize its effect.

Collaborative design requires similar openness, but higher trust because the stakes are higher still. It requires a manufacturer to share product designs with suppliers during the early stages of the product life cycle. This is at a risky time when the sunk costs are burgeoning, and the revenue flow has not yet begun. It could undermine the launch if competitors got wind of the new product, and rushed forward their own campaigns.

SCM is concerned with the upstream side of manufacturing or retailing. Looking downstream, we see end users – our ultimate customers.

CUSTOMER RELATIONSHIP MANAGEMENT (CRM)

What is CRM? It's anything that helps an enterprise to manage its relationship with its customers, of course. It is a blanket term for all those activities at the end-user destination of the supply chain. The objectives are to win new customers, to identify the most valuable customers, and to serve, retain and delight all of them if possible. And that is only possible if you get to know your customers as individuals, each with a unique set of needs and expectations that you aim to meet or exceed.

Most enterprises maintain a database to hold the names and addresses of their customers – for invoicing purposes, if nothing else. Even supermarkets and retail stores know the addresses of their regular customers, the ones who apply for loyalty cards. When customers present their loyalty cards at the checkout, the store can relate their purchases to a particular customer name, and that is valuable marketing information. How do Sainsbury's know to mail me their Pet Club magazine with special offers on pet food? Because I present my Reward Card when paying for Classic Ocean Fish in Jelly cat food. The customer database therefore holds not only addresses of customers, but regularly updated information about their buying habits. The more an enterprise knows about its individual customers, the more it can tailor its approach to suit their individual needs and interests. Well, that's the theory anyway.

In practice, mature organizations may have a hotch potch of legacy systems. For instance there may be a couple of ERP systems and three customer databases generated from mail orders, telephone call centre orders and e-commerce orders via the web site. This makes it impossible for the enterprise as a whole to have a single view of each individual customer. Ideally, in whatever way a customer chooses to make contact with the organization, the person dealing with the contact should have the same complete view of the customer's previous contacts with the organization. It should be possible for me to place an order, and pay for it over the Internet, then call the company and say I want to pick up the order from their retail outlet in Liverpool. For many companies, this just would not be possible. The person taking my phone call would not have access to the e-commerce database, and the retail outlet may not have access to any database.

To summarize then, CRM has two dimensions (again): technology and people. The easy part is the technology for people to deliver excellent service to their customers. But CRM technology such as Computer-Telephony Integration (CTI) and Sales Force Automation (SFA), and data mining, requires people to change the way they work. It's the people dimension that's difficult. Never forget that people will always resist change, unless they see clear and certain benefits for them personally and individually. Then they will embrace change with enthusiasm, and help make it happen.

Now at Work

The Boots Advantage Card and business intelligence tools bring major success

Within 18 months of launch, Boots the Chemists' £25 million investment in their Advantage Card added an extra 4 per cent to turnover. But the real advantage sought by Crawford Davidson, Head of Advantage for Boots, is customer insight. And with 1400 stores in the UK, 11 million card holders, and 12 million customer visits per week, he has plenty of data to work on.

About a terabyte of customer data is stored in a data warehouse built with a DB/2 database running on an IBM SP/2 platform, and analysts use MicroStrategy as one of the main tools to deliver key business information. It was 'the top product we evaluated for heavyweight querying,' said Project Manager Ian Radmore. He wanted to get the structure right from the start, and store data at the lowest level of granularity so that users could build it up to any level during analysis.

The Boots Customer Insight team of 30 analysts, all heavyweight users, use reports in MicroStrategy to do demographic profiling, basket analysis and direct marketing response analysis. 'Considering the amount of data being queried, response times are excellent,' says Ian. Boots run 250 promotions every month, each of which used to take four hours of data manipulation to assess. It now takes five minutes of data input and a report that runs in minutes, freeing the customer insight team to draw insights from the information.

With tight margins and low average spend, direct mail is expensive, so Boots introduced Advantage Point in-store kiosks to deliver a range of personalized offers to card holders. Crawford explains, 'Kiosks take Boots further along the road towards one-to-one marketing with the customer.' In Boots' long term CRM strategy, communication with customers will be via mobile phone, digital TV, Internet, kiosks, in-store, mailing and telephone. 'The consumer will select the way they want to contact the brand. We must ensure that we have a single view of the customer so that however they contact Boots, the brand and their personalized proposition is the same.'

Boots are planning a new campaign for the data warehouse. 'We need a self-learning system,' insists Crawford. 'We need to be able to deliver personalization which can only be achieved through automation, where the consumer is the stimulus for an offer and their reaction to that offer prompts the next offer.' Crawford believes that Boots has the underlying IT infrastructure to do that.

www.microstrategy.com
www.ibm.com

BUSINESS INTELLIGENCE AND DATA MINING

Where do you go data mining for business intelligence? To the data warehouse or data mart, where you drill down to find the information you want. OK, so that's got some of the jargon out of the way – quite a bunch of mixed metaphors, I'm afraid. So let's start again.

One of the fundamentals of all computing is that data entry is expensive, and data storage is cheap. It is true of word processing, where it is always worthwhile saving all but the tiniest of files, and it is true of enterprise-wide systems, where organizations also save and archive files. However, even with your PC it can be difficult finding a file on your multi-gigabyte hard disk, so imagine the problems of analysing terabytes of enterprise data.

A data warehouse is an additional computer system in the enterprise for storing data in a structured manner, to give business decision-makers rapid access to information. The warehouse copies its data from existing systems like order entry, general ledger and customer relationship management, and stores it outside the operational system. The data is intended for use by executives rather than programmers, so there must be a user-friendly interface that does not require highly developed computing skills. Not all data is stored: it would not be practical or useful to record, say, revenue flows minute by minute throughout each day. The data is consolidated and summarized. The warehouse is a large database, and as we discovered earlier, the way a database is designed affects what and how data is stored, and affects the ways in which it can be used later.

A data mart is a small data warehouse of up to 100 gigabytes. If a data warehouse gets too big, its speed of response to queries can fall too far. Twenty seconds for a routine data warehouse query and two minutes for medium drill-down might be just acceptable, but any longer will stop most users from using the system. The solution is to copy data from the data warehouse into two or more data marts that are designed for particular classes of user.

Most ERP systems have the capacity to generate routine reports to answer closed questions like 'How many products did we sell in the SW region last month?' However, they cannot handle the more powerful open business questions that data warehouses are set up to answer, such as 'What kind of customers are most profitable?' or 'What kind of marketing campaign will be most effective?' These are the questions that deliver the greatest business benefit, but finding the answers to them requires a dynamic interaction between the user and the data. Users must be able to explore different possibilities, and reformulate queries on the fly as they do so. This on-line analytical processing (OLAP) requires special tools.

There are two sets of tools for data mining: those for discovery of patterns and trends in the data, and those for verification. Discovery tools include data visualization, neural networks, cluster analysis and factor analysis. Verification tools are the more familiar statistical techniques such as regression analysis, ANOVA, t-tests, correlations and forecasts. Power users will be able to make ad hoc selections from these, but many business managers may prefer to run 'canned' pre-programmed queries.

We have reached the end of four chapters, trawling through the business use of information technology from different perspectives. The purpose has been to understand where we are today, and how we got here. The collapse of the dotcoms at the turn of the century might be interpreted by some that the Internet is a busted flush. Nothing could be further from the truth: the real action is taking place out of sight of retail customers, within and between businesses.

Chapter 5 provides an opportunity to brush up your practical computing skills. It allows a break from narrative and theory before Chapter 6 in which we look at how to change systems that are past their use-by date. Then finally in Chapter 7 we look ahead to see what new developments are emerging, and how they are influencing the design of information systems.

REVIEW AND RELATE

Is this chapter relevant to you at work? Check it out. Relate the material to your own experience by reflecting on the questions below.

1 What business processes do you contribute to at work? You may only be involved in one. Define it (or them) as follows. Category: start point to end point. Here are some examples:

- Manufacturing: procurement to shipping.
- Sales: prospect to order.
- Order fulfilment: order to payment.
- Service: inquiry to resolution.

What sub-processes or stages can you identify inside the business process? Question everything. Can any be eliminated? Are they progressed in parallel or one after the other? Are they all value-adding or essential? How could the business process be re-engineered, using appropriate IT?

2 What computer systems and applications does your organization use internally? How integrated are they? Do you know, or can you find out about the architecture: do you have ERP, EAI or CBD? Do you have systems that connect you with your supply chain partners or customers? What plans are there for such connections, and what preparations are being, or have been, made?

3 How would you feel if it were announced that the main process that you contribute to will be re-engineered? It might result in relocation, use of new technology, require fewer people with wider skills. What assurances would you seek? Would you see it as a threat to your job and income, or an opportunity for personal growth, development and employability? If you were asked to champion the re-engi-

neering, how would you sell it to the present job incumbents? How important to success is an atmosphere of trust? How much should be out in the open, and how much should remain secret?

4 Does your organization have an IT department? Are any applications outsourced to an ASP? Can you think of any applications that might be candidates for outsourcing? What would be the advantages and disadvantages?

5 List the office automation products available on your PC at work. Which of them have you used? Is there one, perhaps PowerPoint or Excel, that you would use if you could acquire the skill without too much effort? How might this benefit you, and your colleagues?

6 Can you think of an application for data mining in your organization? What useful information could it provide? What questions could it help answer? What solutions might it help provide?

REFERENCES AND FURTHER READING

Hammer, M. (1990). 'Re-engineering work: don't automate, obliterate.' *Harvard Business Review* (July–Aug).

Hammer, M. and Champy, J. (1993) *Re-engineering the Corporation: Manifesto for Business Revolution*. Harper Collins.

Smith, A. (1776). *An Enqury into the Nature and Cause of the Wealth of Nations*. Full text available at www.bibliomania.com

Reports and white papers at www.netstore.net and www.csc.com

Hands on, with Microsoft Office

I only took the regular course ... the different branches of Arithmetic:
Ambition, Distraction, Uglification and Derision.

'Alice's Adventures in Wonderland' (1865), Lewis Carroll

IN THIS CHAPTER ...

- Why you really do need adequate computer skills.
- Basic keyboard, mouse and Windows skills.
- Hands on exercises in word processing and spreadsheets.
- Hands on searching for information and preparing presentations.

A CHANCE TO HONE SOME EXECUTIVE SKILLS

How would you manage if by some unlucky chance you were blinded?
I pray it never happens, but you would find ways to compensate and
get back to work. Blindness is no barrier to reaching the highest levels
of office, as David Blunkett has proved. He must find it frustrating,

though, not being able to browse the newspapers, and be dependent on people to select and filter the information he gets.

Inability to use IT is disabling for a manager. You can compensate, and depend on people to select and filter information for you – but having poor IT skills is a voluntary disability.

Data and information are the building blocks for knowledge. In the new economy, information and knowledge have replaced tangible assets as the basis for business success. For executives in knowledge intensive organizations, the ability to share information and act on it are critical skills. In these organizations, information systems play a key role, and IT skills rank in importance alongside personal skills, self-motivation, and the ability to work unsupervised and in teams.

Here is the chance to get an edge – hone up your computer skills.

THE REALLY BASIC BASICS

General notes on hardware and software

Learning to use a computer or some new software is a bit like learning any other skill such as riding a bicycle, for instance. It is impossible for a tutor to 'teach' you how to ride a bike: you see other people do it, and you just have to get on the bike and learn for yourself. It is the same for computers – learning by doing.

Of course a tutor can do something to make learning easier. With a bike, for example, the tutor can lower the saddle so both your feet touch the ground. Also, a tutor can show how to do it, and divide the whole skill into small parts to learn separately. But in the end, it's up to you: you just have to try to do it – and you will certainly make lots of mistakes. No one ever learned how to ride a bike without falling off lots of times, and you should expect to make lots of mistakes while learning new computer skills. When you make a mistake, usually the cost is just a little time to re-do some key presses. So, be brave, take risks, and when you make a mistake, stop and think why it happened and try not to make the same mistake again. That is the way to learn quickly.

A computer, however, is much more complex than a bicycle. When you push the pedals on a bike, you can see how they turn the wheels, but when you press a key on the computer keyboard you can't always see what happens. So in these exercises, try to figure out what is happening inside the box when you are pushing keys on the keyboard, or clicking the mouse. It is important you understand what is happening: you shouldn't just remember a series of key-strokes like learning a telephone number. If you know exactly what each keystroke achieves, you are more likely to remember what you learn.

Hardware and software basics

Hardware is anything you can plug in and switch on. Software is a list of instructions that tells the hardware what to do, and controls the flow of data between the various hardware devices of the computer system.

The main hardware devices are:

- A keyboard (for input).
- A mouse (for input).
- A visual display unit (VDU) or screen (for output).
- A printer (for output).
- A main unit – the box underneath the screen (for processing and storage).

Inside the main unit there are usually at least five smaller devices:

- A central processor unit (CPU).
- A set of memory chips for temporary storage, called random access memory (RAM).

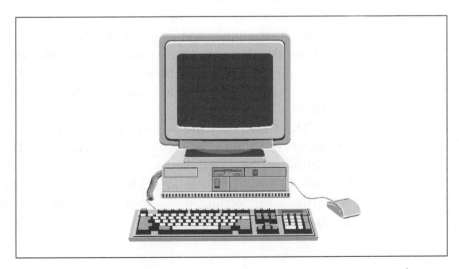

Figure 5.1
Front view of a PC

- A diskette drive, for transportable, semi-permanent storage.
- A hard disk, for large quantity, semi-permanent storage.
- A compact disk read-only memory (CD-ROM) drive, for permanent storage.

The CPU is a slice of silicon, about the size of a book of matches, with millions of microscopic electronic components etched on its surface. A well-known example is the Pentium chip, made by Intel. This is the clever part of the computer that does all the computing.

The RAM chips look similar to the CPU, but the etched circuits are much simpler. These RAM chips form the memory that holds the software you are using, and the data that you key into the computer – but only while the electric power is switched on. When you switch off your computer, the circuits die and all memory in RAM is lost, including the files you have been working on. So if you need to keep your work, save it (copy it onto disk) before closing an application or switching off the computer.

The diskette drive is like a record player for recording, playing back or erasing data on a magnetic disk. The data on a diskette can be software instructions for controlling the computer, or work files such as word processed letters or reports. When you first switch on your computer, most of the RAM memory circuits are empty, but you can load them with software and work files by telling your computer to read the files from the diskette, or hard disk.

The hard disk is a precision made, sealed unit that works the same way as a diskette, but can hold many thousand times more data than a single diskette. It can hold copies of all your software and all your work files. However, the hard disk is a mechanical device that gets used all the time, and may eventually wear out and stop working. When that happens, everything on the disk may be lost. The data on your hard disk may be many times more valuable than the computer itself, so you should make back-up copies of all your important files.

The CD-ROM drive is just like a CD player. Until recently, CD-ROMs could only play back factory recorded CDs, but some combo drives are now designed to record and play back, and handle not only CDs but DVDs as well. The most common use for the CD-ROM drive is for loading new software into the computer and onto the hard disk.

Keyboard and mouse

There is a pointer that you will see on the screen. It looks like a little arrow that moves around when you move the mouse. You can use the mouse to move the pointer and select a command from a menu. Just point and click with the left mouse button. Also, you can point and click where you want to start typing. It's easy.

Typing is fairly easy, too. It's not something that can be taught – you just have to put some hours in, learning and practising. The best way is with an on-line or PC based typing tutor such as 'Mavis Beacon teaches typing'. It is cheap and available at PC World and other retail stockists.

If you really are starting from scratch, mastering touch-typing will save you time in the long run. In touch-typing you use all four fingers of both hands, plus your thumbs for the space bar. You start with your forefingers resting lightly on keys F and J, with the other fingers on the other keys in the middle row of keys. This is called the home position. With a little practice, your fingers soon learn where all the other keys are in relation to the home position, and you can type without taking your eyes off the screen. With a little more practice, you'll soon be able to type with absolutely no conscious effort. Then when you type, you can devote all your thinking to composing what you want to write. All it takes is a little typing each day and you'll achieve that in a month or two.

Microsoft Windows

This is a widely used graphical user interface and operating system that handles all the routine, fundamental house-keeping tasks that computer applications would have to do for themselves if there were no operating system to do it for them. Things like keeping track of where programs and data are stored, scheduling and routing data to and from the central processing unit, and to and from various input, output and storage devices. Some of these things are done automatically, some are triggered by the application package, and some can be instigated by you, the user.

There are versions of Microsoft Windows for use at home, in the small office, and as part of a network, but to the user (that's you), they all have a similar look and feel. There are lots of commands you can execute using Windows, and there are lots of ways of invoking each of the commands. One way of finding out about these – and about the

Microsoft Office suite of programs – is to get hold of the European Computer Driving Licence CD-ROM, and work through the tutorials and tests. When you can do them satisfactorily, you can collect a widely recognized qualification.

You may already be familiar with Windows and another application such as Word, perhaps. Then you just need an introduction to some of the other applications. If so, select from the exercises that follow. For each application there is an easy step-by-step example and some graded exercises to do.

INTRODUCTION TO MICROSOFT WORD

Word is Microsoft's word processor software. Word processors are excellent for preparing documents that consist mainly of words or text. Word processors can also handle numbers, charts, images and photographs to a limited extent, but other software packages are more suitable when the document does not consist mainly of words.

When you start up Word, you see a screen like this:

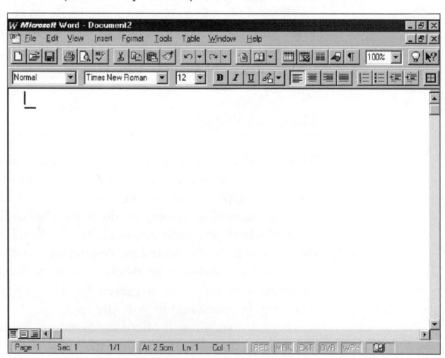

Figure 5.2
Screen shot of blank Word screen

This is a window showing what is stored in RAM, the computer's temporary memory.

Entering text

You can think of the white area as a blank sheet of paper, and you can start typing on it straight away. When you type in a string of characters, the key hits are stored in the order you type them, in RAM. Key hits for invisible characters, such as the <Spacebar> key and the <Enter> key, are also stored in the same way. The <Enter> key acts like the carriage return key on a typewriter: it stops the string of characters appearing on the current line and forces any text after the <Enter> key to continue from the left margin on the next line down. When you hit the <Enter> key, a 'hard' carriage return is inserted at that point in the text. It is called a hard return because it will remain at that point in the string, unless you go back and delete it.

The computer sends the long string of characters to the screen as you type them, and displays them starting at the left margin. When the string reaches the right margin, the computer automatically inserts a 'soft' return, to continue the string of text at the left margin on the next line down. The computer will reposition these soft returns automatically if you decide to reformat the text between narrower margins, or if you decide to use a larger font size with fewer characters on each line.

You should not hit the <Return> key at the end of every line, as you may have done with a typewriter. If you do, the computer will not be able to reformat the text automatically. Only hit the <Return> key when you want to start a new paragraph. This actually makes your task of writing easier: you can type freely to record your flow of ideas, and decide later how to format the text on the page.

Word exercise for absolute beginners

You need some text stored in memory for the exercises, so type in the following extract from 'Jane Eyre':

Mr Rochester flung me behind him: the lunatic sprang and grappled his throat viciously, and laid her teeth to his cheek: they struggled. She was a big woman, in stature almost equalling her husband, and corpulent besides: she showed virile force in the contest – more than once she almost throttled him, athletic as he was. He could have settled her with a well-planted blow; but he would not strike: he would only wrestle. At

153

last he mastered her arms: Grace Poole gave him a cord, and he pinioned them behind her: with more rope, which was to hand, he bound her to a chair. The operation was performed amidst the fiercest yells, and the most convulsive plunges. Mr Rochester then turned to the spectators: he looked at them with a smile both acrid and desolate.

'That is my wife,' said he.

Formatting text

1. Save your text

On the menu bar, click **File**, **Save**... and in the dialogue box that opens, enter the file name **Jane Eyre 01**, and click the Save button. This names the file, and puts a copy of it onto the hard disk. What you see on the screen is the RAM version. Now you can edit and modify the RAM copy, and if you make a mistake and damage or lose it, you still have a copy of the original on the hard disk. However, if you save an edited version, it will update the copy on the hard disk, because they both have the same name. So we must keep Jane Eyre 01 safe, by saving again under a new name.

2. Change the name of the RAM copy

Click **File**, **Save As**... (not just Save) and in the dialogue box, enter the file name **Jane Eyre 02** and click the Save button. This changes the name of the file you are working with, and now whenever you save it, it won't overwrite the original Jane Eyre 01.

3. Change the font style and size

On the menu bar, click **Edit**, then click **Select All**. The text becomes surrounded by black, indicating that it is selected. There is a small window in the toolbar displaying the font style 'Times New Roman'. Click on the button just to the right of the small window, and select Arial from the menu that appears. Now click on the button just to the right of the font size window, and change the font size from 10 to 16. Now deselect all the text by clicking the mouse pointer anywhere on the page. The black surround disappears.

4. Change the left and right margin width

There should be a ruler across the top of the page. If it is not shown, click **View**, **Ruler**. (Repeating this command will make the ruler disappear again.)

> On the menu bar, click **Edit**, **Select All**.
> On the Ruler, drag the left margin and drop it at 3.
> On the Ruler, drag the right margin and drop it at 12.
> On the menu bar, click **View**, **Page Layout** (or in Word 2002, Print Layout).

There is a little window at the right hand end of the toolbar, displaying a percentage figure, probably 100%. Click the button to the right of the window, then click 50%. This does not change the file, only the view you have of it on screen.

Now use Save As ... to save a second copy in this new format, in a file named Jane Eyre 03. Now change the view back to 100%.

5. Open two files at the same time

With Jane Eyre 03 still open, open Jane Eyre 02 as well.

On the menu bar, click **File**, then click **Jane Eyre 02.doc**. Both documents are now open, but you can only view one at a time. You can copy blocks of text from one document to the other, using Copy, and Paste. Try it now:

> Select a paragraph in Jane Eyre 02, by holding down the mouse button and dragging diagonally across the paragraph.
> On the menu bar, click **Edit**, then **Copy**. This places a copy of the selected paragraph onto the clipboard, a temporary storage area for copies in transit, so to speak.
> On the menu bar, click **Window**, **Jane Eyre 03**. Jane Eyre 03 is now displayed, ready for you to paste the contents of the clipboard into it.
> Point and click somewhere in the text, to locate the mouse pointer where you want the clipboard copy to be pasted in.
> Now click **Edit**, **Paste**. The copied paragraph appears at the point selected.

6. Print a file

Choose any one of your three files, and get it displayed on screen.

Make sure your printer is connected, switched on, and loaded with paper.

On the menu bar, click **File**, **Print**... and in the dialogue box that opens, click on the **OK** button.

That's it, you've finished the exercise. I hope you were keeping your eyes open, and noting what was going on. Did you see the descriptive notes that appeared when the mouse pointer hovers over a tool button? Did you notice the little icons next to the menu items under File, and Edit? The icons are the same as those in the toolbar, which are short cuts to the menu items. For instance, you can save your file just by clicking on the disk icon on the toolbar. And did you notice the letters underlined in File, Save? These tell you how to save a file without using the mouse. Just hold the <Alt> key down with your left hand, while you hit first the F key and then the S key with your right hand. There are several ways of doing most common tasks.

You should have the confidence now to experiment on your own. For instance, open Jayne Eyre 01, save a copy as Jayne Eyre 04 (or any other name) and then explore all the menu items and toolbar icons to find out what they all do. If you get into difficulties and all else fails, just click **File**, **Exit** (or Alt F X). That will close Word, and you will lose any work you did not save, but your files saved in previous sessions will be OK. You can start up Word again, and try to figure out what went wrong.

When you feel ready, or even before that, have a go at this next exercise.

Word exercise for rusty users

This exercise requires you to produce, on A4 paper, the letter shown in Figure 5.3. OK, no help here, and you can only award yourself ten out of ten if you produce an exact replica. Oh, all right then, check out 12pt Times New Roman, 36pt Cooper Black, and 14pt Century Gothic.

Your learning should not stop here. Use Microsoft Word at every opportunity at work, for assignments and coursework. Keep experimenting to find out more about the software. It has more functions than you will ever need, or even find out about. But if you think it would be nice for the computer to do something, it probably can, so experiment, and find out how. But before experimenting, save your existing work by clicking the Save icon. Then if things go wrong and

Awesome Rides plc

221b Baker Street
London NW1B 4SH
Phone 0171-843-5252
Fax 0171-843-5000

10 January 2000

Sir Hartley Roderhythe
Devonshire Hall
Harrogate
N Yorks
BD32 5HS

Dear Sir Hartley

Thank you for your hospitality last Thursday. It was a great pleasure to meet you and your charming wife, Lady Roderhythe.

I can now give you a first estimate for our 430m 'Spectre' ride, installed at the site we examined in your theme park at Devonshire Hall.

Materials and services	Time/Quantity	Cost
Consultation and design	200 hours	£20,000
Site clearance and preparation	3 days	£12,000
Materials and equipment	430 metres	£975,000
Assembly and installation	9400 hours	£84,600
Site supervision	30 days	£6,000
Insurance	2%	£21,952

Total: £1,119,552

As discussed at our meeting, it is not possible to give an accurate estimate at such short notice and without a site survey. However, for your purposes, I think it would be safe for you to use a figure of about £1.1 million.

I feel sure you will see this as an attractive proposition, but you will probably want to discuss it with me. I will phone you on Tuesday. Once again, many thanks for your interest in our company.

Yours Sincerely

S Holmes
Sales Director

Figure 5.3
Awesome Rides
letter

you lose or spoil your work, you can always start again with the file as it was just before experimenting.

There is often a quicker way of doing regular tasks. Try to find out about these, and they will save you more time as you learn about them and get faster. For instance, did you know you can select a single word just by double-clicking, and select a whole paragraph by treble-clicking? You can select one or more lines by clicking and dragging down in the left margin.

Use drag-and-drop wherever possible. It is very versatile. Try selecting a word in a line of text, and then try dragging it to another point in the text and dropping it there. Learn how to move around quickly inside your document. Never use the left, right, up and down arrow keys to move the cursor more than two or three spaces, but try using them with the <Ctrl> key depressed. Try using the following keys on the keyboard and see what effect they have: <Page Up>, <Page Down>, <End>, <Ctrl> and <Home>, <Ctrl> and <End>.

Also use Help: there is a huge amount of information there.

Word exercise for more competent users

Another letter for you to do, in Figure 5.4 this time. Apart from the signature, there are no features requiring any special or detailed design work. You don't need to draw the star shape, or insert hard returns at the end of each line to fit the text round the star. Figure out how to get Word to do all the detail work. Check out the toolbars (hold down Alt press V then T).

INTRODUCTION TO MICROSOFT EXCEL

Excel is Microsoft's spreadsheet software. Spreadsheets are excellent for preparing documents that consist mainly of numbers, calculations, charts and graphs. For instance a spreadsheet makes it easy to do sales analysis, tables of figures, charts and graphs, balance sheets, profit and loss accounts, budgets and cash-flow forecasts. A spreadsheet can also handle small amounts of text, but if you need to write more than a line or two, it is probably better to use a word processor.

When you start up Excel, you see the screen shown in Figure 5.5.

Across the top of the window, you see the familiar menu bar and toolbar, and you will recognize some of the menus and buttons. They work in the same way as they do in other applications such as Word.

With Word, at the start you see a blank screen, but with Excel the window is filled with 'cells' where the columns and rows cross, to give each cell its own address. For instance, the cell at the top left of the spreadsheet is cell A1, and on the screen shown in our example, the selected range – a black rectangle – presently surrounds the single cell at B14.

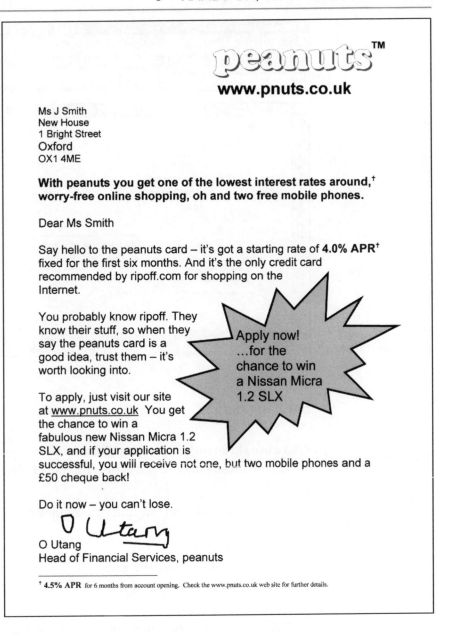

Figure 5.4
Peanuts letter

Each cell can hold a value, or some text. Or a cell can hold a formula with cell addresses as variables. For instance, if the formula = A1 + A2 is entered at A3, the computer will display at cell A3 the sum of the values held in cells A1 and A2.

With Excel it is easy to display tables of figures as charts and graphs. That is why Excel is so useful and popular with managers.

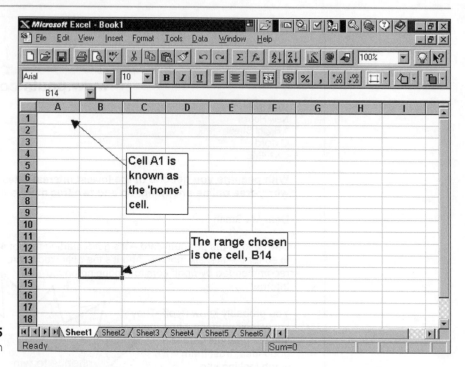

Figure 5.5
Blank Excel screen

Entering data

There are three different types of data you can put into a cell, and the computer must know which type of data is being entered:

■ A number – an amount or a value that can be used in calculations.
■ A formula – an equation or function that the computer will use, and display the solution.
■ A label – a word, or a line of text.

If all the characters typed into a cell are numbers, the computer assumes the cell holds a value that can be used in calculations. If any other character is typed into a cell, the computer usually assumes the cell holds a label, and none of the data in that cell can be used in calculations. If the first character is = or + or −, the computer assumes the cell holds a formula and will display the results of the formula.

Excel has a huge range of special functions that allow you to display instantly, for example, the median or standard deviation of a table of figures.

Of course there is more to learn, but this is enough to get you started on the exercises. Remember to experiment. If you feel it should be possible to get the computer to do something, you can be certain it can do it. You just have to find out how to make it. If you can't discover by experimenting, try the Answer Wizard in the Help menu.

Excel exercise for absolute beginners

1. Move the mouse

See the **cell pointer** travel over the screen.

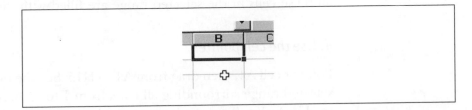

Click on cell B5. See the **selected range**, a black frame round the cell. Move the cell pointer until it rests on the left side of the black frame. See the cell pointer change into the **move cursor.**

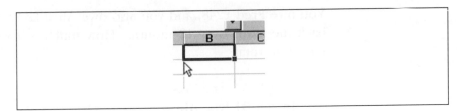

Move the cell pointer until it rests on the bottom right corner of the black frame. See the **fill cursor.**

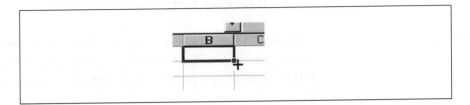

We will use these different cursors in the next exercises.

2. Use the move cursor

Use the cell pointer to select cell D3. Type in the value **100** and hit <Enter>.

Select D3 again. Now use the move cursor to drag the selected range to cell F6.

See the value of 100 has been moved from cell D3 to F6.

3. Use the fill cursor

Select cell F6. Move the cell pointer so that it touches the lower right hand corner of the selected range. When the cell pointer changes to the fill cursor, drag this corner down to cell F10. See the black frame of the selected range now surrounds cells F6, F7, F8, F9 and F10, and all these cells in the selected range are filled with the value 100.

4. Use the cell pointer

Point at cell A1, then drag from A1 to H15. See the black frame of the selected range surrounding all rows from 1 to 15 between columns A to H inclusive. Press <Delete> on the keyboard. See the contents of all the cells in the selected range are deleted.

5. Enter a formula

You owe Fred £248, and you also owe Alice £332. You agree to pay back the loans over 12 months. How much will you pay back each month in total?

In cell A1 type **Fred**.
In cell B1 type **Alice**.
In cell A2 type **248**.
In cell B2 type **332**.
In cell A3 type **Payment** =
In cell B3 type = (A2 + B2)/12

You should now see displayed in cell B3 the value 48.3333. You can improve the display by choosing a currency format for cells A2, B2 and B3. With the cell pointer, drag over cells A2 and B2 to select these cells.

In the menu bar, select **Format**, **Cells...**, **Number**, **Currency**, **OK**.

Select cell B3 and change the format to currency for this cell in the same way. Your display should now look like Figure 5.6.

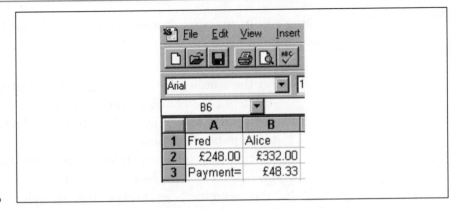

Figure 5.6

6. Enter a table and draw a graph

For this exercise you need to enter the table of figures shown in Figure 5.7, in the range C4 to D16. Excel will help you fill in the months.

> In cell C4 type **Month**.
> In cell C5 type **Jan**.
> In cell C6 type **Feb**.
> Select cells C5 and C6, and then use the fill cursor to drag down to cell C16. Excel fills the rest of the series of months automatically.
> In column D enter the column of sales figures. Excel cannot guess what these are.

To display this table as a graph, you can use the **Chart Wizard** button on the toolbar. Guess which button that might be, and let the pointer dwell over the button. After a couple of seconds, a label will appear,

Month	Sales
Jan	284
Feb	217
Mar	230
Apr	266
May	295
Jun	315
Jul	320
Aug	290
Sep	240
Oct	233
Nov	220
Dec	200

Figure 5.7

telling you its function. But before clicking on the button, first select the range of cells you want to chart, as follows:

Select the whole table, including the column headings, by dragging from the centre of cell C5 to D16.

Click on the Chart Wizard icon in the toolbar. The first of four dialogue boxes appears.

In the first box, select the type as **Line**, and select the first of the sub-types. Click on Next.

In the second box, accept the default choice (Series in: Columns). Click on Next.

In the third box, type **Sales** for the title. Type **Month** for the X-axis. Type **Revenue £1000s** for the Y-axis. Click on Next.

In the fourth box, accept the default (As object in:). Click on Finish.

See your finished graph displayed in a Chart Area.

If the size or proportions are wrong, you can change them. There should be eight small 'handles' at the corners and middles of the four sides. If they are not there, you can make them appear with a single click anywhere in the white Chart Area. Then you can drag these handles to resize or reproportion the graph. Select the **Series 1** legend by clicking on it. It is selected when handles appear. Now delete it by pressing <Delete> on your keyboard.

You can edit any individual feature of the graph. Just click on the feature you want to change, and when the black handles appear that show it is selected, select **Format** in the menu bar, and use the menus and dialogue boxes that appear.

7. Use a function

You can use the Paste Function button in the toolbar to select from a wide range of special functions. To demonstrate how to use them, we will select the AVERAGE function, and use it on the data for the sales graph in step 6 that you have just completed. If you know how to use an available function, you can just type it into the cell where you want it to appear. For instance, if you want the average monthly figure for the sales shown in cells D5 through D16 to appear in cell D18, just type into the cell **=AVERAGE(D5..D16)**. If you don't know the command to type, use the Paste Function button, as follows:

Select D18 as the cell where you want the average figure to appear.

Click the Paste Function button. The Paste Function box opens.

Select Statistical for the function category. Select AVERAGE for the function name.

Click OK. The Average dialogue box opens. If it obscures your data, you can drag it elsewhere.

Select the range of figures for which you want Excel to calculate the average. Either type the range **D5..D16** into the upper space provided, or point by dragging from D5 to D16, and the range will appear in the space automatically. Click OK.

See the answer, which should be 259.1667.

If you want the answer to fewer places of decimals, click the Decrease Decimal button in the format toolbar. This does not affect the accuracy of the value stored there: it just changes how it is displayed.

So there you are. You're no longer an Excel virgin. Go forth and multiply (and divide, chart, analyse ...). Enjoy.

Excel exercise for rusty users

In this exercise you are asked to reproduce a complete spreadsheet. You are given the values, text and formulas to enter, but you should study what you do, and be sure you understand why it should be done that way. The exercise illustrates some of the principles of good spreadsheet design, and gives you an opportunity to learn how to copy formulas. This feature alone can save hours of your time, but make sure you understand when and why you need to include the $ character in some cell addresses.

The spreadsheet you are about to prepare is for finding the level of sales at which a company can break even, the point at which sales revenue is just sufficient to cover the total fixed and variable costs. The company makes a loss below the break-even point, but makes ever larger profits the further it operates above the break-even point.

Figure 5.8 shows how the spreadsheet will print out, except that the values in the Calculation and Output areas are not shown.

Input area: This part of the spreadsheet is where the user will enter basic data to be used in calculations. No formulas will be entered here – only values.

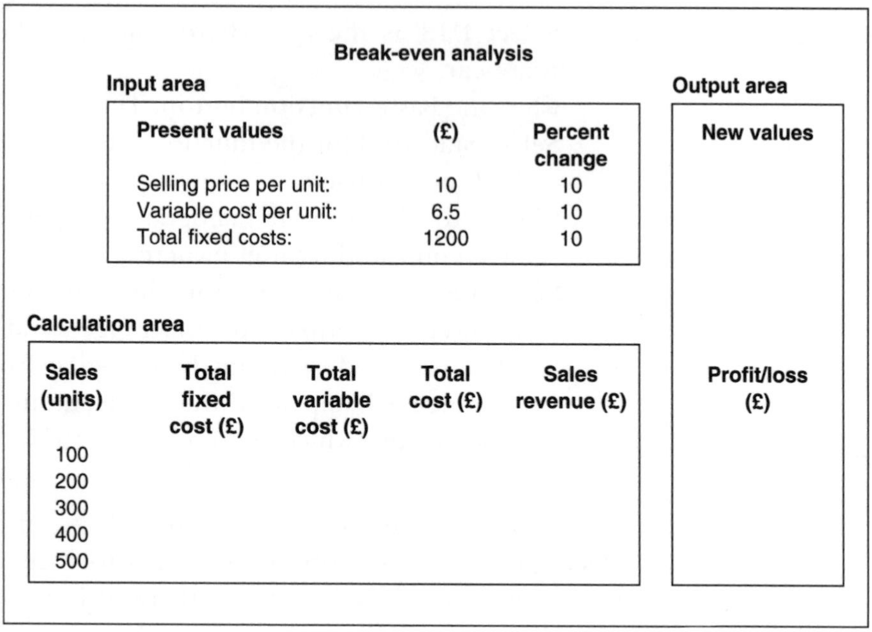

Figure 5.8
Spreadsheet for
break-even 'what
if' analysis

Output area: This is the part where the most important results of calculations will be displayed. The user will not enter any values here. In this example, the top part will show the new values for selling price, variable cost and total fixed cost, when the present values are increased by the percentages shown. The bottom part will show by how much the Sales Revenue is greater than the Total Costs for different levels of sales.

Calculation Area: This is the part where most of the formulas are entered, and the detailed calculations are performed by the spreadsheet. Again, users should not enter any values here.

The formulas to be used are shown in Figure 5.9. At first sight, there seem to be a lot of formulas to be typed in, but most of them can be produced automatically by using Excel's fill cursor. You only need to type in six formulas, and then drag and fill all the other cells where formulas are needed.

You have three tasks: one is to understand what the formulas do. Another is to find out how to enter the formulas without having to do a lot of typing. The $ sign forces copied formulas to refer to one particular column or row. For instance, suppose the original formula takes a value from a cell one row above and three columns to the left. Without the $, a copied formula would take a value in a cell with the same relative position – one above and three to the left of the copied formula, wherever that might be. But with the $, the copied formula is forced to take the value from exactly the same cell that the original formula got it from.

Your third task is to find out how to format your spreadsheet to look exactly like the one in Figure 5.8, but with the values showing of course. There are several ways of changing column width. The simplest is to drag the dividing line between the column letters at the top of the work area.

It is possible to get the spreadsheet to show the formulas instead of the values that users of the spreadsheet need. Figure 5.9 shows the formulas. You wouldn't normally need to do this, but if you want to try it, click the **Tools** menu, then **Options . . .**, **View**, **Formulas**)

You need to type in just one formula in row 6, and five formulas in row 14. Use the fill cursor to get Excel to do all the rest.

Your finished spreadsheet, when printed, should look like Figure 5.10.

To make a profit, more than 300 sales must be made. Try changing the Percent change values in the Input area, to see the effect on PROFIT/LOSS in the Output area.

Now treat yourself to some fun. Use Chart Wizard to prepare a graph of Profit/Loss on the Y-axis against Sales (Units) on the X-axis. Your graph should look like Figure 5.11 initially.

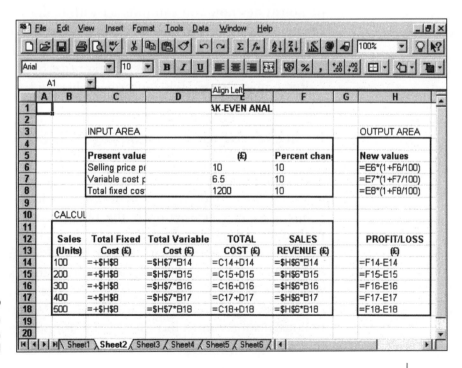

Figure 5.9
Break-even spreadsheet with formulas displayed

Break-even analysis

Input area   **Output area**

Present values	(£)	Percent change		New values
Selling price per unit:	10	10		11
Variable cost per unit:	6.5	10		7.15
Total fixed costs:	1200	10		1320

Calculation area

Sales (units)	Total fixed cost (£)	Total variable cost (£)	Total cost (£)	Sales revenue (£)	Profit/loss (£)
100	1320	715	2035	1100	−935
200	1320	1430	2750	2200	−550
300	1320	2145	3465	3300	−165
400	1320	2860	4180	4400	220
500	1320	3575	4895	5500	605

Figure 5.10
How the spreadsheet appears when printed

Drag the graph to a position where you can see it and the Input area at the same time.

Now try entering some negative percent change values into the Input area, and watch the graph change to reflect the new values as you enter them. This is a simple example of 'What if' analysis. It demonstrates how you can interact with data to understand the sensitivity of the model to changes that you could make. The break-even point is too high? What if you reduced your variable costs by 5 per cent? What if you reduced the selling price by 10 per cent?

Remember to use Help, and remember: to learn, experiment!

Excel exercise for more competent users

This exercise involves the construction of a spreadsheet to help in assessing stock market investment opportunities.

Spreadsheet construction is the province of our more numerate individuals in society. You are unlikely to have aspirations in this field unless you've got a GCSE O-level in mathematics. If you don't have maths at O-level, don't waste time with this exercise – it's not for you. We all have our strengths and weaknesses. Me? I was trained as an engineer, so spreadsheets are a doddle. My problem is I have no political instincts and a terrible memory for people's names. So, if you find maths difficult, want to swap skills with me? I thought not.

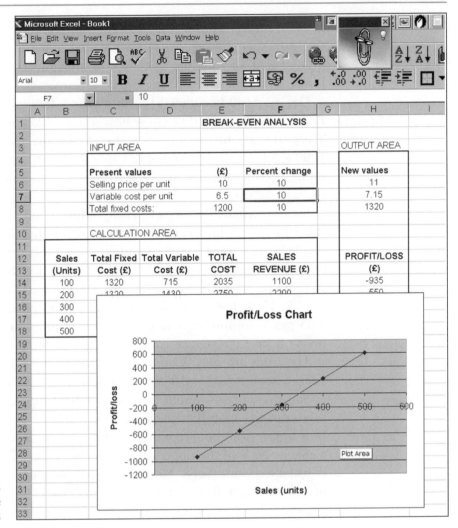

Figure 5.11
The graph changes as you change the input values

Ideally you also need some accounting skills for this exercise, in particular at least a rough idea of the accounting term Net Present Value (NPV). So before we start, here's my instant accountant refresher course.

Question: Which would you prefer to have, £100 now, or £100 in a year's time? Easy, you'd prefer it now. £100 now is worth £100, but you only need about £95 now, to invest and get £100 in a year.

Question: Which would you prefer, £100 now, or £120 in three year's time? Not quite so easy, but do the maths, and you'll find you need about £104 now to invest and get £120 in three years.

What we're doing here is working out the present value of future cash amounts, and then comparing them to see which is worth most. It's not an exact science, because to do the calculation you have to guess at future interest rates, but let's not get into that right now. For the refresher course, let's assume that risk-free interest rates for money lent to building societies or the government are going to hover around 5 per cent for the next few years.

OK, so £100 becomes £105 in a year – that's how interest works. But accountants need to know how much £123.45 becomes in a year. They do it by multiplying by a factor, 1.05 in this case. £100 × 1.05 = £105. And £123.45 × 1.05 = £129.62. What we are doing is compounding forward to find a future amount by multiplying by a factor.

So, to calculate the present value of future amounts we need to put this calculation into reverse. Instead of multiplying by a factor, we divide by a factor. Instead of compounding forward to a future value, we are discounting back to the present value. Let's do it. How much is £129.62 promised a year from now worth today? Easy: £129.62/1.05 = £123.45. It has to be, because that is the figure we multiplied by 1.05 just a minute ago to get the future amount of £129.62. If we divide it by 1.05, we are back where we started.

The rules are easy. Compound forward: for each year multiply by 1.05. Discount backward: for each year divide by 1.05.

So now we know about present values of future cash flows. But to buy a positive cash flow in the future, you have to pay a negative cash flow today. Add them together, and what do you get? The Net Present Value or NPV of the opportunity. The NPV for a risk-free investment is usually around zero. Here's how to calculate it. Pay £100 for an investment: cash flow = minus £100. Receive £105 in a year from now, present value £105/1.05 = £100: cash flow = plus £100. Thus the NPV of the opportunity is the two flows added together: minus £100 plus £100 equals £0.

Stock market investments, however, are not risk free, and no sane investor will risk money without the hope of a greater reward than can be obtained from a risk-free investment. One way to calculate the extra reward for risking money on shares is to calculate the NPV of the stream of cash flows that you are entitled to when you buy shares. When I buy £1000 of shares in the mining company Rio Tinto, I suffer an immediate large negative cash flow of £1000, but then expect to receive a stream of small positive cash flows – the dividends paid each year. And finally when I sell the shares, I receive a large positive cash flow – the sale proceeds. The NPV is what you get if you discount back to the present all these positive future cash flows, and add them to the initial negative flow. If the NPV is positive, say £200 NPV, this is the value of the investment opportunity. It is the extra you might receive beyond what you know you will receive if you just leave the money in the building society.

That, I'm sure you are glad to hear, is the end of the refresher course. Let's now look at the spreadsheet exercise. It could make you rich: you are going to construct an investment appraisal calculator.

You should aim to produce a spreadsheet that looks exactly like Figure 5.12 in every respect.

Here are some design details to help you construct the spreadsheet.

Input area

- Data entry is only possible in the white areas of the input area. All other areas of the spreadsheet are locked, and cannot be accessed by users.
- The white areas are designed to accept values, or text for the Company name.
- The values in Column E are all available from daily newspapers and company reports, or the Internet. Try one of my favourites, www.fool.co.uk

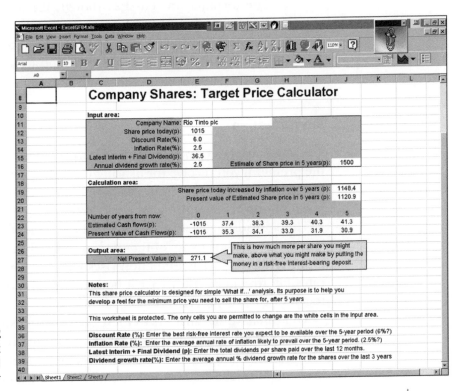

Figure 5.12
Investment appraisal calculator

■ The estimate of share price in Column J is your best guess, after looking at the charts, of where the share price is headed for in five years' time.

Calculation and output areas

■ These areas contain only formulas and cell addresses.

■ The value in cell J19 is the share price today, compounded forward for five years, using the inflation rate that is expected to persist over that time. Using an inflation rate of, say, 2.5 per cent, we must multiply today's price by 1.025 five times over. But a principle of good design is never to construct formulas using values that might change. Instead of values, we should use the cell addresses of where the values are entered in the input area. Thus the formula in J19 should be =E12*(1+E14/100)^5.

■ The formula in cell J20 just discounts the value in J16 back to present value.

■ The formulas in cells F23 through J23 calculate the value in cell E15, compounded forward using the dividend growth rate for the appropriate number of years.

■ The formulas in cells F24 though J24 discount back to present value the values shown in cells F23 through J23.

■ The formula in cell E27 simply adds up all the positive cash flows that occur each year and subtracts the cost of the original investment.

Interpretation

The value displayed in E27 can be interpreted as the present value of the premium you receive for bearing the risk of investing in this stock instead of leaving your money in a building society. That is if all your assumptions in the input area are correct.

This spreadsheet is a model of a real investment. You can play with it to gauge the sensitivity of the outcome at cell E27 to changes in the input variables. What if inflation rises to 4 per cent? What if interest rates fall to 3 per cent? What if both inflation and interest rates rise together by two percentage points?

You can have the answers to these 'What if' questions almost immediately, just by changing the values in the Input area. By playing with your model in this way, you can develop a feel for how the real investment might behave under similar circumstances.

As a manager at work, you can interact with business data by constructing models and playing What if games. Spreadsheet modelling can be a powerful aid to decision making.

A word of warning: don't even think about investing significantly in shares unless you are a net saver. Never put more than, say, £1000 total in shares unless all your savings are greater than all your borrowings, including your mortgage. Risk your money, perhaps, but not your house and family. Spreadsheet models only allow you to gauge risks, not eliminate them.

INTRODUCTION TO MICROSOFT POWERPOINT

PowerPoint is Microsoft's presentation software. It is ideal for preparing multimedia presentations for data projectors or on-line presentations. Also it is great for preparing high quality OHP acetates, 35 mm slides, and handout notes complete with reduced images of the screen presentation.

Preparing a presentation

When you start up PowerPoint, you could see a screen like Figure 5.13.

Your blank screen represents a blank acetate, VDU or 35 mm transparency, waiting for you to type in text, or paste in material from Word or Excel, or any other source, including sounds and movie clips.

However, if you prefer, you can prepare your presentation in outline first, as a set of unformatted headings and body text. This allows you to concentrate on your message and the order in which you present it, and leave till later design features such as layout, colours, backgrounds, fonts and pictures.

You can design everything from scratch yourself, or choose any level of help from PowerPoint, right up to automating everything but choosing the words. As usual, there are presentation designs to choose from, or you can run the AutoContent wizard, that will lead you through every stage. AutoContent asks you to choose from twenty presentation types, according to your purpose. Do you want to motivate a team, sell an idea, deliver information . . .? The remaining steps ask what form of output you require (multimedia, slides, handouts)

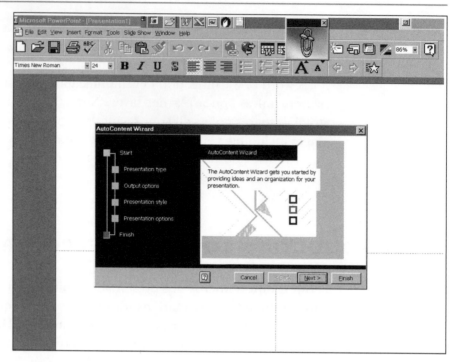

Figure 5.13
One of many ways
to begin

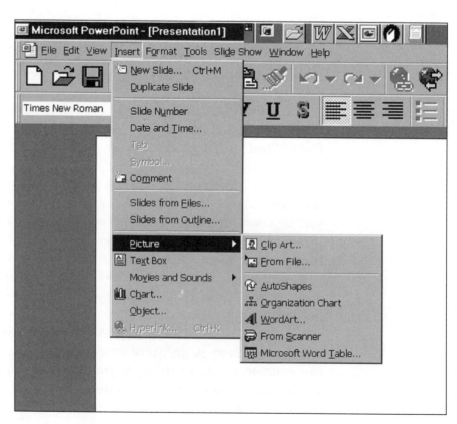

Figure 5.14
Menu, Insert,
Picture

and what you want to appear on the screens. AutoContent even suggests the general content for each slide. Figure 5.15 shows the outline for motivating a team.

All you need do is click on the text and edit it. The rest is automated.

PowerPoint exercise for absolute beginners

In this exercise you will prepare, with the help of AutoContent, a mini presentation of four OHP slides for thanking a speaker. So start up PowerPoint.

1 If there is a dialogue box asking how you want to create a new presentation, click **AutoContent Wizard**, then **OK**. If there is no dialogue box, click **File**, **New**... Then click the **Presentations** tab, **AutoContent Wizard**, then **OK**.

2 The Start dialogue box is the first of six boxes. Click **Next>**. In the 2nd box, click **Carnegie Coach**, then **Thanking a Speaker**, **Next>**.

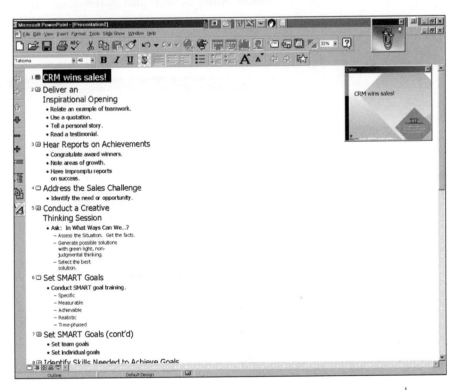

Figure 5.15
Outline for motivating a team

In the 3rd box, click **Presentations, informal meetings, handouts, Next>**.

In the 4th box, click select **colour overheads** for the output, and **Yes** to print handouts.

In the 5th box, type a Title: **History of Amazon**, type Your name: (**Your Name**) and Additional information: **Training Director**. Click **Next>**.

In the 6th box, click **Finish**, and see the Outline view of the presentation. If another view appears, click **View, Outline.**

3 See the Outline view of five slides. The first slide is the presentation title slide. It should already show your presentation title. Click on the number 2 of the second slide, to select it and its contents, and press <Delete> to delete it. You should be left with the required four slides, including the presentation title slide.

4 Edit the remaining slides in outline to look like Figure 5.16.

5 Run the slide show. Click **View, Slide Show**. The first slide appears, full screen. Click anywhere, three more times. The next three slides appear. Click once more to return to Outline view.

6 Run through the four slides in the three remaining views: **Slide, Slide Sorter**, and **Notes Page**. In Slide Sorter, try dragging a slide to a new position. In Slide view, try editing a

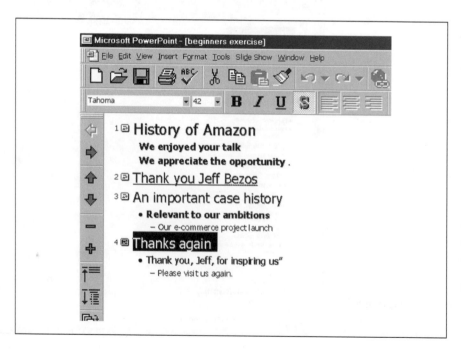

Figure 5.16
Outline of slides
for thanking a
speaker

slide, and in Notes Page, add some notes to the slides as numbered in Figure 5.16, as follows:

Slide 1: Jeff Bezos graduated in Electrical Engineering from Princeton in 1986. He spent two years with a high tech start-up company. In 1988 he joined Bankers Trust Co. N.Y., led the development of computer systems to manage $250 billion of assets. In 1990 became their youngest Vice President, then left to join Wall Street company D. E. Shaw. Became their youngest Senior Vice President in 1992. Left in 1994.

Slide 2: In 1995 Jeff attended a four day introductory course on book selling, covering 'Developing a business plan', 'Selecting opening inventory', 'Ordering, receiving, returning', and 'Inventory management'.

Slide 3: Jeff tapped out his business plan on a laptop while being driven across New York by his wife Mackenzie, and formed Amazon.com later in 1995.

Slide 4: At the first company picnic in 1996, Jeff handed out T-shirts bearing the message 'Get Big Fast'. Amazon never made a penny profit until 2001 Q4, when it reported its first sales greater than $1 billion. The first profit of $35 million was equivalent to about 9 cents per share, which stood then at about $10 each, down from $100 two years earlier.

7 Save your presentation and print your slides. In practice you could print onto inkjet transparencies, but for this exercise print on A4 paper in landscape layout.

8 Print your handout sheet, with the slides and notes on a single A4 sheet. Click **File**, **Send To**, **Microsoft Word.** Select **Notes next to Slides**. Click **OK.** Microsoft Word starts up, and the notes appear as a Word document. The notes run over to a second page, but you can drag the divisions between the slides up the vertical ruler, until all the slides and notes fit onto one A4 page. Print a handout page for photocopying.

PowerPoint exercise for rusty users

In this exercise you can design from scratch a presentation of three OHP slides, with pictures or charts pasted from Excel and the Internet. You should produce handouts showing the three slides on a single page, with explanatory notes alongside, and print the slides and the handout sheet.

Here's the scenario: you work for Chandler Associates, Company Lawyers who have offices in six UK cities. You are allocated five minutes at a head office meeting to make the case for an intranet, and for doing a feasibility study. Your outline should look like this:

Slide 1: The case for an intranet at Chandler Associates, plc. (This slide to get attention and interest) Three compelling reasons:

- ■ Savings: Estimated savings from less travel, better communications.
- ■ Performance: Faster, better service, through teamwork and knowledge sharing.
- ■ Capital Investment: ASPs, the zero capital cost option.

Slide 2: Functions and uses (This slide to create desire):

- ■ Expertise database: Find a partner with specialist knowledge.
- ■ Client database: Who we dealt with, what cases handled, Internet links.
- ■ General: E-mail, meetings, minutes, phone numbers.

Slide 3: The proposal (This slide to get action):

- ■ The project: Feasibility study, Business and systems analysis, Implementation.
- ■ Approval requested for Feasibility study: Cost £x, duration y weeks.
- ■ Questions?

Keep the slides simple. After sending the presentation to Word, you can make more room for the notes by deleting the first column in the table that only contains the slide numbers. If you wish, you can paste charts or pictures into the notes section of the handouts.

PowerPoint exercise for more competent users

Now for the fun. The scenario here is that Chandler Associates are to go ahead with their Intranet project, and the first step is to get everyone up to speed on what to expect. In this exercise you prepare a presentation of 4 slides, complete with sounds and animations. Then you put it on floppy disks using Pack and Go, for mailing to the

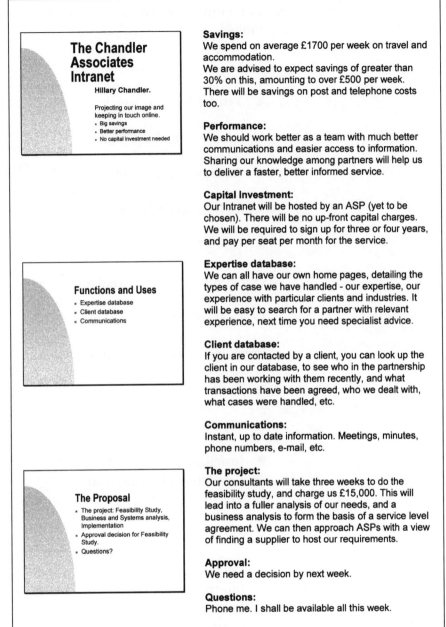

The Chandler Associates Intranet

Hillary Chandler.

Projecting our image and keeping in touch online.
- Big savings
- Better performance
- No capital investment needed

Functions and Uses
- Expertise database
- Client database
- Communications

The Proposal
- The project: Feasibility Study, Business and Systems analysis, Implementation
- Approval decision for Feasibility Study.
- Questions?

Savings:
We spend on average £1700 per week on travel and accommodation.
We are advised to expect savings of greater than 30% on this, amounting to over £500 per week. There will be savings on post and telephone costs too.

Performance:
We should work better as a team with much better communications and easier access to information. Sharing our knowledge among partners will help us to deliver a faster, better informed service.

Capital Investment:
Our Intranet will be hosted by an ASP (yet to be chosen). There will be no up-front capital charges. We will be required to sign up for three or four years, and pay per seat per month for the service.

Expertise database:
We can all have our own home pages, detailing the types of case we have handled - our expertise, our experience with particular clients and industries. It will be easy to search for a partner with relevant experience, next time you need specialist advice.

Client database:
If you are contacted by a client, you can look up the client in our database, to see who in the partnership has been working with them recently, and what transactions have been agreed, who we dealt with, what cases were handled, etc.

Communications:
Instant, up to date information. Meetings, minutes, phone numbers, e-mail, etc.

The project:
Our consultants will take three weeks to do the feasibility study, and charge us £15,000. This will lead into a fuller analysis of our needs, and a business analysis to form the basis of a service level agreement. We can then approach ASPs with a view of finding a supplier to host our requirements.

Approval:
We need a decision by next week.

Questions:
Phone me. I shall be available all this week.

Figure 5.17
Handout sheet for the Chandler presentation

regional offices. Individual partners can run the slide show on their PCs, or groups can view it using a data projector.

1 Click **File**, **New...**, click the **Presentation** tab, and choose a template such as **Generic (online)** if you have it.

2 In Outline view, edit the outline to leave just four slides, as follows:

Slide 1: The Chandler Intranet

■ Project bulletin No. 1

Slide 2: Reasons for Change

■ Business expectations

Faster business cycle creates expectations of faster response

■ Competition

Our competitors are installing Intranets

■ Cost savings

Immediate savings on stationery and travel

■ Further savings in phase 2

Slide 3: Project schedule

■ Installation of computers and network cabling
■ Commissioning and training
■ Termination of paper publications

Slide 4: The next steps: Phase 2

■ Centralized billing
■ Internet home page

3 Animate the text. In Outline view, click a slide icon and add animations. In the menu bar, click **Slide Show**, **Preset Animation** and select from the list. Or if you want more variety, change to Slide view, then in the menu bar click **Slide Show**, **Custom Animation**. A dialogue box opens, allowing you to choose different animations for the title and text. There are too many variations here to describe. Try them, and to see a preview of each, just click on the miniature slide on the right of the screen.

4 Add narration. You need a microphone for this. In Slide view, select **Slide Show**, **Record Narration.** Record your narration on each slide, and save the file when prompted. Now select **View**, **Slide Show** and you can see the results of your work. Do any final editing and save your presentation.

5 Put your presentation onto disk, for sending out to the regional offices. Select **File**, **Pack and Go**. The Pack and Go Wizard launches. Follow the instructions in the six dialogue boxes. You have your presentation on floppies, ready to post.

INTRODUCTION TO MICROSOFT INTERNET EXPLORER

Explorer is Microsoft's browser software for finding and viewing information about anything on the Internet, or on enterprise Intranets and Extranets. It is very simple to use, even if you don't like using a keyboard. You can find your way to interesting, relevant sites simply by pointing and clicking with the mouse.

However, you'll need to develop your skills to get the best from this versatile tool. To make efficient use of your time, be disciplined and stay focused. Explorer has a way of making you feel you're just ten seconds from finding exactly the source you are looking for ... and when you next check the time an hour has passed, and you still haven't found that perfect source. Also, as you progress towards your target, at every turn there are lots of distractions. If you once branch off track, there will be other tempting diversions, and before you know it, you're lost. If it does happen, click the History button on the toolbar, and jump back to a page on your original track. Your motto should be: 'Don't browse (no reading or surveying desultorily here, if you please), search!'

There are three reasons why you should use Explorer and learn about the Internet.

■ First, the Internet is the only widely available source of up-to-date information on fast-moving developments in e-commerce and computing. It takes 12 months to research, write and print a textbook, so the information on e-commerce in this textbook may be seriously out of date within a year of publication.

■ Second, e-commerce is such a hot topic, to understand it fully you need to experience it directly by visiting sites

where e-commerce is being done, and form your own opi-
nions on new developments. It's not enough simply to read
what others are reporting.

■ And third, browsing – sorry, searching – is becoming a
required skill for communicative competence. Internet browsers are used by companies to allow employees to access their
company 'intranet' – a small, private part of the Internet
often containing lots of information managers need for
their jobs. For instance, the employee procedure manuals
and internal telephone directories are often posted on the
company intranet. There are no printing and distribution
costs, and they can easily be kept right up to date. But
more than that, the Intranet and browser enable self-service
for all employees, who can maintain their own Human
Resource files, claim expenses, search for training courses,
for vacancies, or for other employees with particular skills.
Of course this cuts costs, but the main advantage is empowered, motivated staff, and easily accessible, high quality, up-
to-date information.

Finding information

When you start up Explorer, you see a screen like this:

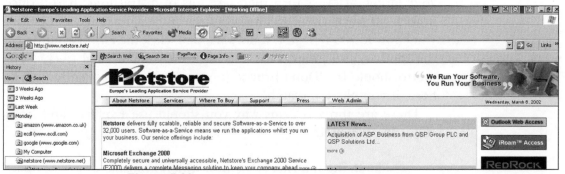

Figure 5.18
Explorer screen

At the top of the screen is the usual Windows menu bar, with the
File Edit View pull-down menus that you are now familiar with.

Below this is the toolbar for finding your way around the millions of pages of the World Wide Web – the biggest and best-known part of the Internet.

And below the toolbar is the address bar that holds the URL – the address – of the page that Explorer is looking for, or displaying. If you know the URL of a site, you can just type it in here, and press <Enter>. However, there are easier ways than typing, as we shall see. First let us examine the toolbar options.

Back takes you back to the previous page you viewed
Forward takes you forward again to where you were before
Stop stops a page loading if it is taking too long, or you change your mind
Refresh re-loads a page if something goes wrong, or you want the latest update
Home loads the home page of your organization or service provider.

The next three buttons on the toolbar, **Search, Favorites, History**, allow you to turn on, or off, a special feature on the left side of the screen. Try them out to see what they do. Click the button once to turn on, and again to turn off.

Search allows you to enter one or more keywords, to direct a search for relevant sites.
Favorites allows you to store the URL of a site so you can revisit it, just by pointing and clicking.
History automatically stores most of the actual pages you visit, so you can view them off-line, just by pointing and clicking. Some pages are not available off-line for security reasons, but even if the page itself is not stored, the URL will be, so when you are next on line, you can still load it again just by clicking.

There may be other tools on your toolbar. You should check them out to see what they do.

There may also be another bar beneath the address bar. For instance I have installed a Google bar there. It's not strictly necessary, but it makes each search using the search engine Google a few seconds quicker. Why use Google when there is a Search button on the Explorer toolbar? Because there are many search engines and directories, and those offered by Explorer are not necessarily the best or fastest.

Search engines and directories

This is a big subject, part of an even bigger one – the Internet and ways of using it. All we have time for here is a brief introduction to get you started on the exercises. It's really important to have a good reference book on how to get the most from the Internet and there are hundreds to choose from. There is one that stands out from the rest, *The Rough Guide to the Internet* by Angus Kennedy, which at £6 would be good value at twice the price. It's written in an amusing, engaging style, not at all like a technical guide, compact but well structured and likely to have the answers to any question you have. Check it out.

The Rough Guide will tell you the difference between a search engine, a directory and a search agent. They all require you to enter key words for your search, which they use to search databases and extract a list of URLs of sites containing those key words. When you launch a search, none of them set off to search the whole Internet – it's too big for that. The database search takes a second or two at most, but displaying the results is often delayed because the page also has lots of pictorial, animated advertisements that take time to load. That's why Google is so popular: no ads, just simple text links. Google's results often spring onto your screen in less than a second of hitting <Enter>.

Enough talk – the best way to learn is to do, so let's get started.

Explorer exercise for absolute beginners

When you start up Explorer, usually a home page loads that has links to other pages. On the Internet, it will be the home page of your Internet service provider, perhaps AOL (America On Line), or Freeserve. On your corporate Intranet, the home page will be a portal, a page with links to information and resources that are relevant to your working environment and that of your colleagues.

There are three ways you can move to another page where you hope to find useful information. You can:

■ Click on a hypertext link.

- Type in a page address if you know it.
- Search the Internet using a search engine or directory.

Clicking on a link will take you to another page, either at the same site, or through the Web to another site, anywhere in the world. A link on a page can be hypertext words, a URL address, or a picture, that will automatically load the new page when you click it. Text that is a link is a different colour, often blue. You can find out if text or a picture is a link. Just move the arrow cursor so that it hovers over the text or picture. If the cursor changes into a pointing finger, it is a link, and if you click on it, the new page will be loaded.

Try it now. Do a little aimless wandering through the Internet maze, but keep an eye on the time. When you get lost, just click on the Home button on the toolbar, the one that looks like a little house. It jumps you straight back to your home page. If you want to return to something you saw somewhere in your wanderings, click the History button on the toolbar, and look down the list of sites that appears on the left of the screen. Click on a site in the list, and it will jump you straight back there.

The page address, if you know it, will take you directly to the page you want to see.

1   On the menu bar, click on **File...**, **Open...** then type the URL address in the dialogue box. You can leave out the http:// as Explorer will add it for you. Check there are no typing errors – the address must be exactly right, including punctuation and case. Then click OK, or hit <Enter>. Try visiting www.tesco.com or any other URL you have seen in the press.

2   Add the site to your Favorites. (You can delete it later if you wish.) Click **F_avorites**, **Add to Favorites...** In the dialogue box, click OK. Now you can return to the site any time you like, just by clicking the Favorites button on the toolbar, and then, from the list that opens on the left side of the screen, clicking the site.

3   For practice, try visiting these sites:

    www.roughguides.com
    www.guardian.co.uk/netnews (if it doesn't load, try omitting
        the netnews part)
    www.internetworld.com
    www.searchenginewatch.com

If you like any of them, add them to your Favorites.

Searching the Web is easy. First go to a site where the free search tool is available to use. Then you just type in a few key words, hit <Enter>, and the tool will bring back a list of links to pages in which these words appear. Sometimes when you do a search, your results are disappointing. If you want to improve your results, read the page of tips and advice for that tool. There are slight differences between the different tools.

Suppose you are asked to update your CEO on collaborative commerce. Do a survey of what's on the Web, like this:

4 Use a search engine. Go to www.google.co.uk (or the USA site www.google.com). The UK site may be quicker to access, especially in the afternoon when America has woken up and started using the Internet.

In the window, type 'collaborative commerce' as shown, complete with quotes. Otherwise, your results will include irrelevant sites containing just the word collaborative, or just the word commerce. When you hit <Enter>, how long does Google take, to fetch your list of results? How many sites in your list? Click on one or two, to see what they contain.

5 Use a directory. Go to www.yahoo.com and try the same key words. Compare the results.

By searching on carefully selected key words, your search should result in a useful number of relevant pages. Poor choice of key words may result in 50,000 or more, mostly irrelevant pages, or none at all.

Explorer exercise for rusty users

You probably use Explorer at home to buy cut price airline tickets, look up your old school chums, find an aerial view of your street ... that kind of thing, so you are comfortable with browsing. In this exercise, you'll have the chance to polish up your search skills. You can download a couple of free search tools onto your PC, and then use them to do a precisely defined search.

1 **Get Google on your PC**. There are several ways of doing it. Type in the URL www.google.co.uk, or if you have been there recently, click History and then click Google in the

list, or if you added it to your Favorites list, click it there. Or, you can make Google your homepage, or add the Google toolbar to your browser. The toolbar is convenient, saves a few seconds on each search, and can be uninstalled in three clicks if you don't like it. Go to www.google.co.uk and take a careful look at all the options and links on the page. If you want the toolbar, click on the Google Toolbar link for more information. It only takes a few seconds to install, and if you decide not to keep it, just click on the Google logo, then click the last menu item, **Uninstall** . . .

Now test drive it. Type into the Google toolbar your town or village name, followed by bed & breakfast.

Now do another Google search. Type the following, replacing the word 'town' with the name of your town or village: +town +bed +breakfast −hotel

2. **Get Copernic on your PC**. Go to www.copernic.com and download the free Basic version as a file to your PC. It takes about ten minutes to download, depending on the speed of your connection. Double click on the file to install the program and put a button on your Explorer toolbar. When you click the button, you see a screen that looks a bit like Explorer. Copernic will run your key word search on all the leading search engines simultaneously.

3 **Choose key words for a search**. Choose your own key words, or if you prefer, try this. Suppose you are asked to write a report on procurement in the UK retail sector. Do supermarkets use Internet exchanges through which they can purchase their supplies? Or do they still rely on EDI? Here are some key words you could use: UK retail supply EDI exchange.

Should you use them all? Or just a couple? You'll find lots of articles on search engines, and how to use them, at www.searchenginewatch.com

Perhaps the best way to improve your results is simply to practise using just one or two engines, and thus develop an instinct for the best approach.

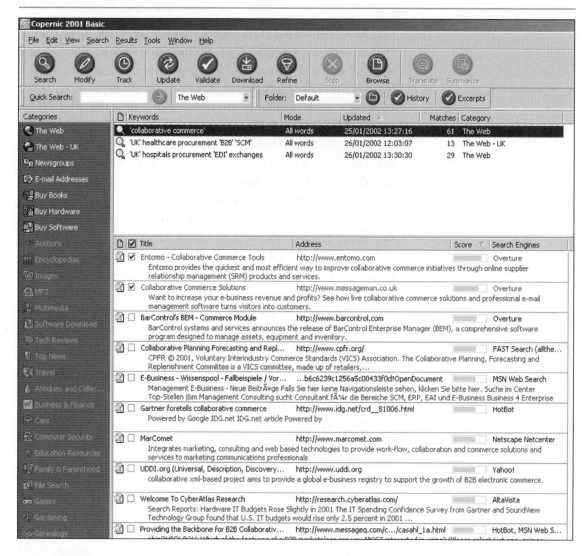

Figure 5.19
The Copernic search agent

Explorer exercise for more competent users

Read this clip from *The Hyperlinked Organization* by David Weinberger
(See www.cluetrain.com):

'You're a sales rep in the Southwest who has a customer with a product
problem. You know that the Southwest tech-support person happens not
to know anything about this problem. In fact, she's a flat-out bozo. So, to

do what's right for your customer you go outside the prescribed channels and pull together the support person from the Northeast, a product manager you respect, and a senior engineer who's been responsive in the past (no good deed goes unpunished!). Via e-mail or by building a mini-Web site on an intranet, you initiate a discussion, research numbers, check out competitive solutions, and quickly solve the customer's problem — all without ever notifying the "appropriate authorities" of what you're doing because all they'll do is try to force you back into the official channels.'

Maybe it's time to learn how to create your personal Web page for the enterprise intranet.

Don't be alarmed – we're only going to dip a toe in the water, just to show how easy it can be. In fact, the less you know about Web page design, the less likely you are to get carried away with all the bells and whistles. As with PowerPoint, there are so many features you could add, but just because you can, doesn't mean you should. Don't let the medium distract from the message. Like salt and pepper, a little adds interest but a little too much spoils the dish.

1 Start up Microsoft Word, and from the menu bar, select **File**, **New,** then select **General Templates . . ., Web Page.** Now you see a blank page. The layout will be as follows:

Your name will be in 26pt bold, centred at the top.
One third of the area on the right will hold a picture of you.
The remaining two thirds of the area on the left will hold
   written information about you.
So type your name at the top.

2 Add the picture. You need a head and shoulders view, in JPEG or other common picture format. You can scan an existing print, and save the image as a .jpg file. Alternatively you can use a digital camera. For this exercise you may prefer just to use some clip art. Then . . .

Click **Insert**, **Picture**, **New Drawing**. A canvas opens up, that you can resize to occupy the right third of the page.
Click **Insert**, **Picture**, **From File**, find your image file, and double-click on it. The image will open in the canvas.

3 Add the text. **Click Insert**, **Text Box**. A text box opens with circular handles at each corner and on each side. Drag and resize it to fit the remaining space on the left of the page.

Click inside it, and type the following, using 16pt bold for headings, and 12pt normal for the rest:

How to find me:
Office: Oxford Branch, Admin Bldg. Room 4.02
Phone: 01865-123456 Ext 78
e-mail: nellg@oranges.co.uk

Current projects:
CRM – Customer Relationship Management
South Midlands Regional Sales

Home interests:
Hill walking
Marmalade making.

4 Do a final check. Your e-mail address should be a hypertext link. Word should do that for you, unless the option is turned off. If it's not a link, highlight it, and then click the Insert Hyperlink button on the toolbar.

And that's it – easy peasy. If you fancy developing your Web designing skills, read the chapter on Creating your own Web page, in *The Rough Guide to the Internet*. And get yourself an HTML editing package.

We have reached the end of another chapter. If you read the earlier chapters, you should be right up to date on what's been happening in the business computing world, and have reached a significant milestone. Beyond here we look into the future and ways of coping with the changes that keep on coming.

REVIEW AND RELATE

1 For each new skill you have learned, list the first two tasks you will apply it to at work. For each task, on what date will you do it, and what will be the first step?
2 Pat yourself on the back. Congratulate yourself for persevering.

REFERENCES AND FURTHER READING

Kennedy, A. J. (2001). *The Rough Guide to the Internet*. 2002 edition for PCs and Macs. Published by Rough Guides Ltd and distributed by the Penguin Group. (A new edition is likely to be published every year, so get the latest edition.)

European Computer Driving Licence CD-ROM. The ECDL is an internationally-recognized standard of competence certifying that the holder has the knowledge and skill needed to use the most common computer applications efficiently and productively. Find out more by visiting www.ecdl.com, or write to The British Computer Society, ECDL Department, 1 Sanford Street, Swindon, Wilts SN1 1HJ, UK. Phone number 01793 417530.

CHAPTER 6

Matching the information system to the needs of your organization

Knowledge is of two kinds. We know a subject ourselves, or we know where we can find information upon it.

Samuel Johnson (1709–84)

WHAT BUSINESS ARE YOU IN?

What service or product does your organization deliver? Do you work for a hotel chain or an airline? Perhaps you work for a Local Authority, or maybe even one of our few remaining manufacturers. But whatever your line of business, the chances are you outsource some activities peripheral to your main business. Few companies own and maintain their fleet of cars. Local Authorities don't own or operate the equipment for collecting refuse or repairing roads. Hotels lease back their buildings, manufacturers hire plant and airlines lease jet planes.

So why does your organization own and maintain its information systems? Probably because:

- No one has thought about doing anything else.
- There were no companies capable of delivering a suitable service.
- The data held by the system is so fundamental to the business that it could not be risked with someone else.
- There were no clear advantages in paying someone to do it.

For most organizations, these reasons are unsustainable now. There are Application Service Providers (ASPs) advertising a wide range of services available via the Internet that they already deliver to growing numbers of clients. The old monolithic systems are being replaced by new systems that can be quickly put together like Lego bricks. ASPs can use Component Based Development (CBD) techniques to offer tailor made solutions to their customers.

Companies never think twice about risking other invisible assets with a service provider. How many companies do their own banking for instance? And during the last century, how many companies have been brought down by a bank failure? Off hand, I can't think of any. But we all know companies that have failed through their own financial mismanagement.

There are three clear advantages of using an ASP.

First, it's the business of ASPs to deliver a first class IT service. It is the only thing they do, there are no other distractions and it's how they make their money. The bigger ASPs have been developing and selling ERP systems for years. They can afford to hire and retain the best staff, and acquire the best hardware and systems. They know they are in a competitive market and their success depends on their reputation. And they know you can transfer to another ASP if you are not satisfied. You are likely get a faster, better IT service from an ASP than you now get from your own IT department.

Second, as collaboration and e-business develops, you will increasingly depend on networks and systems outside your business, that you neither own nor control. It will be the information that you share that will deliver advantage, not the information you keep secret, and your success will depend more on the systems you use than on the systems you own. But your IT department can only fix the few systems inside your business.

And third, for a new service there are no massive up-front capital charges. You pay per month per seat, so you are not locked in to using an expensive system for a payback period measured in years. You sign up initially for three years, but can add and remove functionality and capacity at short notice. This is increasingly important in today's fast moving business environment. It means you can fine tune your system as your needs change.

However, outsourcing part or all of the IT function to an ASP that delivers its service over the Internet is a new option. It only became feasible at the end of the 1990s when standards for Component Based Development (CBD) were emerging, and sufficient Internet bandwidth had been built. Although most organizations have a significant investment in their legacy systems, it seems likely that many will eventually outsource at least some of their systems.

THE LIFE CYCLE OF AN INFORMATION SYSTEM

Before the advent of CBD, business systems consisted of programs containing many thousands of lines of code, written in huge monolithic blocks that could not easily be changed, beyond editing the odd line of code here and there. As the business evolved and technology advanced, systems became outdated, and the only option was to write huge new monolithic blocks to replace the old ones. Big systems could cost millions and take years to pay back, so it was important to get the design right.

An information system must match and serve business needs, and so the design of these big, expensive, inflexible systems had to be based upon a rigorous prior analysis of the business. In the days when business needs changed slowly, the system would remain aligned to the needs of the business for a period of years before needing replacement. But it was important to get the design right, as it would take much of its useful life to pay back the investment in the system.

Of course it is still important to get the design right, but with more flexible CBD systems constructed of interchangeable components, it will never again be necessary to upgrade systems only occasionally in large, risky, discontinuous leaps into the dimly foreseen future. Instead it will be possible to upgrade systems almost continuously, in small, incremental steps that can easily be reversed if necessary. CBD systems are built from hundreds of components, each of which can be removed or replaced without affecting the integrity of the rest of the system. This new architecture allows the system to evolve and keep in step with the business and its changing environment. But most organizations are not at that stage yet, and to get there, they must go through the usual stages of the information system project.

There are three main stages in an information systems project:

■ First, analysing how the whole business is to be run.
■ Then designing on paper a suitable computer system.
■ Then, selecting the hardware, installing and commissioning it.

To these three stages, we can add two more: a preliminary feasibility study before committing to the expense of a full-blown analysis of the business; and a final maintenance stage to keep the system running satisfactorily after it is installed.

The complete systems life cycle therefore consists of five stages:

1 Feasibility study.
2 Business Analysis.
3 Systems Design.
4 Implementation.
5 Maintenance.

THE PROJECT TEAM

If you work in a big organization with its own computing department and you plan to buy rather than hire a system, you may be able to put together a project team entirely from your own staff. Smaller organizations however must get help from independent consultants, or more likely, get a hosted solution from an ASP.

Putting together your own project team will make the project longer, but it may be cheaper. Also, you keep the specialist knowledge in your organization, and that can be useful in the later maintenance phase after the consultants have left. But consultants can provide structure and methodology to the project and they bring expertise and additional human resources, valuable to cover the extra work generated by the project.

Even if you use an ASP or employ consultants, you cannot hand the whole job to them: your staff must be well represented on the project team. The team will be led by a Project Manager, and should consist of:

- System users.
- Business analysts.
- Systems designers.
- Computer programmers and engineers.

Users are at the top of the list. They must get a system at the end that they've had a big say in designing, and they feel they 'own'. A misguided steering committee may be tempted to impose a system without consulting the users sufficiently. This approach is very likely to fail; the best system in the world will fail if users feel it is being used to spy on them or control them, or will make their job more difficult. They will use their ingenuity to find ways to defeat the system or circumvent it.

Another danger is that computer professionals can sometimes get the bit between their teeth and charge off towards a technologically sophisticated dream solution. This too is likely to result in unsatisfactory performance. The users must believe in the benefits of the system and see it as a useful tool to help them do a better job.

It is the performance of the total human–computer system that matters, not just the computers. For the best chance of success the project team must gain total commitment and wholehearted co-operation from the users. Then users will apply their ingenuity to make the system work, even if it turns out to be less than ideal from a technical or ergonomic point of view.

There is only one way of gaining the full support of users: they must be fully involved from the earliest stages of the project, with real influence in its design, all the way through to the end. This inevitably means the project will take longer to complete, but like the ha'penny-worth of tar to stop the ship sinking, it really is essential.

ORGANIZING THE PROJECT

The Project Manager will report directly to a Steering Committee consisting of senior executives.

The total cost of a major systems project will always be large, often a large percentage of annual turnover. Also, the system will handle basic functions like invoicing and budgeting – activities to do with cash flow, the life blood of the organization. There are very real risks if the system does not function satisfactorily, and so the Steering Committee must have the power of veto, to halt the project at the end of any one of the five stages of the project. The project team must therefore prepare a report for the Steering Committee at the end of each stage, with two or three suggestions for the next stage, one of which should be recommended to the Steering Committee for their approval.

We will return to examine how the project is controlled through the five stages of the life cycle, but first, let us review how computers initially came to be used in business. Technology is still developing rapidly and has a big influence on the design of information systems, so to get a feel for where business computing is headed, you should know where it came from.

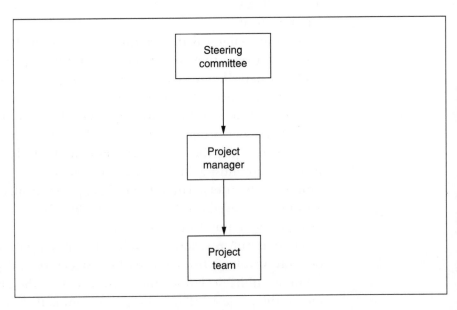

Figure 6.1
Project
organization chart

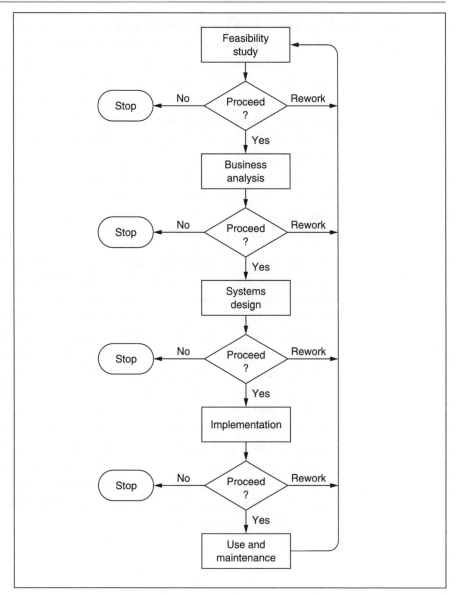

Figure 6.2
Steering
committee
control of project

THE BIRTH AND UPBRINGING OF THE BUSINESS COMPUTER

Conception

In 1958 there were just 160 computers in the whole of Europe, and only the very biggest companies could even think about using them – mostly for scientific applications. All organizations used paperwork systems for recording and distributing the information they needed. These systems were operated by an army of clerks, secretaries, mail boys and teams of girls in finance with the strange title of 'comptometer operator', who spent the day tapping away on adding machines. Information was stored in filing cabinets and plan chests, accessed by asking a secretary to pull out the needed files or drawings, and communicated through circulation lists and the internal mail system.

Embryo

By the late 1950s some businesses were waking up to the potential of these computers operated by scientists. Computers at that time were huge, unreliable monsters consuming so much power that the lights dimmed when they were switched on. They relied on thousands of radio valves that popped and fused like light bulbs. The machines seldom ran for more than a few hours between failures, and needed special premises and a large team of engineers to keep them going.

However, some businesses discovered that they could save on labour costs by buying time on these machines. They got access at economic rates to the number-crunching power of the scientists' computers, which proved ideal for routine accounting functions. The first business uses they were put to were the processing of payrolls and accounts receivable. Big savings were made in labour by automating clerical tasks and one of the first jobs to disappear was that of the comptometer operator.

Birth

During the 1960s organizations began to realize that computers could be applied to other routine tasks such as stock control and production control. Transistors replaced radio valves, making computers cheaper and more reliable, and so bigger companies began to set up their own Data Processing departments and operate their own computers. Thus the central mainframe was borne, operated by DP staff offering a computing service to other department managers.

Infancy

By the late 1970s more and more business tasks were being computerized. The transistor that had replaced the radio valve was itself being replaced, first by the integrated circuit and then by the microprocessor. These developments cut the costs of computing dramatically while at the same time increasing their power and reliability.

Also, many department managers were beginning to get fed up of going cap in hand to the DP citadel to beg small computing favours. They were beginning to find that computers were simple enough to run and had fallen in price sufficiently for them to buy and operate in their own departments, which freed them from being dependent on the DP department. Separate computers were soon arriving in the Design Offices, the Planning Department, the Sales Office and so on.

This piecemeal approach to corporate computing came about because managers could make immediate savings in direct labour at the same time as freeing themselves from dependence on the DP department. Naturally the DP departments did what they could to resist this trend, because they could see their influence waning. But it was too late. The arrival of the PC in the early 1980s reduced even further the significance of the big central mainframe. The low cost and versatility of the PC meant they were popping up like mushrooms, everywhere.

Soon computers were to be found in nearly every organization.

However, this could hardly be called a corporate approach to computing. The PCs were being used to automate the old paperwork systems, faults and all, and were reinforcing departmental boundaries. Each computer held its own separate files. The same information was being held many times over in different computers, with some versions obviously being more up to date than others. And to transfer data from one department to another involved printing out hard copy in the sending department and then re-keying the printed data back into the computer at the receiving department.

Adolescence

In the 1980s these so called 'islands of automation' – separate computers in different departments – were being linked together via communications networks to form management information systems. The intention was that these integrated systems of computers should transcend departmental boundaries and allow data to be held at different points in the network, and yet be available through the network to all authorized users who might need it.

There is a concept known as single data entry for multiple users. In theory it means that each data element held by the total system should only be held once. In practice it is interpreted to mean that there should be the least possible duplication in the storage of data. If data is only entered and held once, in a single common database, there can only be one version of the state of play, available to all who need it. This should eliminate the confusions that can arise when earlier versions of modified records or drawings are allowed to remain in circulation. Even into the 1990s a common violation of the single data entry principle was the holding of two separate databases of employees – one for payroll, and one for the Human Resources function.

During the 1990s, business computing went through a dynamic period of growth and development. The Internet burst onto the scene, and businesses prepared themselves for the Y2K bug, when old software would run out of dates at midnight on the eve of year 2000.

Early maturity

For an industry to be considered mature, the pace of developments should be moderate, there should be a few large companies dominating the industry and there should be a set of standards for all developers and users (like for cars, for instance). The industry is getting closer to meeting these requirements. For instance, the Windows user interface and the Internet protocols TCP/IP have become *de facto* standards for business communications. Operating a computer is becoming intuitive, and plug-and-play hardware is becoming the norm. Although developments are still proceeding apace, in 2002 we can claim that the business computer is beginning to show signs of growing up.

CONTROLLING A COMPUTER SYSTEM PROJECT

The era in which business information systems delivered almost no performance improvements during their life is coming to an end. When a business converts to a system constructed from components, it will never again need to replace large proportions of its systems all

Phase	Team size	Typical proportion of total project costs (%)
Feasibility study	1 or 2 analysts	<5
Business analysis	Project manager + 3 or 4 analysts	10–15
System design	Project manager + analysts + programmers + users	25–30
Implementation	Project manager + analysts + programmers + users	55–60

Figure 6.3
Team size and costs for each project phase

in one go. However, many organizations have yet to componentize, and so they face at least one remaining large computer system project. We will return to CBD shortly.

THE FEASIBILITY STUDY

This is a quick survey of information flows in the organization, to see if they need changing. It can be done by a business analyst or two and a systems designer perhaps. It should cost little more than the cost of the time these guys log on. The project manager and team will not yet be recruited but even at this stage it is important to keep potential users of the new system informed of the purpose of the study, and the opportunities for participation if the project goes ahead.

The feasibility study should deliver a report to senior management, recommending either to stop the project, go back and repeat the feasibility study, or go on to the next stage. The study should also give a rough estimate of total project cost, pay-back period, and return on investment.

Giving the go-ahead for the next stage only commits the organization to doing the business analysis, which incurs the costs of setting up the Steering Committee, appointing a Project Manger, and seconding members onto the Project Team. There may also be consultants' fees and other indirect costs.

Now at Work

Systems project at Comet puts users first

Comet, the UK's second largest electrical retailer, invested heavily in operational systems during the 1980s and 1990s, and thus had huge amounts of data about sales and products. But Michael Cleary, Information Systems Manager at Comet, saw a problem. 'We had a lack of accessible information that the business could use.'

Comet has 265 stores and 8000 employees in the UK. It has a turnover of close to £1 billion and sells 40,000 different white, brown and multi-media products direct to consumers. But the systems in use were very unfriendly, with green screens and product codes instead of names. Also, Cleary says, there was no single version of 'the truth' about sales and products, and when managers asked for reports from IT, they were often too busy to create them.

Comet responded to these challenges with a data warehouse project, based on Sequent Numa-Q hardware, an Oracle database and MicroStrategy analysis tools. By June 1998 much work had been done, but the project was technology focused and had not delivered its business objectives. 'We knew we had to regroup to ensure the project became business led once more,' Cleary recalls. And thus Project Edison was launched. Phase one was to regain support from the business community, and deliver accurate historical data.

Phase two would prioritize the business intelligence requirements of different units and ensure that everyone saw how Edison would improve business processes and decision-making across the company. There was a newsletter, a quick reference guide to the new systems, e-mail technical support, and training courses using real-life data.

By July 1999, users in marketing and stock planning were adjusting reports from the system to suit the changing needs of the business. Decision-making was quicker and more profitable. Fewer paper reports were being used, and there was just one version of the truth, no matter who was looking at it, or for what purpose. Today there are 110 users of the system, including 15 power users who can set up their own templates and filters.

Cleary believes there are three lessons to learn from this project. First, start small, and grow from success. Aim to deliver 80 per cent of requirements from the first 20 per cent of effort, not the other way round. Second, always have the user in mind when developing technical solutions. There's no point in having the most elegant system, if it fails to do the things the business wants it to do. And third, include a diverse team of people working on the project to guarantee the system delivers business benefits.

Comet plans to continue using MicroStrategy software and extend the range of users with web-based delivery, but only in response to requests for particular projects from the business. Cleary concludes: 'Technology must always be used to satisfy business requirements, not implemented for its own sake.'
www.microstrategy.com
www.oracle.com

THE BUSINESS ANALYSIS

This will not involve any capital costs. The project is still at the investigation stage and can be thought of as a re-run in more detail of the feasibility study. The business analysis will focus on:

- Business objectives and philosophy.
- What is done now, and how it is done.
- What should be done, and how it could be done.

An experienced manager with business skills is required for the first phase. Is there a mission statement? Does the organization deliver high spec. at high price or mid-range spec. competing on price? And how are these objectives to be achieved? By keeping tight control of bad debts? By monitoring sales volumes and adjusting prices? Answers are needed to questions such as these, to use as system design criteria.

A systems analyst with interviewing skills is needed to find out what is done now, and what procedures are used. What are the inputs to the organization system and what are its processes and outputs? The inputs may be information, raw materials, products ... The analyst should collect a full set of all forms and paperwork used for running the organization, and all user manuals and system documentation. Talks with staff will determine what is actually done, and any reasons for not following standard practice.

Experienced business analysts who also know about computers must decide what should be done and how. If any business process reengineering is needed, it should be done at this stage. The business is analysed as a set of systems: those the business uses – and could or should use – are analysed.

The results of the business analysis lay the groundwork for the next stage of the project, which must be approved by the steering committee. By giving the go-ahead for systems design, they will approve expenditure for perhaps a third of the total team hours during the life of the project.

SYSTEMS DESIGN

The project will gain further momentum, requiring input from programmers and engineers.

All investigations are now complete and the results are contained in the reports or 'deliverables' from the previous business analysis stage. These form the basis for the systems design stage. At this stage the design should not close off options that will be considered at the next, implementation stage. The design should not be hardware or software specific. It should be a theoretical representation of the data flows, the data inputs and outputs, the data storage and processing requirements. The actual software and hardware will not be chosen until the implementation stage.

The deliverables from this stage should include a full technical specification, so that during the next stage, implementation, different vendors can be invited to tender against the specification.

IMPLEMENTATION

This is the major part of the project and it is when the largest expenditure occurs. Half the total project team hours may be used at this stage, and there will be large capital costs for hardware and software. Also, there will be training costs which typically may be similar in size to the hardware costs.

Now at Work

ERP shock

In 1999 Deloitte Consulting reported the results of their survey of 62 US organizations about their implementations of SAP, Oracle, PeopleSoft or Baan packages. Almost all confirmed that their business performance had fallen for between three and nine months after implementations were completed.

'It was a shocking discovery and not one we expected to make,' said Steve Baldwin, a senior partner with Deloitte who headed up the research. 'But when we interviewed businesses four out of five said implementing ERP software hurt the business in the first six months,' he said. Baldwin stressed that the dip is only temporary, and that businesses recover afterwards.

InformationWeek, 17 Feb 1999
www.informationweek.co.uk

This is also the stage at which the major risks occur. Up to this point, there has been no interference with the basic procedures that the organization uses to conduct its affairs. But now operations will be transferred to the new system. Inevitably there will be a 'J-curve' effect where output dips during and immediately after the transfer. This must be expected, but if all goes well, output should quickly recover to a new higher level, and this too must be anticipated by making sure production inputs are adequate to sustain the new higher level of business output.

The big risk of course is that all may not go well, and the Steering Committee must be very confident that the system will work. They may require the project team to confirm that all is well before authorizing transfer of operations to the new system.

The main phases of implementation are:

- Hardware purchase and installation.
- Software purchase and writing.

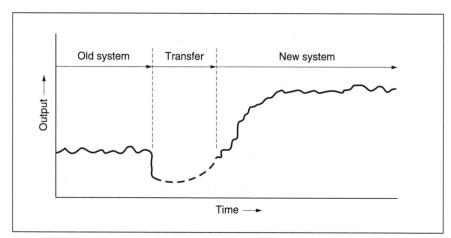

Figure 6.4
The output 'J-curve'

- Systems and software testing.
- User training.
- File conversion and transfer to the new system.
- Switch to the new system and stop using the old system.

Hardware purchase and installation

This will involve inviting suppliers to tender against the technical specification, but inevitably suppliers will emphasize their strengths, and not dwell on the short-comings of their tender. The project team must make sure that no important areas of weakness are overlooked.

Installation is bound to cause some disruption as ceiling panels are taken down and floors lifted to install communications cabling.

Software purchase and writing

Comparing and assessing the suitability of different packages is quite a complex business. Technical conformance to the specification is obviously important, but the user-friendliness of the human–computer interface is extremely important. The computer experts, because of their familiarity with the way computers work, are sometimes not aware of the difficulties new users have with new systems. These difficulties can be overcome by training, but an inherently difficult system will from the start cause irritation and will never endear itself to the users.

Even standard off-the-shelf software must be installed on the hardware and set up to produce the type of output required. However, users are not always able to describe exactly the type of support they require from the system, until they start using it. Then, they can recognize it when they see it.

If software has to be specially written, prototyping is appropriate. The programmer uses a fourth generation programming language, a 4GL, to produce very quickly a limited package with keyboard inputs and screen outputs which can be easily changed. Then when the user is satisfied, the programmer can go away and write the full version. This will take longer to do than the prototype version, but will have adequate speed and capacity to meet the design specification.

Now at Work

How Littlewoods became a European leader in the deployment of retail technology

In the run-up to the new millennium the big UK high street retailer Littlewoods launched a re-engineering project of revolutionary scale. Over three years, Project Merlin would change everything: the way people worked, the command and control culture, the business processes and the IT systems. 'The main thrust was to save in excess of £20 million per annum by re-configuring our supply chain, and that involved everybody. We had to look at the way we worked and then re-define the processes and change the systems that supported these processes,' said Steve Lock, Head of IT. The aim was to move from command and control to collaboration, sharing information with everyone, internal customers and suppliers, to become more efficient and increase profits by 3 per cent of sales within two years.

So, out went the legacy Bull mainframes, replaced by a new Sun E10,000 Starfire box (17 UltraSparc 250 MHz processors, 4GB memory) at the Liverpool Headquarters. In the high street stores, web-enabled client-server networks were installed around Compaq 5000 Proliant servers (dual Pentium P200s, 256 MB memory, 8 GB drives). All 130 high street stores had to be re-cabled and equipped with standard Compaq PCs (16 MB memory and Windows 95, or 32 MB and NT for power users). The new architecture makes easy work of deploying new releases or applications. No need for IT staff to visit every PC : new versions are automatically downloaded when users log on in the morning.

Software had to be standardized too. Steve commented: 'We made a major shift from being application developers to system integrators. We selected the best packages around at the time – Oracle for the database, ComShare as our planning tool, Retek for merchandise management – and underpinned this with the data warehouse solution of MicroStrategy. The aim was to mould these core packages into our business model so that they became key industry solutions.' Everything was made simple and intuitive. All applications were web-enabled and users only need to know about Microsoft Windows and Internet Explorer 3.

Eric Turbeville, Business Champion for the project, is confident Littlewoods have the right strategy and tools. 'The technical implications of choosing web technology did add to our headaches, but it has put us in the right position to gain competitive advantage. The only change I would have made is perhaps to have fought harder for the project in the early days, and to have got it underway sooner.'

www.oracle.com
www.comshare.com
www.retek.com
www.strategy.com

Systems and software testing

When the hardware and software for all the component sub-systems have been installed and tested, the whole system including all computerized and manual procedures must be tested to ensure it operates in an integrated fashion.

In a big system, project testing can never guarantee perfection because of the almost infinite number of multiple interrelationships that can arise between program modules. However, common human and physical failures can be anticipated and so these are purposely introduced. During a test run, erroneous transactions are processed and hardware failures are simulated to check that the system can handle the problem and recover from the failure.

User training

Skimping on training is a false economy, and yet, if the project budget is under pressure, training is more likely to be cut than hardware. The technology cannot work without people: people form the most important part of the total system.

The trouble lies deep in management attitudes which are reinforced by our financial accounting conventions. Hardware appears as assets on the balance sheet, whereas people don't, so despite claims from the top that 'people are our most important asset', training is not seen as an investment. Hardware cannot walk away, whereas people can. Some managers believe that if you give people training, they are sure to leave because they can use it to secure a better job. This is in stark contrast to the experience of Nissan who have big budgets for on-going training. They know that people will actually decide to stay because there are opportunities for training, rather than move and get stuck in a job where there is no training. When Nissan opened a plant in Tennessee, USA, they spent $30,000 per employee on training before the plant started operation.

If money spent on training is not money down the drain, then what is the payoff? There's the rub: the benefits are very difficult to estimate, even with specific operator training. The costs of training are up-front and known exactly, but how can you ever know whether it was worthwhile? All you can do is rely on the advice of consultants with experience of systems projects where greater and lesser amounts were spent on training. They should be able to estimate the savings that arise from shorter start-up and improved system effectiveness.

The documentation produced during the analysis and design stages of the project will provide a rich source of training material.

File conversion and transfer

Before the new system can operate, the files of standing data used by the old system must be copied over to the new system. For instance, the file of customer addresses and the file of product prices are needed before the system can produce invoices. It is seldom as simple as loading a tape from the old system and getting the new system to read it. Usually the new hardware and software will be incompatible with the old, and special programs have then to be written to translate the old tapes into a form understandable by the new system.

The transfer of files must not take too long, however, because life goes on during the transfer and the old system will continue to be used for business until the final switch-over. Thus the state of play on the old system will advance, and the taped data put into the new system will soon be out of date. This will make switching over to the new system difficult because it is not up to date.

Switching to the new system and stopping the old system

Wherever possible a phased implementation should be adopted, with different sub-systems brought on-line one at a time. Thus the Accounts module could be implemented and tested first, say. Then only when it is operating correctly, the Production module could be brought on-line. However, with big real-time systems which rely on a single database – an airline ticket reservation system for instance – it is not possible to reduce the risks in this way: the whole system must be started at the same time.

Another way to reduce the risks is to use a period of parallel operation as a safeguard to check that the new system is functioning correctly, before switching off the old system. This should be for a strictly limited period, because maintaining both systems doubles the workload for the users with every transaction having to be input twice. Also, it prevents the users from gaining confidence in the new system. With both systems running, users will revert to the old system whenever there is a difficulty.

The project team should encourage ownership of the system by the users, and should reduce support to normal maintenance levels soon after the old system is abandoned.

MAINTENANCE

This is included as one of the stages in the life cycle of the system, but it is not part of the project, because it will last for years, up to the time when a new feasibility study marks the beginning of the next systems project.

The purpose of system maintenance is not to maintain the status quo, like car maintenance for instance. Maintenance in the context of

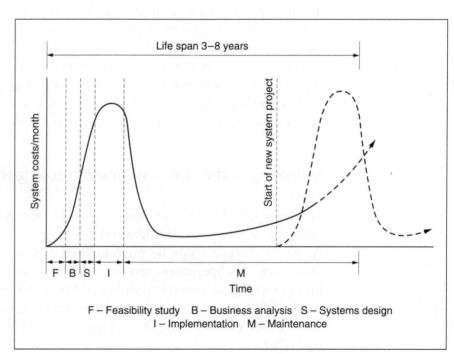

Figure 6.5
Bathtub curve of
system life time
costs

F – Feasibility study   B – Business analysis   S – Systems design
I – Implementation   M – Maintenance

information systems means maintaining a system which is appropriate to the business needs of the organization. There will be occasions when a system 'bug' requires fixing, but for the most part, maintenance is more a question of adjusting the system to suit the changing needs of the organization over time.

A change in the rate for value added tax is one example of the kind of influence that may result in a need for system maintenance. The program that computes the amount of VAT charged on invoices would need to be edited.

One of the project team's last responsibilities is to conduct a post-implementation review. The purpose of this is to compare the performance of the system with what was originally specified in the systems design documentation. As a result, before finally being disbanded, the team may be asked by users to do some post-implementation fine-tuning of the system.

Apart from acting as an important control activity, the post-implementation review is a valuable opportunity for team members to learn from the experience of being involved with the project. It will add to their value as team members on the next project.

COMPONENT-BASED DEVELOPMENT (CBD)

OK. It's time to get a handle on this CBD term. Let's answer a few questions, in simple business terms.

What is a component?

It is a piece of software that delivers a set of services, via a defined interface. Components can be put together to form larger components, and complete applications. Put together the right components and you get a finished product, just the same as for a car or a dish-washer.

What are the advantages of components and CBD?

1 Applications built from them can be adapted easily to meet changes in business or technology. Components can be

removed or replaced without compromising the rest of the system.

2 Components can be re-used. They improve programming productivity, quality and speed of delivery. It's quicker to build from components than from lines of code. Also, it is inherently less error-prone, especially when the component is being reused and has been tested and used before in other applications.

3 CBD allows monolithic chunks of legacy code to be wrapped in an interface, so that from outside, the legacy behaves like a large component, and only communicates via the interface. This allows organizations to convert to components in stages, without having to dump all legacy code in one go.

4 Componentization has the capacity to commoditize the software market. A market may eventually arise, in which it will be possible to build, buy and sell software components, in much the same way as components in any other industry.

Where did components come from?

The software industry has long been seeking an escape from the rigid and expensive monolith. In the early 1990s there was much talk of using 'objects' as modules that could be clipped together like Lego bricks to form an application. Objects had been used by computer scientists for decades, mostly for research in artificial intelligence, long before they started being used to construct business information systems. Objects are software modules consisting of part procedures and part data, that could represent real-world business objects such as products, customers, orders and accounts.

Objects can therefore be used to model the way a business works, and to build a system to manage the business. So this is where the overall framework came from. In fact many components are objects, but objects on their own tend to be too fine-grained. Also, there was a need to find a way of incorporating legacy code, and thus the general idea of a component was born, that could consist of a single object, or a collection of objects grouped together inside an interface, or an old legacy application inside an interface.

There are three major standards in the component market: Microsoft's COM, or Common Object Model, Sun's EJB, or Enterprise JavaBeans, and CORBA, the Common Object Request Broker Alliance. They each have their own Interface Definition

Language (IDL) and as usual in the software industry, they are incompatible and each is vying to dominate the market.

Why are components now so important?

Because they are the key to collaborative commerce, source of the next big surge in business for the software industry.

For 40 years, software resided in the computer you operated with your terminal, or in the PC on your desk. Then in the 1990s Sun proposed a new model: client-server LAN networks with thin clients that only stored a graphical user interface. When you used software, you accessed it through the network. Now, in the 2000s collaborative commerce applications stretch beyond the boundaries of the organization. Managers are participating in SCM and CRM processes, and using applications that they no longer wholly own or control. Applications are breaking free of the local computer and becoming distributed across the Internet. The old software languages and architectures are no longer appropriate for these conditions.

In Chapter 7 we will examine the shape of these new languages and architectures that are in development. But first, to round off this chapter, a little light relief.

DATA FLOW DIAGRAMS

Systems analysts use DFDs to analyse and develop information systems. You may be shown a DFD by an analyst at some stage. So, here are some brief notes, an example and an exercise. Try them. They're easy, and then sometime soon when that analyst tries to bullshit you, you won't be phased.

DFD notes and example

DFDs are widely used for cataloguing all the data flows in a system. A complete description of a system would require a levelled set of data flow diagrams, starting at the top with a context diagram. The context diagram at Level 0 shows no detail inside the system. All it shows is the inputs and outputs crossing the system boundary. Level 1 shows the major processes. Level 2 splits the Level 1 processes into sub-processes, and so on. For simple systems Level 1 is as far as you need go, and that's the case in our example.

The purpose of the DFD is to describe in theory the data flows that must occur for a business process, without any reference to how the flows may be achieved in practice. That will be decided later when a system is being designed. A data flow could be a price automatically extracted from a database of prices, or it could be a verbal order placed by a customer in a restaurant. The DFD can tell us nothing about people, machines, cables, electric signals or software. There are just four symbols used in DFDs, shown in Figure 6.6. Every symbol must be labelled.

Now here is a simple example. You go into Sweaty Betty's fish and chip shop. There is a chalk board on the wall with menu items and prices. Betty is behind the fish friers with her husband Fred, who is smoking a cigarette. You order haddock and chips with mushy peas,

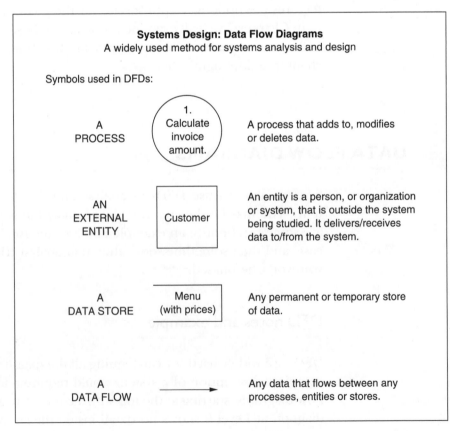

Figure 6.6
Symbols used in
Data Flow
Diagrams

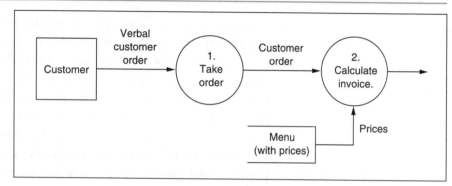

Figure 6.7
Processing an
order at Sweaty
Betty's

to take away. Betty lifts fish out of the fat to drain. Fred glances at the menu and adds up your bill ... Figure 6.7 shows the DFD for that situation.

The DFD is a dispassionate analysis that focuses on the business process. There was a news item recently about a vending machine for dispensing freshly fried chips. The DFD for the vending machine would be the same as that in Figure 6.7, except the customer order would not be verbal. Get the idea? Try the examples below.

The final chapter focuses on the Internet: the way it is transforming the business environment and driving the design of new computer architectures. The goal is to enable a global electronic market place with new business opportunities and threats. We will identify the trends, and try to guess where they will lead.

REVIEW AND RELATE

1 Have you been involved in a big system project? If so, can you identify the five stages in the life cycle of that project? How meticulous was the planning? How meticulous does it need to be, now that systems are becoming more adaptable?

2 Do a quick search on the Internet, to discover ASP organizations that could possibly host your systems at work. Check out NetStore and CSC plus two others.

3 Write a ten-line memo to your boss in answer to the question: 'What are software components, and why do we need to know about them?'

4 Draw the DFD for updating records in the following situation.

Points cards are one type of loyalty card used by petrol companies such as Shell, BP and Fina. In the Fina scheme the points can be exchanged for vouchers for spending at Argos. When a customer pays for petrol, the card is put into a read/write device. It reads and displays the number of reward points already stored on the card, and then adds the new points to the total on the card for the latest purchase. When the card is full and holds the maximum allowable points, a new card is just given to the customer. No customer details are recorded.

5 Draw part of the DFD for a supermarket such as Sainsburys, to show the data flows that occur when a customer presents a loyalty card to the check-out operator at the store.

Loyalty cards allow customers to collect points for vouchers, like the Fina scheme, but the card only holds the customer identity and address. The points earned are recorded on the store system, and the balance adjusted when purchases are made or a voucher is issued. On your DFD, show just one process (Update records) and two data stores (the card, and company files). Make sure you show and label all data flows into and out of the process. Assume that when the card is swiped, it is a 'read only' operation.

REFERENCES AND FURTHER READING

Cameron, B. (2000). *The Death of IT. The Forrester Report*. Forrester Research Inc. www.forrester.com

Harry, M. J. S. (2001). *Business Information: A Systems Approach* (3rd edition). Pearson Education Ltd.

Maynard, J. (1999). *ASP – Making Sense of Application Service Provision*. A NetStore white paper. www.netsore.net

Schaaf, J. M. (1999). *Users' Guide to Hosting. The Forrester Report*. Forrester Research Inc. www.forrester.com

Sprott, D. and Wilkes, L. (1999–2000). *Using Componentised Software*. CBDi Forum – The Forum for Component-Based Development and Integration. www.cbdiforum.com

CHAPTER 7

Information around the world and into the future

> Now this is the Law of the Jungle – as old and as true as the sky;
> And the Wolf that shall keep it may prosper, but the Wolf that shall
> break it must die.
>
> 'The Law of the Jungle', Rudyard Kipling (1865–1936)

IN THIS CHAPTER ...

- The Web: opportunities and threats on the superhighway through the jungle.
- Business Process Management – architecture for the 21st century?
- Managing across organizational boundaries.
- Collaborative Commerce – who can hack it?

TRADE, INFORMATION, TRUST AND COLLABORATION

'On a political map, the boundaries between countries are as clear as ever. But on a competitive map, a map showing the real flows of financial and industrial activity, those boundaries have largely disappeared. Of all the forces eating them away, perhaps the most persistent is the flow of information.' Thus wrote McKinsey consultant Kenichi Ohmae in *The Borderless World*. Back then in 1993, three years before Jeff Bezos started Amazon, few people had heard of the Internet, but the invisible international exchange of digital information was already well established.

Trade requires participants to exchange information which allows better understanding and trust, which feeds back to more trade. It takes time for the virtuous circle to close, but what is true of countries is also proving true for enterprises. Just as the boundaries between countries are dissolving, so too are the boundaries between enterprises. In *The Agenda*, Michael Hammer, of process re-engineering fame, now urges managers to 'push past your boundaries' to lose your identity in an extended enterprise and to streamline the processes that connect you with customers and suppliers.

We now realize that business processes don't stop at the boundaries of enterprises, but extend all along the value chain. And once again, by fortunate coincidence, the computer industry has arrived just in time with a new technology to support these extended business processes. The 1990s was the decade of Business Process Reengineering but the 2000s seem set to be the decade of co-opetition, collaborative commerce and business process management. That is the theme for this chapter, but before looking to where we're headed, let's see where we are coming from.

GLOBAL NETWORKS

Long before businesses first gained access to the Internet in 1990, many separate private networks had already been set up which still exist today. For instance, the world's major banks belong to a private network, the Society for World-wide Interbank Financial Transactions (SWIFT), that allows subscribers to make a transaction half way round the world and have it acknowledged within a few seconds. The system still handles transactions worth hundreds of billions of pounds on a typical day, and this is just one network amongst several serving the banking sector, such as the Clearing House for International Payments (CHIPS) and the Clearing House Automated Payment System (CHAPS).

There were, and still are, hundreds of other leased lines and private networks to handle all manner of different information types. For instance networks for airline seat reservations, for meteorological data, for international news services, and for electronic data interchange (EDI). We should look at EDI in more detail, as it paved the way for e-commerce and collaborative commerce.

ELECTRONIC DATA INTERCHANGE (EDI)

EDI is defined as the computer to computer exchange of structured data, sent in a form that allows for automatic processing, with no manual intervention. It exists as a set of standards for setting up connections between the computers of purchasing organizations and those of their suppliers. By getting rid of paperwork, it speeds up the process of making enquiries, placing orders, invoicing and settling accounts. The digital purchasing information from the purchaser's computer system passes automatically into the supplier's computer system. It is cheaper, faster and less prone to typographical errors. However, the attraction for purchasers was that it provided a mechanism for requiring suppliers to deliver materials at the same rate at which they are consumed. The purchaser, receiving just-in-time deliveries, can then operate with lower stock holdings and reduced working capital, to achieve more flexible, higher quality production.

For instance, in the early 1990s Rover at Longbridge used EDI to arrange just-in-time deliveries of colour sequenced parts to match the colour sequence of Rover 220 Coupe bodies advancing along the assembly track. Rover kept inventory to a minimum by sending schedules automatically to suppliers via AT&T EasyLink EDI. Some suppliers would get just forty minutes to schedule and deliver parts for the Rover 220 Coupe, but most would get between 12 hours and one weeks' notice.

To ensure a metallic blue Coupe didn't get fitted with red wing mirrors, sequenced delivery had to work round the clock, sometimes every two hours. Bar codes were fixed to the body shells as they went onto the track, which a PC scanned and translated to an EDI message sent to the supplier for parts needed usually 12 or 13 hours further down the track. Colour co-ordinated wing mirrors, however, were scheduled after the paint plant, just 40 minutes ahead of 'trim and final'.

EDI is the reliable, utilitarian, unglamorous side of networking. It has been around in the UK since the 1980s and saved big users millions of pounds every year. For instance, in 1990 British Coal held stocks of 200,000 different products to support their operations, sent out 600,000 purchase orders and received 1.6 million invoices every year. But they had EDI links with 500 suppliers, and one third of their orders – 200,000 of them – were placed electronically. Shorter lead-times between placing orders and receiving goods allowed reduced stock levels, which released £1 million, and lower administration costs saved a further £50,000 each year.

For computers to be able to exchange messages the 'protocols' – that is, the language, codes and routines for the exchange – must be agreed. In the early days, setting up direct communications between computers was tricky, because there were many different languages, codes and routines in use, and if the protocol used by the receiving computer differed even slightly from that used by the transmitting computer, then communications could not be established.

Setting up 500 separate connections between British Coal and its 500 suppliers would have been impossibly expensive and time consuming, but there were third party network operators who were eager to act as electronic clearing houses between groups of purchasers and groups of suppliers. Different network operators focused on different industries, and performed a valuable service in setting standards for each industry. They became known as Value Added Network Services, or VANS for short.

The VAN service consists of a computer database between the customer and supplier that allows each company to have its own electronic mailbox through which it can send and receive commercial messages. Thus, before sending off a message, a company had only to translate it into the format required by the VAN computer, a task performed by software provided by the VAN service. On receiving the message, the VAN service reads the address and places it in the intended recipient's mailbox. The recipient then downloads the message from the VAN service into its own internal computer system, but before it can be used, the data must again be translated, from the VAN format into the format required by the recipient's computer system. The software for communicating with the VAN computer is supplied by the operator of the service, and once set up, messages can pass through the service quite rapidly.

The four main EDI VANS networks in the UK are:

- GEIS who offer Tradanet and EDI*Exchange.
- IBM who offer Global Network Services.
- AT&T who offer EasyLink.
- BT who offer EDI*Net.

These four global network providers are 'closed', or private, networks managed by the operators and available only to subscribers, in contrast to the Internet which is not managed (but operates to agreed standards) and is open to anyone. The VAN operators guarantee delivery, integrity and security – features which are valued highly by their customers.

GEIS serves the retail and distribution, pharmaceuticals, automotive and several other sectors. IBM serves the insurance, health and many other sectors, and these two companies between them carry well over half the EDI messages in the UK. The rest are carried by AT&T, BT and other smaller providers.

There are several industrial groups who have agreed messaging standards for electronic trading:

- CEFIC in the chemical industry.
- EDIFICE in the electronics industry.
- ODETTE in the automotive industry.
- EDICON in the construction industry.

World wide there are three leading standards:

- In the UK it is the TRADACOMS (Trading Data Communications) standard, as they have the biggest customer base of over 2000 users.
- In the USA it is ANSI ASC X.12 (American National Standards Institute).
- Internationally it is EDIFACT (Electronic Data Interchange for Administration, Commerce and Transport).

EDI, as supplied by the VANS, has always been a rich company club, because a big purchasing organization as the main beneficiary could coerce each of its suppliers into paying the heavy joining fee and monthly subscription. Pay up, or give up the contract to supply us, was often the message.

However, in 1997 UK retailer Tesco Stores volunteered to take part in a European initiative to promote Efficient Consumer Response (ECR). It was a trial to see if the Internet could be used to bring EDI to smaller companies. Tesco's VAN service was provided by GEIS, who agreed to convert Tesco's EDI messages into a form suitable for sending over the Internet and for reading with a browser such as Navigator or Explorer. In this way, EDI was opened up to a tiny supplier, Kingcup Mushrooms, who employ 30 people growing and packing mushrooms for Tesco. They paid a few hundred pounds' joining and subscription fees, and used only a compost-stained PC and modem with Windows 95 and Navigator. This trial heralded the beginning of the end for conventional VAN service EDI. Companies can now exchange messages conforming to EDI formats via the Internet, without the need for a VANS operator, at a fraction of the previous cost.

The VANS operators may survive for a while, but their technology is expensive, slow and inflexible. Their proprietary networks will never achieve the reach of the Internet, and their only remaining advantage is cast iron security. E-commerce via the Internet seems certain to prevail.

THE INTERNET

The Internet is an amazing phenomenon which burst onto the scene in 1995 apparently from nowhere, but it was born in 1969 as a private network for the US Advanced Research Projects Agency, for scientists working on Department of Defense projects. This small network grew and linked with other networks, at first just in the USA, but by 1990 world wide after the Defense agency relinquished control.

For four years the general public showed no interest in the text files, and the growing number of Web sites on the Internet. Then, in 1994 Jim Clark and Marc Andreessen launched Mosaic, quickly renamed Netscape Navigator, the first browser. At a stroke it dynamized the Internet, and converted it into a consumer product. It became a colourful, user friendly resource requiring no special computer skills, and suddenly the world woke up to the business potential of this network of networks.

It grew astonishingly fast, attracting millions of new users annually, and offered new developments almost daily. For a year,

Microsoft dismissed it as a distraction, and Netscape Navigator claimed over 80 per cent market share. In 1995 Microsoft launched Explorer, a product with a very similar look and feel to Navigator, but with one difference – it was free of charge. Browser wars broke out for eighteen months. Microsoft and Netscape both offered updates and new versions almost weekly, but gradually Microsoft gained market share, and in 1998 Netscape, with its share down to 30 per cent, was forced to stop charging for its product, thus losing most of its revenue. A few months later Netscape was bought by AOL.

History and architecture

The Internet is a network of networks, which operates without any centralized control, other than conformance to the same TCP/IP communications protocols. The initials stand for Transmission Control Protocol/Internet Protocol, the name for the set of open, non-proprietary conventions which underpin the remarkable robustness of the Internet.

TCP/IP requires a communication to be split into 'packets', each with its own address so they can be routed individually through the network. The originating computer then sends them off, looking each time for a line to another computer in the network nearer to the packet's destination address. If a line is busy or otherwise unavailable, the computer will send the packet via the next available line going in the right general direction. Packets get passed from computer to computer through the network, with the packets of a message perhaps taking different paths to their destination. On arrival they are re-assembled in their correct order.

It is often said the network was designed this way so it could still function with large parts of it knocked out by a nuclear attack. However, in the 1960s computers were slower and less reliable, and the switched packet solution was probably the only practical way of ensuring messages got through. In fact solid state devices are vulnerable to the magnetic pulse radiated by a nuclear explosion. The pulses would wreck computers far beyond the range of blast damage, and a national network would probably not survive a nuclear attack.

The Internet grows up

1969	ARPANET formed. A 4-node network.	An ARPA-controlled network of university, military and defense contractors, to aid researchers in sharing information. It allowed remote log on, file transfer, and e-mail.
1974	TCP/IP developed.	A system of protocols developed for wide area networking.
1981	CSNET allowed to connect to ARPANET.	CSNET – for linking university Computer Science departments in several states. The first autonomous network that DARPA allowed to connect to the ARPANET.
1983	MILNET splits from ARPANET, leaving just 45 nodes.	ARPANET for research into networking. MILNET for military communications.
1987	10,000 hosts now linked.	
1989	CSNET merges with BITNET. 100,000 hosts linked.	BITNET – a network for academic discussion between faculty members of all disciplines at universities.
1990	ARPANET decommissioned.	Commercial networks allowed to link.
1991	World Wide Web launched.	
1993	600 web servers linked.	Internet in 100 different countries. 10 million users.
1995	100,000 web servers.	40 million users. Navigator and Explorer available.
1998	3,700,000 web servers.	100 million users estimated.
2001	36,300,000 web servers.	Over 300 million users worldwide.

The Internet only emerged as a consumer product after the World Wide Web was launched in 1991. The Web is a set of protocols that allow Windows, hyperlinks, and user friendly browsers. Before then, the Internet belonged to the computer scientists, who worked with text only, on green screens, typing obscure commands and cryptic addresses. That underworld still exists today, but it is dwarfed by Web traffic using point and click protocols. Although the consumer uses of the Web are the best known, it is business uses such as e-commerce that will have greatest impact on the way business is done.

E-COMMERCE

E-commerce includes all commercial exchanges of information via the Internet from business to business (B2B) and business to consumer (B2C). In other words, e-commerce includes all digital exchanges between all links in the value chain from extraction and growing of raw materials, through processing, manufacturing and distribution to the ultimate consumer. Of course B2C is what the public is most aware of, but that is just the tip of the iceberg. Beneath the pavements, cables hum with the growing flow of B2B traffic.

So if the Internet was opened up to commerce in 1990, why did nearly a decade pass before business started taking it seriously?

There were five reasons: reliability, security, accessibility, vested interests and standards. The Internet was designed as a private research network, for exchanging files, reports and messages amongst a closed group of users. If a file could not be located, or a copy of a report dissolved in cyberspace, or a message took a day to arrive, it did not matter too much. The users knew the system was secure from outsiders, and would just try again another day. But for commercial users, problems such as these would be intolerable, and the reliability and security of the Internet was questioned.

Also, for EDI there was a reliable, secure alternative system with a twenty year track record, already providing a healthy revenue stream for organizations with the skills that would be needed to make EDI work for free on the Internet. They were in no hurry to work themselves out of a nice big earner. And finally, although EDI standards could be used over the Internet, technically they were not ideal for it, and in any case there were just too many different proprietary, national and international standards in use to fulfil the wide scale promise of the Internet.

All of these problems are now being solved. The Holy Grail is universal inter-operability between disparate business systems. The stakes are high, and all the usual suspects are jostling for position, regularly announcing significant developments. It is reminiscent of the browser wars of the mid-1990s, but with many more players in a much bigger field. By the time you read this, the picture may be more settled, but here are some of the main advances that contributed to inter-operability.

1976 ANA established. The Article Number Association set UK standards for bar coding and VANS EDI.

1987 EDIA established. The EDI Association was formed by the VANS EDI business community.

1996 ECA established. The EDIA was reborn as the Electronic Commerce Association, with an interest in the Internet as well as VANS EDI.

1998 e.centre launched. e.centre is the trading name of EAN UK Ltd, the Association for Standards and Practices in Electronic Trade, formed by the merger of ANA and ECA.

2001 IBM and Microsoft announce web services technology that was claimed to be universally interoperable through standards such as simple object access protocol (SOAP), the universal description, discovery and integration (UDDI) register, and the web services description language (WSDL). All were developed in collaboration with various standards authorities and other software vendors.

2002 WS-I formed. IBM and Microsoft form the Web Services Interoperability Organization. The new organization will help software vendors and users with web services and XML standards. It will also certify new web services as officially interoperable.

It may be years before the ideal of universal interoperability and integration is achieved. There are many stakeholders with something to say on standards, and somehow their views must be reconciled. WS-I must involve software vendors such as Siebel, PeopleSoft, Sun and i2, and integration vendors such as Vitria and SeeBeyond. Also, there are other standards organizations working on the problem. They include RosettaNet that has already implemented trading standards for high-tech industries, the World Wide Web Consortium (W3C), the Organization for the Advancement of Structured Information Standards (OASIS), UDDI.org, the Global Commerce Initiative (GCI), the UN/EDIFACT Working Group (EWG), ebXML.org and the Business Process Management Initiative (BPMI).

Now at Work

United Technologies dumps slow EDI for speedy RosettaNet

Indiana-based UTEC is the Electronic Controls division of the $26 billion United Technologies Corporation. Until October 2000 they used EDI to order components from Arrow Electronics, the $13 billion components supplier that maintains an on-site store at UTEC's assembly plant. UTEC operates close to just-in-time manufacturing, sending an order for parts to Arrow about every six hours. But the EDI system was too slow.

UTEC's orders were routed to an EDI mailbox at Arrow, but the EDI batch processing of messages was too slow for Arrow to fulfil the order on time. 'By the time the EDI process allowed Arrow to see the orders, the delay was too long,' explains Pam Webber, the MIS Manager at Arrow. 'The Arrow Sales Rep who supports UTEC in the on-site store had to go into UTEC's system, see what was ordered, and then manually re-enter the orders in the Arrow system. When the orders transferred through EDI finally reached Arrow, they were manually cancelled. The EDI transaction information was no longer required.'

'The EDI process for UTEC had been set up years ago and it just wasn't working because of the time delays,' says Webber. Arrow and UTEC decided to move the whole process over to RosettaNet standards for e-business over the Internet. The standards are specialized XML-based dialogues that define business processes between trading partners.

Arrow believes successful implementation starts with communication. Staff identify the people involved, and send them guides to define their objectives from an e-business perspective. 'Communication is also important because changing business processes often has a rippling effect within an organization. Job responsibilities will change and daily routines may be transformed. These changes need to be defined and clearly mapped so that people aren't surprised by the effects of automation.'

Arrow's IT staff needed to discover the business rules for no-touch order processing. They sat with the on-site Arrow employee and observed her daily routine. 'You don't find out what people do, really, until you sit next to them, because they often don't realize the intricacies of their own processes,' says Webber. 'We came up with about ten business rules that we felt would give us about 80 to 90 per cent no-touch throughput. In fact the implementation yielded over 93 per cent no-touch throughput.'

Other advantages of RosettaNet compared to EDI were inventory turns doubled, order response time reduced from eight hours to 20 minutes, with manual exceptions only taking two hours. Real time, 24×7 ordering was achieved, with improved order accuracy, and increased return on working capital through better inventory management.

Arrow will continue using EDI where it already works well, but as RosettaNet transaction costs continue to fall, existing EDI installations may be re-evaluated.

You can view the full case study, from which this summary is derived, at www.rosettanet.org

The standardization initiatives taken since year 2000 represent a significant development. Prior to 2000, the emphasis was mainly data-centric, considering only standardization of how the data should be represented for stable pairings of trading partners. Since 2000, however, standards groups have started taking a more process-centric approach, considering how the data will be used, by temporary groupings of several trading partners, to manage business processes that extend along the value chain.

BUSINESS PROCESS MANAGEMENT SYSTEMS

Business Process Management (BPM) is going to be big, really big. It will radically change business systems, adding a fourth layer to the architecture, and should provide a revenue stream for software companies and consulting partnerships for the rest of the decade.

BPM is a tool with the potential for massive first mover advantage if used appropriately. It is the next logical step, building on the technologies of Business Process Re-engineering, Componentization, Enterprise Application Integration, B2B e-commerce and Collaborative Commerce. In the right hands, BPM promises to bring major cost savings, dramatic improvements in customer service and the greatest possible agility in response to changing business conditions.

Interested? OK I'll explain, but bear in mind that BPM is embryonic and still evolving rapidly. The destination is agreed but the route details have yet to be hammered out.

Remember Mike Hammer and BPR back in Chapter 4? He explained how businesses operate according to rules, some of them written, some entirely unarticulated, and many based on assumptions that are no longer appropriate. He described how Ford Motors changed the rules and converted to invoiceless processing of accounts payable. That, of course, required big changes to the accounting software which was still required to print a cheque, but according to different rules. The accounting package consisted of functions, such as print cheque, and rules, such as pay on receipt of goods.

Remember also that applications packages still tend to support the old departmental disciplines, like finance, manufacturing, human resources and sales, for instance. This is still the case, even for organizations that have abandoned purely departmental structures and reorganized as process-focused multi-disciplinary teams. As a result, business systems have been left behind by the revolution in management methods that we reviewed in Chapter 1. Our business systems remain locked in a departmental structure that was designed in the industrial age of departments and specialists. Far from supporting organizational change, they hinder it.

Even after a decade of BPR, our existing systems architectures are too inflexible to reflect the big organizational changes that have occurred and will continue to occur. ERP promised more flexibility by integrating the separate packages, but as extra modules were bolted onto the core, they solidified like concrete. Integration didn't increase agility: the more you did it, the less agile the system became. But with all those billions of lines of legacy code, there was no alternative – until now.

The big problem with BPR is that business processes are constructed from business rules, and many of these rules were baked inside the software when it was first cooked up. Thus, BPR always required extensive software engineering to delve into the code and change the rules. It involved significant risk and investment in a full systems project, to analyse, redesign, modify and implement the software changes.

The big central idea of BPM is to go into applications packages and separate once and for all the rules from the functions. The rules can then be held in a new pan-disciplinary layer, above the remains of the applications packages. The applications now only contain a bunch of componentized functions. The new layer will hold the rules in computer readable form, assembled into the business processes of the organization, and these processes will orchestrate the functions in the layer beneath to implement the processes.

This then provides an architecture that can truly support business strategy, and instantly reflect changes made to meet emerging opportunities and threats. A new business process can easily be created by writing, copying, reusing and rearranging rules. The new process can be loaded into the business process layer, and tested before it is adopted. At a technical level, switching to the new process then becomes as simple as switching from Word to Excel on your PC. Thus, as process teams form, dissolve and reform, they can expect full system support from day one.

Now at Work

The nuts and bolts of BPMS

The BPMS resides on a Process Server, and has the following parts:

- a Process Repository – a place to store the business processes that the organization has used, is using or developing or testing.
- a Business Process Modelling Language – for writing and editing business processes that are executable by computer.
- a Process Engine for executing the business processes.
- a Business Process Query Language – to provide an interface for managing the BPM system, in the same way that SQL provides an interface for managing a database management system.

The BPMS has eight support capabilities:

- Discovery – to make explicit all implicit rules and processes, and to bring embedded rules and processes into the process management environment.
- Design – to create processes from sub-processes, activities, participants and rules.
- Deployment – to roll out new processes to all the participants, including people, applications and other processes.
- Execution – to ensure that the new process is carried out by all participants: people, other organizations, systems and other processes.
- Interaction – to allow humans to manage the interface between automated and manual processes.
- Operation – to allow humans to manage exceptions, for instance to change participants, or reallocate process steps.
- Optimization – the ongoing activity of process improvement.
- Analysis – to measure process performance and devise improvement strategies.

> More generally, the BPMS should allow business users and process engineers to use the eight capabilities to integrate systems and automate routines, to design processes on-line and deploy them immediately, and to observe and control processes from end to end across multiple applications and business partners.
>
> (Distilled from a report by CSC Research Services, 'The Emergence of Business Process Management', January 2002, available as a PDF file at www.bpmi.org)

Hey, how cool is that! But there's more. The new architecture won't be restricted to managing internal processes. It will be possible to manage processes that extend beyond the corporate firewall to support collaboration and include suppliers, partners and customers. BPM seems perfectly matched to the present and future needs of business. You can see why everyone in computing and software is getting excited. It sounds great, and some important first steps have been made, but there are daunting problems ahead before we attain system nirvana.

It is their bespoke and legacy software that will cause problems for organizations. In some cases it may prove impossibly expensive to extract the business rules, and packages may need to be reconstructed using components. In fact this would prove more satisfactory technically, but is a big bang solution with higher risks and rewards. Generally, managers would prefer an incremental upgrade path. Managers who were disappointed after their big investments in ERP won't want to risk big single investments in BPM.

Organizations that have componentized their systems should face fewer problems. It may be possible to expose rules in an ERP system to the BPM system, so they become assets that can be integrated into processes, though standards to enable this have yet to be developed. It may also become possible to automate the extraction of rules. In January 2002, CSC Research Services produced a report on the emergence of BPM, in which they list 180 software companies with a stake in the development of BPM. Their collective intelligence is likely to produce a number of ways of smoothing the upgrade path.

As with any powerful tool, the results obtained will depend absolutely on the motivation and skills of the users, no matter how technically perfect the installation. In a survey of organizations a year after they installed ERP, only around one third claimed to be well satisfied with their systems. Whose fault is that?

Having dealt with the opportunities of pushing beyond the safety of the firewall, now let us turn to the threats.

KEEPING RECORDS SECURE AND CONFIDENTIAL

Clearly there are potential problems with using a public medium for transferring sensitive or valuable information. Individuals, enterprises and the State can be at risk. There are a variety of remedies. Users should follow good security practices and the Law empowers monitoring and policing through statutes, for example, Computer Misuse Act 1990, Data Protection Act 1998, Regulation of Investigatory Powers Act, 2000. There are hardware remedies, including firewalls, fault tolerant computing and mirror sites, and software solutions such as antivirus scanners, encryption, authentication and virtual private networks (VPNs).

Some of these topics require a specialist technical treatment that is not appropriate here. Look them up in the glossary at the end of the book, and if you want a fuller treatment, Google will find you lots more on the Web. Meanwhile, read on.

What would you think if you were refused life insurance though perfectly fit? Or inexplicably refused credit? Or failed to get a job because the interviewer somehow knew of your past membership of a political party or trade union? If you phoned a company for the first time, would you be surprised to find the salesman knows who you are without being told? Would it upset you if he also knows your age, the credit cards you use, and that you are often away in Brighton at weekends?

You would rightly be outraged and extremely alarmed. You would be at risk if details of your medical, financial and personal life were in general circulation. Technically this Big Brother scenario is possible now, but we are protected by the Data Protection Act, which by curious coincidence was first passed in 1984. It was extended in the Act of 1998 with full effect from March 2000.

It has always been possible to use technology for good or evil, and the growing power of database technology must be channelled in the right direction. Organizations use databases to keep records of their customers, clients, patients, members, shareholders, employees, students etc. together with their addresses and details of transactions of various types. Every time you join a professional association, buy shares, register to access a Web site, fill in a guarantee card or book a holiday, your name and address and details of transaction are added to a database. On their own these records pose no threat but if they are brought together, cross-referenced and compared, they reveal a detailed picture of your habits and lifestyle which should remain private.

Databases are stored on disk and in computer memory, and the cost per kilobyte of storage has roughly halved every 2 years since business computers were first used. This phenomenon shows every sign of continuing, and it is now economic to store millions of records, all instantly available. One application is the running of creditworthiness checks. When you pay with your Access or Visa card, the salesperson may phone up to check the status of your account. It takes seconds to access your details from amongst the millions of others.

A common application is database marketing. By buying and selling lists of different types and bringing them together into a single database, selective searches can be made to produce lists of potential customers who conform to some desired profile. There is no point trying to sell to a person who hasn't the money or use for your product. So when selling compact disks, you can improve response by mailing just to prospects who have recently bought a CD player (and filled in the guarantee card), and also have lots of disposable income (they buy shares). By comparing lists of guarantee holders and registered share holders, you can mail just to those who appear on both. You should get a much higher response rate.

There are lots of companies that buy and sell mailing lists. You can even download lists from the Internet.

The Data Protection Act is intended to safeguard against the improper use of personal data. The Act conforms to the Council of Europe Convention on Data Protection. The Convention was agreed to ensure that data can flow freely between all European countries. It therefore helps protect our international trade.

Data controllers who process personal data must notify the Data Protection Registrar, and conform to eight data protection principles. Personal data shall:

1 Be processed fairly and lawfully.
2 Be obtained only for specified lawful purposes.
3 Be adequate, relevant and not excessive for the purposes.
4 Be accurate and kept up to date.
5 Not be kept for longer than is necessary for the purposes.

6 Be processed in accordance with the rights of data subjects under the Act.

7 Be guarded against unlawful processing, and accidental loss, destruction or damage.

8 Not be transferred outside the European Economic Area without ensured rights for data subjects.

Databases can be used in the public sector too. They can remove a huge administrative burden from healthcare teams, and allow them to focus on individuals in the community who need it most.

A modern general practice may have six to eight doctors serving 15,000 to 25,000 patients. Patient records are still held in the old brown medical record envelope (MRE) in some practices, but they are beginning to be replaced by computer records. Old practices often employed more receptionists than doctors, and the office where they maintained the MRE filing system was often bigger than the patients' waiting room. With the records held in a database, doctors in their surgeries could access patient records for themselves in seconds, and the records could be maintained by two or three people and a PC in a small office.

Also, the same profiling techniques used in marketing can be used to identify patients more prone to certain diseases. We know, for instance, that some people have a greater risk of heart disease. Men are affected more than women, overweight people more than those of correct weight, people with high blood pressure and cholesterol levels more than those with low values, people who smoke more than those who don't, and people from families where the disease has struck before more than those from families where it hasn't.

Database searches can list those especially at risk, who could then be offered appropriate life-style counselling and preventive treatment. Effective disease prevention could reduce suffering, hospitalization and NHS costs.

HACKERS AND UNAUTHORIZED ACCESS

The Computer Misuse Act 1990 made hacking illegal, but it didn't help much, as few hackers are ever caught. After a survey of 4,900 IT professionals in 30 countries, PriceWaterhouseCoopers estimated the cost of hacking and viruses to the world economy at $1.6 trillion for

2001. (In $100 bills that would weigh 160,000 tonnes, and be enough to buy Microsoft Corporation five times over.)

As organizations grow more dependent on the Internet, the opportunities for breaking into systems illegally, or hacking, must also grow. It is worth knowing a bit about how it's done – not so you can try it, but so you can avoid inadvertently helping a hacker.

There are three main ways of gaining unauthorized access:

- Wire-tapping methods.
- Trial and error methods.
- Password stealing.

WIRE TAPPING METHODS

Remote access to a central computer often involves the use of ordinary telephone lines. One way of getting hold of the password of a legitimate user is to tap into the telephone wires, perhaps in the same building before the wires go out under the street.

Masquerading

When a user phones up the central computer but before the user logs on, our hacker will switch the line to his own PC where he has written a little program to present a counterfeit screen display inviting the user to enter his or her password. The PC will record the password and then send a simulated error message and break the connection. The unsuspecting user will try again, log on successfully this time, and not think twice about the minor irregularity experienced during the logging on.

Later the hacker can log on using the legitimate user's password saved in his PC.

Piggybacking

In this method our hacker's PC is introduced into the line so that the communications from the legitimate user pass through it before being passed on to the central computer. While the legitimate user is logged on, messages can be intercepted and modified. For instance files sent from one bank to another could be intercepted and additional credits added to the hacker's account.

TRIAL AND ERROR METHODS

Search-and-try programs

Hackers often write simple programs to help them log on to remote computers. A program can be written to automate the logging on procedure, trying a different password each time. With an auto-dial modem and a search-and-try program a hacker can leave the program running all night and look in the morning to see if any attempts have been successful.

Psychological clues

Hugo Cornwall, author of *The New Hacker's Handbook*, gives a list of passwords that crop up time and time again. They include: HELP, TEST, SYSTEM, LOVE, SEX, REMOTE, PHONE and FRED.

People usually choose passwords they will find easy to remember, so if you know something about the user, you can often guess a likely password. For instance, have you ever chosen for a password your date of birth, or the name of your spouse or children or the football team you support perhaps? If so, with a little bit of research a determined hacker could very quickly discover these and try them out.

PASSWORD STEALING

Overlooking

When you enter your password, the characters are not usually echoed on the screen. That would make it too easy; the password would stay on the screen long enough for any passer-by to read. Instead the screen remains blank, but that won't stop a hacker looking over your shoulder and watching which keys you press, especially if you are a one-fingered hunt-and-peck typist.

Scavenging

Some hackers will even go to the trouble of going through the piles of rubbish thrown out by the computer department, looking for discarded code on print-outs, system documentation, memos and reports – anything that may be helpful in narrowing the search, such as a particular length or format recommended for the password.

TAMPERING WITH DATA

There are three distinct groups of individuals who may try to get at the data in your system to steal or damage it.

One group, hackers, do it for fun and kudos; the intellectual challenge and accolade from fellow hackers is the only motivation. Hackers often contribute to, or run, bulletin boards on the Internet. Hackers' bulletin boards are easy enough to set up with a PC and a modem. The culture is quite subversive – like in the early days of citizens' band radio – with hackers exchanging dial-up numbers of big systems, passwords and information on how to break in.

Now at Work

Denial of service attacks

DoS attacks make their target Web sites unavailable to customers and visitors for hours or a day at a time. Amazon, eBay, CNN, Buy.com, E*trade and Yahoo have all been attacked.

The attackers are a group of malicious hackers, some as young as 13 years, who use remote control zombie/bot programs previously installed unbeknown to their owners on unprotected high bandwidth Windows machines that are normally on. On receiving a signal, hundreds of bot programs start deluging the target with billions of IP packets, consuming all the bandwidth and denying access to anyone else.

University of California San Diego researchers found 4000 DoS attacks made per week during a three week period in 2001. Half lasted less than ten minutes.

Find out more at www.grc.com

Another group of potential troublemakers are dissatisfied employees or ex-employees who may break into the central computer for revenge, or to restore a loss they believe they have unfairly suffered. Often they have inside information which makes it easier for them to get in. They may have worked in the computer department, or have knowledge of passwords, and their motivation may be theft or vandalism.

The third group are just plain criminals who happen to know something about computers. They are motivated by personal gain, and may use any of the traditional methods: fraud, illegal transfer of funds, forgery, ransom demands, espionage, blackmail... The computer versions of these crimes have produced a colourful vocabulary of popular terms.

The salami method

When an accounting system calculates employees' paycheques, it does so only to the nearest penny: any small fractions of a penny are simply cut off and not paid. The salami method involves writing and inserting a few lines of code to collect all these tiny slices and transfer them to a separate account. The slices are too small for most businesses to notice, but can quickly add up to a considerable amount.

If the organization makes payments through the Banks Automated Clearing System (BACS) the payments could be made automatically to a bank account in a false name by electronic transfer of funds, and then the funds could be withdrawn from any of the bank's hole-in-the-wall machines. The irregular lines of code may never be discovered but even if they are, there can be no fingerprints to link them to any particular individual. Thus for the perpetrator the risks of being caught are very small.

Time bombs and logic bombs

Again, these are irregular lines of code inserted into a legitimate program, which will be activated automatically at a particular date, or when certain conditions are met. Computer criminals can use them in several different ways.

A computer criminal could insert a logic bomb into the central computer of an organization, which would cause the whole system to 'crash', that is, fail in a comprehensive manner, losing data and corrupting programs so that all the system software would have to be set up and reloaded to get the system running again.

Alternatively the logic bomb could be designed to display a ransom demand and then cause the program to 'hang' – lock up and not respond to any inputs until a particular password is entered to unlock the system again.

Legitimate software writers have sometimes used logic bombs to make sure they get paid for the work they were contracted to do – but in more subtle ways than crudely demanding payment. The software may be coded to start malfunctioning in a less extreme manner, giving the software writer an opportunity to ask for payment of amounts owing before agreeing to correct the malfunction. This is, of course, illegal.

The Trojan horse

In Greek mythology, the well-defended city of Troy was invaded by deceiving the Trojans into thinking that a large wooden horse left outside the city walls was a gift from the gods. They pulled the horse inside the city and during the night soldiers climbed out and opened the gates. Similarly, an apparently innocent computer program could contain some extra mischievous lines of code, to release inside your system. For instance, you may be tempted to load a disk with a computer game on your computer at work. If so, don't. It may not be all that it seems.

Data diddling

This is the simplest form of computer crime. It simply involves changing data or entering incorrect data. Examples might be a student hacking into the college computer system and changing the record of their grading, or an employee gaining access to the payroll system and granting themself a pay rise. Data diddling is the most common form of computer crime.

Viruses

Just as a program can be written to copy a file from disk into memory, for instance, so a program can just as easily be written to copy itself into a free area of memory. Then the two copies will copy themselves to give four copies. The four will become eight, then sixteen and so on. Very soon the whole memory will be filled with copies of a program which has no purpose other than to reproduce itself. At this point the computer will stop, completely disabled.

Any program that can replicate itself automatically is called a virus. It can be attached to a seemingly innocent program that acts as a Trojan horse to carry the virus, or you might receive it by e-mail. When you open it, it mails a copy of itself to everyone in your e-mail address book. Just like real viruses, they are infectious and damaging.

In 1988 a student at Cornell University unleashed a virus into the forerunner of the Internet, Arpanet, the computer network that connected university and Department of Defense research laboratories across the USA. It did damage which cost close on $1 billion to put right, and the student, Robert Morris, was found guilty and sentenced to four hundred hours of community service and a fine of $10,000 dollars. Thirteen years later, in 2001, the Love Bug worm (a virus that attacks operating systems) was estimated to have cost businesses up to £8 billion.

COMPUTER SECURITY METHODS

There can never be a 100 per cent secure system. If enough people are determined to break in, sooner or later someone will find a way. Part of the problem is that the more secure you make a system, the less easy it is for bona fide users to use. There has to be a compromise, and the costs of the inevitable breaches must be budgeted for. For instance a few years back, Visa International, the credit card organization, budgeted for a loss of more than £130 million in fraud. However, they said that was acceptable because it represented less than 1 per cent of turnover. In 1995 the UK banks lost £83.3 million from plastic card fraud, some £3.5 million attributable to fraud involved with the UK's 22,000 ATM cash machines.

Computer security depends on a combination of physical barriers, software defences and security procedures.

Barriers, software and procedures

Physical barriers consist of making sure that computers and terminals are locked up and only accessible to legitimate users. It is also important to make sure that disks and tapes are similarly protected. All disks from outside the organization should be regarded as potential sources of infection, and should be checked and if necessary disinfected, on a stand-alone 'dirty' machine set aside for the purpose, before being loaded onto the organization's mission-critical networks and machines. The risks are real, and companies regularly go out of business within 12 months of a virus infection, if vital files such as outstanding invoices or customer databases are lost.

Now at Work

Secure connections tunnel through the Internet

A Virtual Private Network (VPN) is a private connection between two networks or computers using the public Internet. VPNs can be used to connect two separate organizations for e-commerce, or to enable remote access to the corporate Intranet.

Normally, Internet data packets are in clear text that anyone could read, so tunnelling technology is used. First, data packets are encrypted, and then they are wrapped in Internet Protocol so they can be carried by the Internet.

There are three classes of VPN for different applications:

- Intranet VPN, or real time service. This provides remote users the same service that on-site users expect. Takes priority for bandwidth, delivers a fast two-way service for video conferencing and up to the minute data.
- Extranet VPN, or non-real time, mission critical service. This provides sufficient bandwidth to support many Intranet services, but is not-real time. It is satisfactory for most SCM and collaborative commerce applications.
- Access, or Standard – for non-real time applications such as file transfer, web surfing and e-mail.

They should all provide the same high level of security.
www.networkmagazine.com

Networks make physical barriers difficult, because telephone wires cannot be completely protected physically. However, for extremely sensitive telecommunications links, such as those connecting military computers to missile launching facilities, physical barriers are used. The cable is passed down a pipe containing a pressurized gas. If any attempt is made to break into the pipe, the pressure drop will be detected and trigger an alarm.

Software defences usually depend on passwords, Personal Identification Numbers (PINs) in conjunction with cards, and cryptography.

Passwords should be changed regularly. If you are ever responsible for systems security, make sure users choose passwords which are not proper names or real words, preferably a random mixture of letters in upper and lower case, numbers and punctuation marks, to make it difficult for hackers to guess. The danger then of course is that legitimate users will forget their numbers, or worse still, write them down in accessible places. Often a satisfactory compromise is to choose an easily remembered word or number, with one or two random characters introduced somewhere in the middle.

Cards and PINs similar to those used with credit cards can be used, and cryptography can be employed to code transmissions across networks in such a way that only the intended user can decode the message. The growth in commercial use of the Internet has led to the development of so-called 'firewalls', which are designed to protect a company's internal networks from infection or intrusion from external networks.

And finally, procedures should be in place to ensure that codes and passwords are changed regularly, and that audits of system performance are regularly carried out. The system should maintain files of all transactions, so that an audit trail can be followed by an auditor to check that no irregular transactions have occurred.

TRENDS: MANAGING INFORMATION IN THE FUTURE

There are four trends which we can identify and use to anticipate how managing information in the future may develop:

- Advances in technology.
- Cheaper computers.
- More costly humans.
- Continuing change.

Advances in technology

ENIAC, the forerunner of modern computers, cost millions of dollars. It weighed 30 tonnes, could hold just 200 digits in memory, and processed at a speed of 5000 Herz. By comparison, my PC has five billion times the memory, and processes 400 million times faster.

In 1965, cofounder of Intel Corporation Gordon Moore made a remarkably prescient forecast, now known as Moore's Law. He predicted that the number of transistors per integrated circuit would double every 18 months, at least until 1975. In 1975 the Intel 8080 had 5000 transistors. In year 2000, the P4 had 42 million transistors. All Moore got wrong was how persistent the trend would be: it looks set to last beyond 2005.

One measure of performance is the amount of RAM, the main memory available in a computer. Take a look at the way main memory and secondary storage in the PC has increased over the years. The trends have persisted for decades.

Memory, storage and speed all apparently follow Moore's Law. We can expect more powerful computers every year, certainly for the next few years.

Figure 7.1
The ENIAC computer in the 1950s. US Army photograph

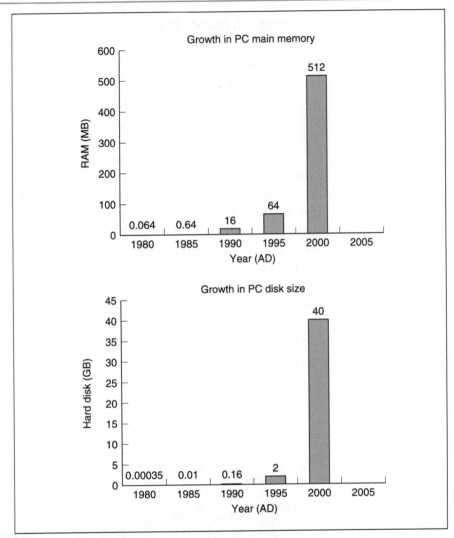

Figure 7.2
Advances in PC
memory and hard
disk storage

Cheaper computers

This exponential growth has caused exponential decay in the price of
a given level of performance – the price of a given level of performance drops by about half every two years. Thus if you can make do
with technology a year or two old, you can buy a new computer at half
the price of a top of the range specification.

In 1968 the Univac 1108 computer operated with just 256 KB of
memory, and cost over $2 million. By 1980 it could be duplicated on a
single circuit board costing less than $500.

In 2002, the PC on which this book was prepared operates with 1 GB of memory, and cost about £2000. That's 4000 times the memory, at one six hundredth of the price.

More costly humans

People on the other hand are becoming more expensive to employ. Standards of living continue to rise, and so too do people's expectations. Someone earning £2000 per annum in 1970 would expect £50,000 in 2002 for the same job. As a result, services are tending to get more expensive in real terms, at a time when many manufactured goods, especially computers, have fallen in price.

Continuing change

Everything seems to indicate that the period of change we are now experiencing will continue at least for some years to come.

Buyers' markets are likely to prevail with product prices falling as more and more sectors of world markets become oversupplied. The consumer is firmly in the driving seat, and is unlikely to give it up. Services and products will sell on quality, delivery, variety and price. White collar unemployment may start to rise as more clerical and information processing roles are either automated or exported to cheaper regions via the Internet. Jobs that remain will require higher and increasing levels of skill, as organizations strive towards the triple targets of instant, perfect and free. To survive, organizations will need to get closer to these ideals than most of the competition. Those that get closest will be the big winners in this information age.

Only a major catastrophe of world-wide proportions could halt these trends.

So what are the implications? What should organizations do? The same technology, materials and other resources are available to all, and they are all falling in price – except for skilled human resources, and that's the key. If you want effective, efficient processes, you need good people to design, implement and improve the processes. So, organizations must hire the best people they can get, then arrange for them to work together effectively, efficiently and happily.

Studies by Sackman *et al.*, into programming performance in 1968, found that the best programmers work 20 times faster than the poorest, to produce programs that are five or ten times smaller and faster running. These are enormous differences. Can you imagine a manual worker in a factory surviving for long by producing only one twentieth of the output of the best worker? If the Sackman results apply to other knowledge workers, organizations can gain a big, invisible advantage by hiring and holding onto the best people.

Working effectively and efficiently means not wasting people's time by having them do things that can be automated, or having them do non-core things that can be outsourced to experts. Then, forget command and control. Inform and entrust your people to work in multi-skilled, self-managing teams, equipped with the best tools. They will be happy and want to stay because they are doing the things they are good at, and for which computers are quite useless. Organizations need people, not computers, for the creative, imaginative, inquisitive roles that are essential in good design, research and development. We need people to make value judgements, to develop their inspirational and intuitive abilities to forecast trends and tune in to customer needs. And above all we need people to push forward, to motivate, to switch on the computers and keep them running, and to carry the organization forward towards its goals.

It's easy, see? Communicate, collaborate, and automate. It's just a question of managing information.

REVIEW AND RELATE

1 Write a 20-line memo in response to a question from your boss: 'What is Business Process Management? Is it as brilliant as it is made out to be, or can we ignore it for now?'

2 What are you going to do about your passwords? Think of some easy names or dates that you can remember easily. Now think of a non-numeric, non-alphabetic character that you could introduce in the middle somewhere, perhaps in place of a letter. For example, Basil could become b@s!l, or b*asil.

3 How far do you agree with the trends outlined at the end of this chapter? Identify the parts you agree with, and decide what you are going to do about your career. Which organizations and industries are likely to benefit? What skills will be in demand? How should you position yourself to benefit from the trends?

REFERENCES AND FURTHER READING

Cornwall, H. (1986). *The New Hacker's Handbook*. Century.

Hammer, M. (2001). *The Agenda: What Every Business Must Do to Dominate the Decade*. Crown Business.

Sackman, H., Erikson, W. J. and Grant, E. E. (1968). 'Exploratory experimental studies comparing online and offline programming performance.' Communications of the ACM. January.

Smith, H. *et al.* (2002). *The Emergence of Business Process Management*. CSC Research Services. www.CSC.com www.bpmi.org www.cscresearchservices.com/process

Appendix: Some interesting Web sites

Here are a few of the sites I visited while researching for this book. I have reservations about quoting site addresses for two reasons. First, they change so frequently. Probably a quarter of them will move, change or disappear within a year or two. And second, if you are looking for information you should do a google search. If you want information on EAI or hacker news, just type those words into google.co.uk and in 0.1234 seconds you will have a screen full of interesting and relevant sites.

Anyway, here they are, in no particular order. If you are researching a particular topic, many of the PDF files and White Papers are free (though you may have to register) and they often deliver material that takes another year to appear on library shelves.

For the following sites, type www then the address as shown. For instance, to visit the site ibm.com, type www.ibm.com

ibm.com
brint.com
attbusiness.net
cbi.cgey.com
yankeegroup.com
informationweek.com
checkpoint.com
infowar.com
ecommercetimes.com
iib.com
gbd.org

dw-institute.com
cognos.com
strategy.com
computerworld.com
ebizq.net
monster.co.uk
peoplesoft.com
communityb2b.com
northernlight.com
internetworld.com
optimizemag.com
cio.com

For the following sites, do not type www. Just type the full address as shown.

http://news.zdnet.co.uk
http://totalsearch.ft.com
http://w.moreover.com

Glossary

If you do not find what you are looking for in this glossary, try visiting one of these sites:

http://whatis.techtarget.com/
www.webopedia.com

ABC analysis – see Pareto analysis.

Alphanumeric characters – all the upper and lower case letters of the alphabet, and the numbers 0 to 9.

ANSI – American National Standards Institute. The American equivalent of the British Standards Institute.

ASCII – American Standard Code for Information Interchange. A set of codes that uses eight bits for each alphanumeric character, plus a range of punctuation marks and simple graphics characters. Originally used for teletypewriters and punched paper tape storage of keystrokes, and now widely used for computer communications.

Authentication – a checkable digital signature attached to a message to assure that it has come from the source it claims to come from.

B2B – commercial transactions between businesses via the Internet.

B2C – commercial transactions between a business and a retail customer via the Internet.

Binary code – a coding system that uses binary numbers to represent alphabetical letters and decimal numbers.

Binary numbers – a number system like the decimal system, but instead of using ten digits, it only uses two: 0 and 1.

Bit – contraction of the term 'binary digit'. It means a single element or figure in binary code – a 0 or a 1.

BOM – Bill of materials. A structured parts-list for a finished assembly. The BOM has the finished assembly at level 0, the main sub-assemblies at level 1, the parts required for the sub-assemblies at level 2, the materials required for the parts at level 3, etc. The BOM therefore contains information not only about what materials and parts go into the product, but also information about the order in which the parts are put together during manufacture.

BPM – Business Process Management. A proposed new architecture for computer systems, in which the business rules embedded in applications are extracted, and placed in a separate layer. It then becomes easy to re-engineer business processes without any major software engineering being necessary.

Byte – a set of eight bits. This is the practical minimum number of bits handled by a computer at any one time. In ASCII, one byte is required to represent each of the alphanumeric characters.

CAD – Computer-aided design. Special software that allows a computer to be used for preparing designs and drawings. New designs can sometimes be produced very quickly by calling up a previous similar design onto the screen and 'editing' it.

CAM – Computer-aided manufacture. A catch-all term to describe any production machinery that runs under computer control.

CFPR – Collaborative Forecasting Planning and Replenishment.

CIM – Computer-integrated manufacture. A comprehensive network of computers and CNC machines which allows a factory to be controlled digitally, without the use of production paperwork, from design all the way through production to delivery.

Client-server – a network consisting of a server, which is a central PC with extra memory and processing power, and one or more thin clients, which are PCs with less memory, and sometimes no local disk storage. The client downloads programs and data from the client, to run them as required, and store the results back on the server.

CNC – Computer numerical control. A system of programs and hardware used to control the tool paths, speeds and feed rates of production machinery used for cutting and forming parts made usually of metal.

Collaborative Commerce – the systems and activities that enable different organizations in a supply chain to work together with a shared infrastructure and shared files. The objective is to achieve fast, efficient consumer response with the minimal stocks held anywhere in the chain.

CRM – Customer Relationship Management.

CTI – Computer telephony integration. A computer system connected to the telephone system that will display customer details, when triggered by an incoming call from an existing customer phoning from home. It can only operate when the system recognizes the caller line identification number.

Digital – binary coded data held in electronic or magnetic form.

E-business – commercial transactions between a business and a retail customer.

E-cash – electronic cash. Cash held on a plastic 'smart' card, similar to a credit card, but payments are instantaneous, with no subsequent billing. When the card is empty, it can be re-filled from your bank account.

E-commerce – commercial transactions between businesses via the Internet.

EDI – Electronic Data Interchange. The exchange of commercial information between customer and supplier in digital form, directly between their respective computers, or via an intermediate third party computer service.

e-mail – electronic mail, sent through a network from one computer screen to another or many other screens. Almost instantaneous communication, far quicker than snail-mail, the old postal system.

Encryption – coding of a message so that it cannot be read by anyone other than the intended recipient who has the key to unlock the code.

Expert system – a database of expertise with a search engine, to allow lesser experts access to the knowledge of more experienced experts. Often constructed using 'If ... then ...' rules, and object oriented programming.

Extranet – a private corporate network using Internet protocols that extends beyond a single enterprise, to give selected partners and suppliers access to predetermined content.

e-zine – an electronic magazine, published only, or primarily, on the World Wide Web.

Firewall – hardware or software installed on an organization's internal network at the gateway to the Internet, to protect it from unauthorized intrusion or virus infection. Named after the firewall installed in early aeroplanes between cockpit and engine compartment to protect the pilot from engine fires.

Gantt chart – a horizontal bar chart, with calendar dates across the top, advancing to the right. Down the left side is a list of orders, or people, or machines or tasks. Thus, bars can be drawn in to represent periods of time when orders are being worked on, persons are on holiday, machines are occupied or tasks are being performed.

The length of a bar represents its duration and the ends show its start and finish dates.

GB – gigabyte. A measure of memory or file size equal to a thousand million bytes. That is enough space to store the whole of this book 500 times over.

Groupware – software to encourage co-operation between the members of a group. It usually offers members a common view of the data being worked upon, and depends on communications and database facilities.

Histogram – a diagram in which columns or vertical bars, side by side and touching, are used to represent frequencies of various ranges of values of a quantity.

Hypermedia – similar to hypertext, but the top file and its linked files may all be multimedia files. For example, you might click on a photo of a bird to hear its song.

Hypertext – a text file which contains highlighted words which act as hot links to other text or files. By clicking on the hot link, the connected text is displayed. For example, you might click on a jargon term to see its glossary definition.

IM – the Institute of Management, the UK professional body for managers, the largest such body in the whole of Europe.

Internet – the network of networks that started as an academic network for scientists in the 1960s, but has created huge interest since it was opened to the public and made more user-friendly. Dubbed the information superhighway by the media, it is often just called the Net by users.

Intranet – the name given to any private network for employees using the Internet hypertext protocol and browsers. Intended primarily for internal users, it can also be accessed through the Internet from outside by authorized users only.

Intrapreneuring – the encouragement of an entrepreneuring spirit inside the organization, amongst managers and employees. Progress through the taking of small risks is encouraged and rewarded.

Inventory – another name for stocks of materials, WIP and finished goods.

ISDN – Integrated Systems Digital Network. This is a communications standard for new networks being set up by British Telecom and Mercury to handle high-speed, real-time digital communication. These networks can also carry voice and moving video, and so are ideally suited for teleconferencing.

Ishikawa diagram – a fishbone diagram for analysing the root causes of some observed effect. Invented by Kaoru Ishikawa, the Japanese professor.

ISP – Independent Service Provider. Someone who controls a mainframe node in the Internet, and offers a dial-up gateway into the Internet for a fee. The fee may also cover a disk allocation for subscribers to prepare their own Web page.

IT – Information Technology. This term covers all the hardware and software used for storing, processing or communicating information. It includes computers, telephones, satellites, fibre optics, videos, etc.

JIT – Just in Time. A system of production where products are transferred from process to process in transfer batches of one, with almost no buffer stocks between processes. When a process somewhere in the middle of the production routing finishes its processing and passes an item to the next process downstream, it should receive another item from the process upstream 'just in time' to keep it busy. The system depends on tight scheduling, and the highest levels of manufacturing quality.

JPG – or JPEG, stands for Joint Picture Expert Group. This group agreed file format has standards for saving picture files in compressed format, often only one tenth the size of a bitmap file. These files carry the .jpg file extension.

Kaizen – the Japanese word for continual improvement.

LAN – Local Area Network. A term used to describe the network of communications links connecting up the computers on a single site.

LCD – Liquid Crystal Display. The type of display used for digital watches, with black characters against a greenish grey background, sometimes backlit. Large LCD displays are commonly used for portable computer screens.

Lead-time – the time that elapses between ordering the manufacture or delivery of something, and subsequently receiving it.

Legacy – legacy software is software that has been retained through one or more information system projects, because of its uniquely tailored design that was deemed unjustifiably expensive to replicate using more up to date methods.

Lorenz curve – this is another name for the Pareto curve. See Pareto analysis.

MB – megabyte. A measure of file size or memory space, equal to one million bytes of 8 bits (binary digits) each.

MIS – Management Information System. A network of computers, usually linked to a central large computer and database, for accessing, storing, processing and communicating management information within an organization.

Modem – a contraction of the term 'modulator-demodulator'. It is a piece of gear that translates computer binary signals into sounds for transmitting through the telephone network. When the sounds arrive, the modem at the other end converts the sounds back into binary code that the receiving computer can understand.

MPS – Master Production Schedule. A statement of the total requirements of finished products to be produced week by week for the next six months or so. It is the final result which the production planning department should be aiming to achieve, and is derived from sales forecasts and orders received.

MRP – Materials Requirement Planning. Computer software for working out when parts should be made, and when materials should be ordered. It takes the Master Production Schedule, which is a statement of the weekly requirements of finished goods, and then works backwards in time to find out when the parts and raw materials should be scheduled to be delivered.

MRP-2 – Manufacturing Resource Planning. MRP software which has been developed and enhanced to take in the scheduling of all manufacturing resources for a given MPS, not just materials and parts, but also the acquisition of finance, machinery, personnel, etc.

Multimedia – computers and programs that deliver not only text and numbers, but also photographic images, moving video, and stereo sound.

Normal curve – a symmetrical bell-shaped curve, which often crops up when the histogram is plotted for a set of figures which tend to cluster around a central or average value.

OASIS – Organization for the Advancement of Structured Information and Standards. A group formed to decide on standards for Web Services.

Objects – are modular software entities that also contain data. They model real-life objects such as 'account' and 'customer' and can relate to each other just like the real-life counterparts. They can be used to construct an information system to model the business of the organization. Quality and speed of coding is increased through re-use, and inheritance (the objects 'Personal Account' and 'Savings Account' both inherit characteristics from the object 'Account'). Object-oriented information systems take between half and one tenth the time to build, and are easily fine-tuned to the needs of the business.

P2P – Peer to peer. A network link between two computers of equal status.

Parallel communications – a system of communications in which the eight bits of a byte travel in parallel down eight parallel wires to arrive simultaneously at their destination. Thus, it is eight times as fast as an equivalent serial link.

Pareto analysis – also known as ABC analysis and 80/20 analysis. It is used to sort out the important few items from amongst the less important many other items, and is named after Vilfredo Pareto, an Italian economist who discovered that 20 per cent of the population of a country will typically own 80 per cent of the wealth of that country. The analysis is performed by ranking the individuals in order of descending wealth, then finding the worth of the first 20 per cent.

PDF – Portable Document Format. A file format that allows any document to be opened and viewed in a form that resembles a paper document. PDF files carry the .pdf file extension and can only be created by purchasing and using Adobe Acrobat software. However, Adobe make copies of their Acrobat Reader widely available free of charge.

PERT – Project Evaluation and Review Technique. This is a project planning and control method that involves representing all the various component tasks as arrows arranged in their logical order. Some tasks can be carried out in parallel, and some tasks cannot start until other tasks have been completed and so must be chained in sequence. The result is a network, and the longest chain – or critical path – through the network determines the minimum time required for completion of the whole project. The underlying method is also known as critical path analysis.

Portal – corporate portals are like Internet home pages, but located on the corporate Intranet. They are a user-friendly interface with dozens of single-click hyperlinks to launch files or applications that employees may need.

Project – a project is the work that must be done in order to achieve some future goal. The work is split into tasks to be performed by specified personnel, which are scheduled before the start of the project, to achieve the goal by the due date.

Protocol – a set of rules and procedures to allow computers to communicate. There are many different protocols in use, for instance File Transfer Protocol (FTP), Transmission Control Protocol/Internet Protocol (TCP/IP).

Quality Circles – a group of workers who meet outside normal working hours to discuss ways of improving the way things are done at work. The groups, also known as quality improvement teams, are paid for their extra efforts and encouraged by management to study and acquire any skills they may need. These groups of up to ten workers are often led by a supervisor, who acts as coach, mentor and adviser.

RAM – Random Access Memory. In theory, this means memory where an item of stored data can be accessed without the need to read through all earlier items to find it, as is the case with serial access media such as magnetic tape. In practice, RAM is now only used to describe the memory circuits of a computer that hold data and programs while the computer is switched on. Each item of data has its own address in memory and can be accessed directly.

R-chart – a continuous graph of the range of values found in samples of n items (usually four or five) taken from the output of a process. If the ranges charted begin to grow, an upward trend will begin to show, indicating that variability is on the increase. This may not affect the average size being produced if the variation causes values to increase both above and below the average. Without the R-chart, an increase in variation may thus go undetected.

Revenue – the total income of an organization before any costs are deducted.

ROM – Read-Only Memory. A form of computer memory that cannot be erased or changed, and which is not lost when the computer is switched off or re-set. It is used for instance to hold the small set of coded instructions telling the computer where to look for the operating system when it is first switched on or re-set.

Run chart – a continuous graph for monitoring samples of one item taken from the output of a process. If there is any drift or gradual change taking place, it will eventually show up as a trend on the graph.

Serial communications – a communications system in which the eight bits of a byte travel in series, one after the other down a single wire. It is a simple system that can use telephone wires for long-distance communications.

SFA – Sales Force Automation. Software to aid sales people in the field, by supporting the creation and circulation of customer contact reports and schedules. Keeps people informed and avoids situations where two reps arrive on consecutive days offering the same product.

Spreadsheet – a computer program that divides the screen up into columns and rows. At the intersection of each column and row is a cell, which can contain a value or a formula that the computer will compute. Thus, for instance, a column of figures can be entered, and the total automatically found by entering a formula at the foot of the column. It is also possible to sort figures into order, present the figures in the form of a graph etc.

Standard deviation – a measure of scatter, or variability, in a set of figures. The simplest measure of scatter is the range – calculated by subtracting the smallest value from the largest value – but this is unreliable because it is derived from just two figures. The standard deviation however is derived from every figure in the set. The first step in its calculation is to find the deviation, or distance, of every figure from the average for the set.

TB – terabyte. A measure of file size or storage space equal to one million megabytes, or a million million bytes. If you can count up to 200 in one minute, it would take you 10,000 years to count the bytes in a terabyte.

Teleconferencing – users on a network, accessing a central database and communicating with each other in real-time by text messages, and sometimes also by voice and video pictures. The users share a joint view of their work, which may be in the form of text, graphics, scanned images and hand drawings.

Teleworking – using a phone, fax and computer communications to work from home instead of commuting to work every day.

TQM – Total Quality Management. A management philosophy that trains, encourages and empowers everyone in the organization to apply a systematic approach to manage their own work and solve their own problems. Whoever receives the output of your work becomes your 'customer', and exceeding his or her needs should be paramount.

VANS – Value Added Network Services. The services of a network provider who does more than just carry messages. It is usually taken to mean EDI services.

Voice-mail – a system for storing voice messages for retrieval by the addressee(s). It works in much the same way as e-mail, and the messages may be stored digitally and reconstituted only when the addressee logs on to collect mail.

Virus – a malicious piece of code that spreads from computer to computer by reproducing and attaching itself to messages passed across networks.

VPN – Virtual Private Network: a secure communications link via the Internet, using authentication and encryption.

WAN – Wide Area Network. The network of communications links used to connect up computers that are located on several different sites, sometimes on different continents.

Web Services – services catalogued and made available by service providers for delivery via the Internet.

WIP – Work in Progress, or Work in Process. It consists of partly completed work: sub-assemblies for building into finished goods, partly machined products, etc.

World Wide Web – the tool known as the Web that allows hypertext access to the Internet, only introduced around 1993, and now by far the most popular choice for business and domestic users. Other tools on the Net include Telnet for remote log-in, and FTP, the file transfer protocol.

W3C – World Wide Web Consortium.

$\bar{X}$ chart – a continuous graph of the average values of small samples of fixed size taken from the output of a process. It is at least twenty times more sensitive than the run chart in detecting small changes in the output.

XML – Extensible Mark-up Language. A language for tagging data so that when it is received and read by another computer, it will know what type of data it is, and what it is to be used for.

Index